CUSTOM CURRICULUM

Can I Really Relate?

Parent Pains

Darrell Pearson and Marv Penner

Extreme Friendship

Kara Eckmann, Duffy Robbins and other youth experts

Which Way to God?

Darrell Pearson and Jan Johnson

NEXGEN®

Building the New Generation of Believers

An Imprint of Cook Communications Ministries
Colorado Springs, Colorado

Can I Really Relate?

© 2003 Cook Communications Ministries

Published by Cook Communications Ministries
4050 Lee Vance View
Colorado Springs, CO 80918
www.cookministries.com

Editorial Manager: Doug Schmidt
Product Developer: Karen Pickering
Series Creator: John Duckworth
Series Editor: Randy Southern
Cover Design: Granite Design
Interior Design: Becky Hawley Design, Inc.

Unit 1: Parent Pains
© 2003 Cook Communications Ministries
Editor: Randy Southern
Writers: Darrell Pearson and Marv Penner
Option Writers: Randy Southern, Nelson E. Copeland, Jr., and Ellen Larson
Inside Illustrator: John Hayes

Unit 2: Extreme Friendship
© 2003 Cook Communications Ministries
Editor: Rick Wesselhoff
Writers: Kara Eckmann and Duffy Robbins
Option Writers: Rev. Nelson Copeland, Jr., Saundra Hensel, Ellen Larson, Jim Marian, Paul Miller, Mark Oestreicher, Darrell Pearson, Susie Shellenberger, and Joel Walker
Inside Illustrator: Kathy Badonsky
Special thanks to Mark Oestreicher and Paul Miller for additional ideas, and to Saundra Hensel, who wrote the paraphrase of the Good Samaritan.

Unit 3: Which Way to God?
© 2003 Cook Communications Ministries
Editor: Randy Southern
Writers: Darrell Pearson and Jan Johnson
Option Writers: Eric Potter, Nelson E. Copeland, Jr., and Ellen Larson
Inside Illustrator: John Hayes

Printed in the U.S.A.

Contents

Unit Three: Which Way to God?

How to Customize Your Curriculum

We know your time is valuable. That's why we've made **Custom Curriculum** as easy as possible. Follow the three steps outlined below to create custom lessons that will meet the needs of *your* group. Let's get started!

 Read the basic lesson plan.

Every session in this book has four to six steps designed to meet five goals. It's important to understand these five goals as you choose the options for your group.

Getting Together

The goal for Getting Together is to break the ice. It may involve a fun way to introduce the lesson.

Getting Thirsty

The goal for Getting Thirsty is to earn students' interest before you dive into the Bible. Why should students care about your topic? Why should they care what the Bible has to say about it? This will motivate your students to dig deeper.

Getting the Word

The goal for Getting the Word is to find out what God has to say about the topic they care about. By exploring and discussing carefully-selected passages, you'll help students find out how God's Word applies to their lives.

Getting the Point

The goal for Getting the Point is to make the leap from ideals and principles to real-world situations students are likely to face. It may involve practicing biblical principles with case studies or roleplays.

Getting Personal

The goal for Getting Personal is to help each group member respond to the lesson with a specific action. What should group members do as a result of this session? This step will help each person find a specific "next step" response that works for him or her.

Consider your options.

Every **Custom Curriculum** session gives you 14 different types of options. How do you choose? First, take a look at the list of option categories below. Then spend some time thinking and praying about your group. How do your students learn best? What kind of goals have you set for your group? Put a check mark by the options that you're most interested in.

 Extra Action—for groups that like physical challenges and learn better when they're moving, interacting, and experiencing the lesson.

 Media—to spice up your meeting with video, music, or other popular media.

 Heard It All Before—for fresh approaches that get past the defenses of students who are jaded by years in church.

 Little Bible Background—to use when most of your students are strangers to the Bible or haven't yet made a Christian commitment.

 Extra Fun—for longer, more "festive" youth meetings where additional emphasis is put on having fun.

 Fellowship and Worship—for building deeper relationships or enabling students to praise God together.

 Mostly Girls—to address girls' concerns and to substitute activities girls might prefer.

 Mostly Guys—to address guys' concerns and to substitute activities guys might prefer.

 Small Group—for adapting activities that might be tough with groups of fewer than eight students.

 Large Group—to alter steps for groups of more than 20 students.

 Urban—for fitting sessions to urban facilities and multiethnic (especially African-American) concerns.

 Short Meeting Time—tips for condensing the meeting. The standard meeting is designed to last 45 to 60 minutes. These include options to cut, replace, or trim time off the standard steps.

 Combined Junior High/High School—to use when you're mixing age levels but an activity or case study would be too "young" or "old" for part of the group.

 Sixth Grade—appearing only in junior high/middle school volumes, this option helps you change steps that sixth graders might find hard to understand or relate to.

 Extra Challenge—appearing only in high school volumes, this option lets you crank up the voltage for students who are ready for more Scripture or more demanding personal application.

Customize your curriculum!

Here's a simple three-step plan to customize each session for your group:

1. Choose your options.

As you read the basic session plan, you'll see icons in the margin. Each icon represents a different type of option. When you see an icon, it means that type of option is offered for that step. The five pages of options are found after the Repro Resource student pages for each session. Turn to the option page noted by the icon and you'll see that option explained.

Let's say you have a small group, mostly guys who get bored if they don't keep moving. You'll want to keep an eye out for three kinds of options: Small Group, Mostly Guys, and Extra Action. As you read the basic session, you might spot icons that tell you there are Small Group options for Step 1 and Step 3—maybe a different way to play a game so that you don't need big teams, and a way to cover several Bible passages when just a few kids are looking them up. Then you see icons telling you that there are Mostly Guys options for Step 2 and Step 4—perhaps a substitute activity that doesn't require too much self-disclosure, and a case study guys will relate to. Finally you see icons indicating Extra Action options for Step 2 and Step 3—maybe an active way to get kids' opinions instead of handing out a survey, and a way to act out some verses instead of just looking them up.

2. Use the checklist.

Once you've picked your options, keep track of them with the simple checklist at the end of the option section (just before the start of the next session plan). This little form gives you a place to write down the materials you'll need too—since they depend on the options you've chosen.

3. Get your stuff together.

Gather your materials; photocopy any Repro Resources (reproducible student sheets) you've decided to use. And...you're ready!

Unit One: Parent Pains

Talking to Junior Highers about Parent Pains

by Darrell Pearson

It was 4:45 on a Monday afternoon. The office seemed unbearably hot. I was tired from a long ministry weekend. And yet here I sat in the most dreaded of situations.

I was counseling a mother and her teenage son.

Maybe some youth workers enjoy such situations, but I've always found them to be very taxing on my life and ministry. Some call it "hopeless" counseling. It's not like the joy of premarital counseling with an infatuated couple. Instead, there's a sadness in talking with a motivated mom and a disinterested kid. It's discouraging, frustrating, and tiring.

But it's good. The more I talked with the two of them, the more I realized that, with me present, they were able to do what was impossible by themselves. They could *talk*.

Is there a more helpful role that the youth leader plays in this world than helping bridge the gap between parents and their teenagers? Probably not. Above all, we are often mediators between people caught in a classic struggle. But we can make a difference.

The sessions that follow will help you as you work with students trying to understand and communicate with their parents. I thought a few guidelines about the parent-child situation as it pertains to a youth worker might help, so the next few paragraphs are thoughts, principles, ideas, and suggestions to make your role more productive.

You Are an Extension of the Parents.

Face it: You're an adult. You *look* like a parent, you *act* like one (most of the time)—you might even *be* a parent. And the parents of your group members have entrusted you with the care of their children (even if that care extends only for a few hours a week). Many of these parents probably have strong expectations that you're going to deliver the same message that they would deliver if they were working with these kids.

Sometimes you might live up to these expectations; sometimes you might not. Either way, you need to remember your role. Whatever you teach your group members needs to be delivered from the perspective of an adult, a person who generally supports what the parents are doing.

It's not helpful to play the role of the "teenage sympathizer," who sees everything from the kid's point of view. You may be the closest thing to a parent some of your group members have. And with the credibility you most likely have with your group members, the parents need to be comfortable that you're a trustworthy person with whom to leave their sons or daughters for a while.

Parents Don't Own Their Children.

On the other hand, you can't play the parents' role only in the way parents want. Junior highers are not puppets of their parents. They are distinct individuals who deserve to be treated as such. (Remember, not all parents treat their children well.) Part of your mediator role is understanding that you won't always side with the parents. You must be willing to take a stand sometimes to support the kids' perspectives. Parents don't own their children; they are entrusted by God to take care of His children, just as they entrust you to do the same.

Communicating with Parents Is Critical to Your Ministry.

It's an unwise youth leader who purposely steps on parents' toes to make friends with students. Parents are the lifeblood of your existence—so take steps to make sure you treat them like VIPs. Communicate accurately with them, listen to their concerns, and respond to them. A lot of youth ministry involves "parent ministry."

Since you're about to embark on a study about parents, why not take a moment to write a note to parents to tell them what you're about to do? They'll greatly appreciate the information. Perhaps they'll want to quiz their junior highers about the sessions in the series. Invite parents to drop in for a meeting, or perhaps include them in a panel discussion. Involve them in the process and you'll be amazed at how many of them are willing to help.

You Are "Jeremiah" to Parents and Teens.

The Old Testament prophets often found themselves in an uncomfortable role—challenging wayward people with the true claims of the living God. It often got them in deep trouble, but it brought people into a closer relationship with God. Playing the "prophet" with parents and teens can be a big help to them as they seek to grow together in their relationships with Christ and with each other. When group members raise concerns about parents (particularly unfair concerns) during your meeting, carefully challenge kids to consider the other side of the problem. Find creative ways to explore this. For instance, you might have a "guest" parent in your group show up to answer questions or roleplay the parental perspective. You'll also need to be prepared to challenge parents, too, when they need to be confronted.

Parents and Teens See Things from Their Own Perspective.

Both parents and teens believe their perspective to be completely accurate. When one tells you his or her side of a story, you think you know every detail and truth that's needed. But you don't.

When a mom recently came to me to explain her family's problems, I thought I had an accurate picture of what was going on. When I talked to the daughter, however, she gave me a whole new perspective. After my conversation with the daughter, I thought I knew what was *really* happening, so I made a few judgmental comments about the mom to the daughter. The mom then came back to me to see if what her daughter had said I said was true, and . . . you get the picture. When I talked to both of them together, I formed a *third* opinion of the situation. Be careful not to trust one side or the other too much for truth. Every individual is convinced that he or she sees the whole issue accurately. Don't be swayed by a convincing argument, but instead by your own observations and feelings after exploring the issue as completely as you can.

Don't Be Defensive about the Parent Role.

This is especially easy to do if you are a parent yourself. It's understandable to feel defensive when a junior higher makes an outlandish remark about his or her parents, but allow the person to vent his or her feelings and opinions. A youth group meeting, Bible study, or Sunday school class is a perfect place for kids to talk about parents without feeling like they have to hold things back. A defensive response on your part will just cause them to shut up and stop sharing. As you discuss the topic of parents, fight the urge to "defend the parental flag"; instead, be willing to listen with an open mind.

Talking with junior highers about parent pains is no easy task. In John 9, the Pharisees found themselves in the midst of an interesting parent-son issue. The blind man that Jesus healed was summoned by the Pharisees to explain what happened, and when he failed to satisfy them, they called in his parents. The parents' only comment was that their son was old enough to speak for himself. Their interest was in themselves—they just didn't want to get in trouble with anyone, and didn't seem to care much about the fact that their blind son was healed.

Such is life with young people and parents even today. Many teens and parents are motivated by self-interest, so healing wounds between the parties doesn't happen easily. But Jesus can and will heal people and relationships today—and He can use us to help do it. We can be instrumental in bridging the gap between parents and junior highers. Let's do a better job than the Pharisees did, and put our own self-interest aside, trying our best to help our group members understand and live with their parents.

Darrell Pearson is co-founder of 10 to 20, an organization dedicated to presenting high-involvement events for teenagers. Formerly youth director at the First Presbyterian Church in Colorado Springs, Darrell spent most of his eleven years there directing the junior high program. He's co-authored Creative Programming Ideas for Junior High Ministry *(Youth Specialties), and written and presented the national-touring program* Next Exit. *He also speaks frequently to youth groups and leaders around the country. He lives with his wife and three daughters in Colorado Springs, Colorado.*

The images on these two pages are designed to help you promote this course within your church and community. Feel free to photocopy anything here and adapt it to fit your publicity needs. The stuff on this page could be used as a flier that you send or hand out to kids—or as a bulletin insert. The stuff on the next page could be used to add visual interest to newsletters, calendars, bulletin boards, or other promotions. Be creative and have fun!

Ever Feel Like Your Parents Are a Pain?

If you've ever had trouble loving or even understanding your parents,
please join us as we begin a new study called *Parent Pains.*
You'll be glad you did—and so will your parents!

Who:

When:

Where:

Questions? Call:

Unit One: Parent Pains

Follow the rules.

For kids only.

Did you hear me?

Most Valuable Parents

SESSION
1

Living with Imperfect Parents

YOUR GOALS FOR THIS SESSION:
Choose one or more

☐ To help kids recognize that most parents are at least somewhat aware of their weaknesses and really want to be better parents.

☐ To help kids understand that their shortcomings are every bit as responsible for family problems as their parents' shortcomings are.

☐ To help kids feel secure in the fact that they have a heavenly Father who can consistently provide what they need, even when their earthly parents fail them.

☐ Other:_____
_____

Your Bible Base:

Psalm 27:10
Matthew 7:1-5

Building the Perfect Parent

(Needed: Cut-apart copies of Repro Resource 1, chalkboard and chalk or newsprint and marker)

OPTIONS

EXTRA **ACTION**

SMALL GROUP

LARGE GROUP

HEARD IT ALL BEFORE

MOSTLY **GIRLS**

MOSTLY **GUYS**

EXTRA **FUN**

MEDIA

JR. HIGH

HIGH SCHOOL

COMBINED

Ask: **How many of you have ever wished you had parents other than the ones you have now?** If group members seem hesitant to answer, rephrase the question: **How many of you have ever wished you could change some things about your parents?** Probably most of your group members have wished this at one time or another. To "break the ice," you might want to share something about your parents that, when you were younger, you wished you could change about them.

Then ask: **If you could create the ideal parents, what would they be like? What attributes would you give them? What are the most important traits good parents should have?** Get responses from as many group members as possible.

Before the session, you'll need to cut apart copies of "Parent Traits" (Repro Resource 1). Distribute one set of cards from Repro Resource 1 and a pencil to each group member. Instruct group members to arrange the cards according to how important they think each parent trait is. (There are a couple of blank cards provided in case group members want to write down some parent traits of their own.) For instance, if they think being wealthy is the most important trait a parent can have, they should put the "Wealthy" card first. If they think being laid-back is the least important trait a parent can have, they should put the "Laid-back" card last.

Give group members a few minutes to work. When everyone is finished, have each group member read aloud his or her top three parent traits. Keep a tally on the board of group members' responses.

Then ask several volunteers to explain why they chose the traits they did as being important. Note which group members chose superficial qualities (like being wealthy, good-looking, well-dressed, etc.) as being important and which group members chose "deeper" qualities (like being forgiving, patient, and understanding).

Keep in mind that many of your group members may come from single-parent families or families in which they're not experiencing healthy parenting. For some of them, just thinking about the qualities of a great parent will be a painful exercise. Be sensitive to this.

Top Ten Parent Pains

(Needed: A large sheet of newsprint or poster board with graffiti written on it, tape, markers, index cards, pencils)

Before the session, you'll need to prepare a large sheet of newsprint or poster board. Write some of the following statements "graffiti-style" on the sheet.

- "My parents don't trust me."
- "My mom sees only my mistakes."
- "My parents have unreasonable expectations."
- "My dad is too busy for me."

The statements should be scattered randomly across the sheet. However, make sure you leave plenty of space on the sheet for more comments to be added later.

At this point of the session, bring out the sheet and tape it to the wall. Distribute markers to your group members. Explain to them that the newsprint or poster board on the wall is a graffiti sheet for "parent pains"—things about parents that upset or irritate their kids. Then have group members come up to the sheet and add their own parent pains.

After a few minutes, have group members take their seats. Briefly go through the parent pains they wrote down, allowing group members to comment on each one. Probably most of the comments you'll get will be ones of hearty agreement.

Distribute an index card and a pencil to each group member. Instruct group members to create their own "top ten lists" of parent pains—the things about their parents that upset or irritate them.

Group members may choose from the "pains" written on the graffiti sheet or they may add some of their own. They should list the pains in reverse order—from #10 to #1 (with #10 being the least irritating or upsetting and #1 being the most irritating or upsetting).

When everyone is finished, have group members form teams of three or four and read their lists to each other. Walk among the teams as group members share their lists. Pay attention to the parent pains they identify as being most irritating or upsetting.

Afterward, say: **It seems like we put up with a lot of "parent pains," doesn't it? But what if the tables were turned? What if we had your parents in here, listing their top ten "kid complaints"?** What do you suppose their top complaints would be? Most group members will probably give answers like not cleaning up

their rooms, watching too much TV, not taking care of their stuff, fighting with their brothers and sisters, etc. [NOTE: Some group members may give more serious, disturbing answers like "My parents complain that I'm too stupid" or "My parents complain because they don't want me around." You may want to offer to meet with these young people after the session to discuss their problems at home more thoroughly.]

Family Log Jams

(Needed: Copies of Repro Resource 2, pencils)

Say: **When we have conflict at home with our parents, it's pretty easy to spot the things they are doing wrong. It's not always so easy to spot our own faults.**

Have someone read aloud Matthew 7:1-5. Then ask: **What does Jesus mean when He says to "take the plank out of your own eye" before you "remove the speck" from someone else's eye?** (Before you start confronting others about their faults, you should work on your own faults.)

Why is it so much easier to recognize other people's faults than it is to recognize our own faults? Get responses from as many group members as possible.

How does it make you feel when other people see only your faults and fail to recognize your good points? Again get responses from as many group members as possible.

Say: **When we have problems with our parents, it's like we create a "log jam" in our families. Very little positive communication or healthy interaction can get through the log jam. Unfortunately, blaming our parents for the problems doesn't get rid of the log jams. We have to focus on our own faults as well.**

Distribute copies of "Log Jam!" (Repro Resource 2) and pencils. Give group members a few minutes to complete the sheets. When everyone is finished, ask volunteers to share some of their responses.

Then ask: **How might the things you identified about yourself contribute to log jams in your family?** Get several responses.

Ask group members to keep these sheets handy and refer to them when they notice "log jams" in their families. Encourage them to take the first step in eliminating the log jams by working on the faults they identified on the sheet.

STEP 4

Parenting 101

(Needed: Chalkboard and chalk or newsprint and marker)

Ask: **Did you know that every day you are learning some valuable lessons about how to be an effective parent? By watching your own parents, you're learning good things that you'll put into practice and bad things that you'll avoid later on in your lives when you have kids of your own.**

What are some things you've learned from your parents that you want to make sure to do just like them when you get to be parents? What are some things about your parents' styles that you're going to make sure to eliminate from your lives when you become parents?

Make two lists on the board and write down group members' responses as they are given. You might use the following headings for the lists: "Things about My Parents I'd Like to Copy" and "Things about My Parents I'd Rather Not Copy."

Try to emphasize the positive things group members identify about their parents. In doing so, you may help eliminate some bad attitudes group members have toward their parents. On the other hand, don't ignore group members' negative comments. It's important for kids to have an understanding adult hear some of their complaints. Try to bring some mature balance and wisdom to your group members' enthusiastic evaluations.

One Perfect Father

OPTIONS

Say: **Today we've discovered that the people we call parents are less than perfect. For some of you, this might come as a surprise. Others of you may have already made this discovery. Like all human beings, parents have flaws and make mistakes.**

Have group members refer to the top ten "parent pains" lists they made earlier. Then say: **I know that many of you are a little disappointed when you think about mistakes your parents have made in raising you. But let's not end our time on a depressing note. I have some good news for you from God's Word.**

Have someone read aloud Psalm 27:10. Explain: **This verse tells us that even if our parents were to make the biggest mistake of all and completely abandon us** (be aware that for some kids this is a reality), **we have a heavenly Father who will always be there for us!**

Give group members an opportunity to silently thank God for His consistent love and to pray for their parents in the tough job they have of being moms and dads.

NOTES

PARENT TRAITS

WEALTHY	**EXPRESSIVE** (often hugs me, kisses me, and says "I love you")	**LAID BACK**
GOOD SENSE OF HUMOR	**GOOD-LOOKING**	**FORGIVING**
CONCERNED ABOUT ME	**LIKES MY FRIENDS**	**LIKED BY MY FRIENDS**
ALLOWS ME TO BE INDEPENDENT	**PATIENT**	**UNDERSTANDING**
WELL-RESPECTED IN THE COMMUNITY	**YOUNG**	**ATHLETIC/ PHYSICALLY FIT**
WELL-DRESSED		

Log Jam!

One rule in my house that's often hard for me to obey is

A habit I have that sometimes annoys my family is

Of all of my assigned chores, the one I forget to do most often is

Something I often forget to say "thank you" to my family for is

One area of my attitude that could use some improvement is

STEP 1

Before the session, list the parent traits on Repro Resource 1 according to how important you think each one is (with #1 being the most important and #16 being the least important). Don't let any group members see your list. To begin the session, form two teams. Have the teams line up behind a start/finish line. Place two sets of cards from Repro Resource 1 on the floor on the other side of the room. When you say go, the first person for each team will run to his or her team's set of cards, arrange them according to how he or she thinks you listed them, and run back. You will then check the order of the cards against your list and mark the ones that are in the correct position. Then the second person in line will attempt to arrange the rest of the cards in the "correct" order. Continue until one team correctly lists all of its cards. Afterward, have group members comment on your list. Do they agree with the order in which you placed the traits? Point out that everyone has different ideas about what traits are important for parents to have.

STEP 2

Rather than having group members write down their parents' top kid complaints, ask volunteers to do impressions of their parents' complaining. They can mimic their parents' voice, appearance, mannerisms, facial expressions, and "pet phrases." Encourage volunteers not to be mean-spirited in their impressions. You may want to set the tone for the activity by doing an impression of one of your parents. If your group members are hesitant to perform in front of the group, try another approach. Call out some typical parental complaints; instruct group members to jump to their feet if their parents have ever had similar complaints. Among the complaints you might use are not cleaning your room, watching too much TV, not doing assigned chores, talking back, and picking on your brother or sister.

STEP 1

As a group, build the "perfect" parent. Have each person call out a characteristic of a perfect parent. These might include things like patience, forgiveness, understanding, love, etc. Write the characteristics on the board as they are named. Then have group members decide what kind of job a perfect parent would have, what kind of car he or she would drive, where he or she would live, what he or she would do in his or her spare time, etc. Afterward, discuss the downfalls of the various characteristics. For instance, if a parent had a job that required a lot of travel, he or she wouldn't be able to see his or her kids' ballgames and school activities. Point out that there is no such thing as a perfect parent. All parents have good points and bad points.

STEP 4

Rather than having group members list things about their parents they would and wouldn't like to copy, take advantage of your group's smallness by having members form pairs. Instruct the members of each pair to come up with two (one per person) brief roleplays demonstrating what they'd like to copy about their parents. For instance, if one member of a pair appreciated his father's encouraging nature, he might come up with a roleplay in which the father is encouraging his son after a tough loss in a basketball game. After all the pairs have presented their roleplays, discuss as a group some parental characteristics your group members wouldn't like to copy.

STEP 1

Depending on the size of your group, have group members form ten to sixteen teams. (A team may be as small as two people.) Give each team one of the parent trait cards from Repro Resource 1. There are sixteen cards you could use; if you have fewer than sixteen teams, choose the cards that seem most applicable to your group members' families. Give the teams two or three minutes to come up with explanations for why their assigned parent trait is the most important trait a parent could have. (Group members don't actually have to believe that their trait is most important; they just have to come up with a convincing argument for it.) After a few minutes, have each team make its presentation. You may want to award a prize to the team with the most convincing argument. Afterward, discuss as a group which parent traits are really important.

STEP 5

Use the anonymity of your large group to your advantage as you wrap up the session. Have someone read aloud Psalm 27:10. Point out that not only is our heavenly Father always there for us, He is also willing and able to help us with problems we have with our earthly parents. Distribute index cards and pencils. Instruct your group members to write down one problem they have with their parents that they'd like God's help with. Group members should not write their names on the cards. As you collect and shuffle the cards, have group members form teams of four. Distribute four index cards to each team, and instruct the members of each team to pray together for the requests written on the cards.

STEP 1

On the two blank parent trait cards on Repro Resource 1, write the following traits: "Concerned about my spiritual life/church attendance" and "Allows me to believe and worship however I choose to." Distribute the cards and have group members rank them according to how important they think each one is. Afterward, focus your discussion on the two traits you wrote earlier. Find out how much influence parents have on your group members' beliefs and church attendance/involvement. Use the following questions as needed to guide your discussion.

• **On a scale of 1 to 10, how concerned would you say your parents are about your spiritual life? How does that make you feel?**

• **If your parents gave you the freedom to believe and worship as you choose, how would it affect your church attendance? How would it affect your involvement with this group?**

STEP 3

In discussing Matthew 7:1-5 with kids who've "heard it all before," use the following questions.

• **When do we have the right to point out another person's faults and weaknesses?** (When our motive is love or concern for the person.)

• **After having read Matthew 7:1-5, would you say we have the right to point out our parents' faults and weaknesses? If so, under what conditions?** Get opinions from as many group members as possible.

STEP 3

If your group members aren't familiar with Scripture, they may be confused by Jesus' use of figurative language in Matthew 7:1-5. As a group, brainstorm some modern-day figures of speech or expressions that might be confusing to people two thousand years from now. Among the suggestions you might come up with are "Excellent!" (from Wayne's World); "Get off my back"; "Chill"; "Hasta la vista, baby"; etc. Point out that Jesus was communicating in terms His immediate audience (His first-century followers) would understand. Have your group members brainstorm some modern ways to express the "Judge not, lest you be judged" message of Matthew 7:1-5.

STEP 5

As you wrap up the session, distribute index cards to your group members. Have them write down the following Scripture passages: Psalm 139:7-12; Matthew 28:20; and Hebrews 13:5. Explain that these are other verses of assurance that the Lord will always be there for us. In addition to the references themselves, group members should write down the page numbers in their Bibles where these verses are found. Encourage group members to look up these passages when they feel ignored or neglected by their parents.

STEP 4

Turn over the sheet of newsprint or poster board you used for the graffiti exercise in Step 2 (or use a new sheet). Write at the top of the sheet "Here's why I'm thankful to You, Lord, for my parents." Then distribute markers and have your group members write at least one thing they're thankful for concerning their parents. Comments may include the following:

• "My parents care enough about me to worry when I get home later than I'm supposed to."

• "My parents say my friends are always welcome at our house."

• "My parents bought me a puppy after my dog died."

Encourage group members not to just write down something nice about their parents, but to direct their comments to God and to thank Him for their parents.

STEP 5

Distribute index cards and pencils. Instruct group members to pair up, preferably with a friend (or at least someone they're comfortable with). Have them share with their partners one thing about their relationship with their parents that they'd like their partners to pray about in the coming week. It might be something as specific as "Please pray that my parents will let me go to the basketball game on Friday instead of making me go to my cousin's birthday party." Or it might be something as general as "Please pray that my mom and I will stop arguing so much." Group members should write down their partners' requests on the index cards and keep the cards handy as prayer reminders. To begin next week's session, have the partners pair up and update each other.

MOSTLY GIRLS

STEP 1

After you've made a tally of the top three parent traits, ask the girls to read aloud the three traits that they considered *least* important. Make a tally of these traits and discuss some of the reasons these things don't seem very important. Ask: **Have some of you put too much emphasis on some qualities that really aren't very important? How can seeing others' perspectives help you?**

STEP 4

As the girls are talking about the lessons they're learning from their parents, ask them to name some frequent expressions used by one or both of their parents. Give them some examples, such as "If I've told you once, I've told you a million times …," "When I was your age …," and "It doesn't matter why, I just said to do it!" List group members' responses on the board and then talk about the expressions. Ask: **Which of these expressions might have an element of truth? Do you often have to be reminded about things? Which ones are just results of frustration? How should you respond to these expressions? Which expressions do you think you will use when you're a parent? Why?**

MOSTLY GUYS

STEP 1

Rather than having group members fill in the two blank cards on Repro Resource 1, fill them in yourself with the following traits: "Plays sports with me" and "Spends time with me." Explain that "Plays sports with me" includes things like a father throwing a football or baseball with his son in the back yard; a father taking his son golfing; a father teaching his son how to play basketball, soccer, or chess; etc. "Spends time with me" includes things like going out to dinner with a parent for "one-on-one time"; going to a ball game, movie, play, or concert together; etc. Afterward, discuss how important sports- and entertainment-related activities are in a father-son relationship.

STEP 2

If you have guys in your group whose fathers don't live at home, ask them to write down some of the pains of being the "man of the house." (However, be sensitive as you do this! Make sure that you don't put anyone on the spot or embarrass anyone.) You might initiate this by writing some of the following statements on the graffiti sheet:

• "My mom expects me to watch my little brother/sister while she's at work."

• "If there's a spider or bug in the house, my mom always makes me kill it."

• "My mom makes me rake leaves in the fall, shovel snow in the winter, water the grass in the spring, and mow the lawn in the summer. She never makes my little brother do anything!"

EXTRA FUN

STEP 1

A few days prior to the session, you'll need to take pictures (using instant-developing film, if possible) of three of your group members' parents. If it's a guy in your group, take a picture of his father; if it's a girl, take a picture of her mother. Also, if possible, bring to your meeting the clothes the parents were wearing in the pictures. You'll also need to bring makeup, disguise props (fake beards, mustaches, glasses, etc.), and hairstyling items (curling iron, gel, mousse, etc.). Have group members form three teams. Assign to each team one of the group members whose parent's picture was taken. Each team's goal is to make its assigned group member look as much like his or her parent as possible. Working with the photos as a guide, the teams will use the clothes and various costume supplies to do their make-overs. Give the teams several minutes to work. Afterward, hold a "fashion show" for each team to show off its work.

STEP 2

Distribute paper and pencils to your group members. Write "Parents for Rent" on the board. Have group members imagine that they're going to rent out their parents for a week. Instruct your group members to write a classified ad that could appear in the "Parents for Rent" section of your local newspaper. (You may want to have some actual newspaper classified ads available for group members to refer to.) Encourage them to be truthful in their ads, identifying both strengths and weaknesses of their parents in their ads. For instance, someone might write "Parents for rent. Father— hard working & strong, but often grouchy. Mother—loving & concerned (sometimes too concerned); also an experienced chauffeur." After each group member shares his or her ad, discuss as a group what kind of person might respond to the ad.

STEP 1

Before the session, you'll need to record several video clips of various TV and movie personalities and characters. To begin the session, play the tape and have group members vote as to whether each character would be a good parent or a bad parent. Among the personalities and characters you might use are Ward and June Cleaver (from *Leave It to Beaver*), Mike and Carol Brady (from *The Brady Bunch*), Hulk Hogan (professional wrestler), Steve Urkel (from *Family Matters*), and Homer and Marge Simpson (from *The Simpsons*). After each vote, have several group members explain why they voted as they did. Encourage group members to be as creative and humorous as possible in their explanations. For instance, Hulk Hogan might be a good father because he could protect his children from bullies.

STEP 2

If possible, without your group members' knowledge, record some of their parents complaining (good-naturedly) about their kids. Try to get the parents to give personal, but non-embarrassing, information about their kids in their complaints. (For example, one parent might say, "My son hasn't changed the water in the fishbowl in his room for so long that his goldfish is now a blackfish.") However, the parents should not mention their kids' names. Play the recording for your group members and have them guess whose parents are speaking.

STEP 2

Instead of having group members come up to the board to write, have them call out their "parent pains," while you write them on the board. After you get about eight or nine suggestions, distribute index cards and pencils. Have group members choose their top three (as opposed to ten) parent pains and write them on the cards. Then, rather than having group members form teams to talk about their lists, ask volunteers to read their lists aloud. Pay attention to the pains they identify as being most irritating or upsetting.

STEP 3

Rather than distributing Repro Resource 2 and waiting while group members fill it out, have volunteers call out answers to the following questions:

- **What's a rule at your house that's hard for you to obey?**
- **What's a habit you have that sometimes annoys your family?**
- **What chore or job around the house do you most often forget to do?**
- **What one thing do you most often forget to say thank you to your family for?**
- **What's one area of your attitude that could use some improvement?**

If your group members are hesitant to respond, you might want to be prepared to "break the ice" by sharing answers from your own life.

STEP 2

If a lot of your group members come from troubled home situations, you might want to change the sample statements on the graffiti sheet to reflect their concerns. Here are some statements you might use:

- "I've never seen my father."
- "My mother is a crack addict."
- "Nobody's ever around when I get home from school."

STEP 4

Add a third list to the board, under the heading "Code Red Eliminators." Explain that Code Red Eliminators are things that parents do that are illegal and/or massively destructive to the family bond. Among the Code Red Eliminators you might list are the following:

- *Sexual abuse (incest)*—Molestation or any sexual activity with a parent (or relative).
- *Physical abuse*—When discipline is not given to correct, but to hurt and harm.
- *Substance abuse*—A parent (or sibling) who has a drug or alcohol problem that will affect the family.
- *Verbal abuse*—When parents curse and yell at children and make no attempt to build a child's self-esteem.
- *Neglect*—When parents do not parent, but show no love or concern for their children.
- *Divorce*—Both parents can no longer get along and decide to end the marriage.

Distribute paper and pencils. Separate group members so that they have room to write without anyone else reading their comments. Explain that you are going to begin an intervention policy for group members who have family problems and need your help—but that you need their suggestions as to how to go about it. After group members have written their suggestions, mention that if they need you to intercede for them in some fashion, they should write their initials in the upper corner of their papers. [NOTE: Don't do this activity unless you really plan to help.]

STEP 1

Separate your junior highers and high schoolers into two teams. Give each team a set of parent trait cards from Repro Resource 1 and a pencil. Instruct the members of each team to work together in ranking the parent traits according to how important they think each one is. (There are a couple of blank cards provided, in case team members think of some additional traits.) Give the teams a few minutes to work. Then have each team share its list. Note the differences between the junior high team's list and the high school team's list. For those traits that are in significantly different positions on the two lists, ask each team to explain its reasoning in ranking them as it did.

STEP 4

Separate your junior highers and high schoolers into two teams. Distribute paper and pencils to the junior high team. Instruct your junior highers to come up with five difficult situations a parent might face with his or her kids. (Situations might include finding out your son is taking drugs, having to tell your daughter she's too young to date, making your kids keep their bedrooms clean, etc.) After the junior highers have come up with five scenarios, they should read the scenarios one at a time to the high school team. At least two high schoolers should respond to each scenario. In responding, a high schooler should explain how he or she would handle the situation if he or she were a parent and then explain how his or her parents would handle the situation. Use this activity to lead into a discussion of what group members would and wouldn't like to copy about their parents.

STEP 2

Compared to junior highers, most sixth graders still have a relatively compatible relationship with their parents (although they may be well aware of the conflicts of others). As you distribute the index cards, ask your sixth graders to write a shorter list—perhaps their top *five* parent pains. If you don't think that would work with your group members, have them (as a group) come up with a list of the top five problems their older siblings or older friends have with their parents.

STEP 3

As you discuss Matthew 7:1-5, ask your sixth graders to think of examples of things that could be planks and specks in their own lives and relationships. Ask: **How do you know about these negative areas of your lives? Who pointed them out to you? How did you feel when they were pointed out to you?**

DATE USED:

Approx. Time

STEP 1: *Building the Perfect Parent* _____
- ❏ Extra Action
- ❏ Small Group
- ❏ Large Group
- ❏ Heard It All Before
- ❏ Mostly Girls
- ❏ Mostly Guys
- ❏ Extra Fun
- ❏ Media
- ❏ Combined Junior High/High School

Things needed:

STEP 2: *Top Ten Parent Pains* _____
- ❏ Extra Action
- ❏ Mostly Guys
- ❏ Extra Fun
- ❏ Media
- ❏ Short Meeting Time
- ❏ Urban
- ❏ Sixth Grade

Things needed:

STEP 3: *Family Log Jams* _____
- ❏ Heard It All Before
- ❏ Little Bible Background
- ❏ Short Meeting Time
- ❏ Sixth Grade

Things needed:

STEP 4: *Parenting 101* _____
- ❏ Small Group
- ❏ Fellowship & Worship
- ❏ Mostly Girls
- ❏ Urban
- ❏ Combined Junior High/High School

Things needed:

STEP 5: *One Perfect Father* _____
- ❏ Large Group
- ❏ Little Bible Background
- ❏ Fellowship & Worship

Things needed:

The Fifth Commandment

HONOR THY FATHER AND THY MOTHER

when you think they're right.

YOUR GOALS FOR THIS SESSION:

Choose one or more

☐ To help kids recognize that honoring our parents is a commandment from God—not an optional suggestion.

☐ To help kids understand that there are times when we must choose to honor our parents even when we think they're wrong.

☐ To help kids choose one way to show honor to a parent this week.

☐ Other:_____
_____

Your Bible Base:

Exodus 20:12
Colossians 3:12-21
Philippians 2:1-4

STEP 1

"P" Is for Parent

(Needed: Seven large pieces of paper, marker, pencils, masking tape)

OPTIONS

SMALL GROUP

LARGE GROUP

EXTRA FUN

SHORT MEETING TIME

Before the session, you'll need to prepare seven large pieces of paper. Each piece of paper should have one of the letters of the word "P-A-R-E-N-T-S" written on it. Tape the signs on a wall of your meeting area so that it's obvious to group members as they arrive that the signs spell out "parents."

To begin the session, distribute pencils to your group members and instruct them to write at least one word or phrase on each of the signs that starts with that letter and describes something about parents.

Encourage group members to write down as many words and phrases as they can think of. The more words you have to work with, the more effective the outcome of the activity will be. Point out that the words do not necessarily need to describe their own parents—just parents in general. Let group members have fun with the activity and don't be alarmed if it seems that they're venting some "bad attitudes."

After a few minutes, divide group members into seven teams. If necessary, a "team" can be made up of one person. Assign each team one of the signs on the wall. Instruct the teams to evaluate all the words and phrases on their signs in the following manner:

- They should *underline* all of the complimentary or positive words and phrases (e.g., "patient").
- They should *circle* all of the uncomplimentary or negative words and phrases (e.g., "pain in the neck").
- They should *ignore* all of the neutral words and phrases (e.g., "people").

Give the teams a few minutes to work. When they're finished, ask each team to give a total count for each category. Chances are pretty good that you'll have a majority of negative words and phrases. Take a minute or two to review some of the words and phrases that were given.

Ask: **Why do you suppose there are so many negative words and phrases on these sheets? Are things really that bad at home?** Allow time for a couple of group members to respond.

Then say: *As unpopular as it may sound, today we're going to talk about what it means to honor our parents.*

[NOTE: If, in the previous activity, the positive comments outnumbered the negative ones, you might want to check the Kool-Aid to see if it had too much sugar. If not, congratulate your group members on their mature insights. Then continue with the rest of the session. There's still plenty your group members can learn from this study.]

Pressure Pounds

(Needed: Paper, pencils)

Ask: **What do you suppose it feels like to be a parent?** (Some group members may say it probably feels good not having anybody tell you what to do. Others may say it probably feels good to be able to boss around your kids. Still others may say that being a parent is tough because of the pressure of being responsible for your kids.)

Say: **I'm sure you've heard your mom or dad say it a thousand times, but the truth is that being a parent isn't easy. A lot of the responsibilities your mom or dad live with must feel like weights they carry around with them all day. Let's take a look at some of the loads parents carry and see how yours are doing.**

The purpose of this activity is to give group members an understanding of the wide range of everyday things that can put pressure on parents. Perhaps it might also help group members develop an appreciation for what their parents go through as parents.

Give each group member a piece of paper and a pencil to calculate the "responsibility load" of one of their parents. Instruct group members to think of the parent they have the most difficulty getting along with. Then, as you read the following list, have them add up the "pressure pounds" their parents are experiencing.

- **For each kid in your family, add 10 pounds.**
- **For each kid that is a teenager or preschooler, add 5 pounds.**
- **If your parent is working at a new job—let's say less than a year—add 15 pounds.**
- **If your parent is unemployed (this doesn't count homemakers), add 25 pounds.**
- **If your parent recently had a loved one die, add 10 pounds.**
- **If your parent is divorced, separated, or widowed, add 50 pounds.**

OPTIONS

EXTRA ACTION

LARGE GROUP

FELLOWSHIP & WORSHIP

MOSTLY GUYS

EXTRA FUN

URBAN

SIXTH GRADE

- **If your parent's favorite team is on a losing streak, add 1 pound.**
- **If your parent travels a lot, add 10 pounds.**
- **If both of your parents work, add 15 pounds.**
- **If your parent has an illness, disease, or disability, add 20 pounds.**
- **If your parent is going to school or taking classes, add 10 pounds.**
- **If your parent argues or fights a lot with his or her spouse, add 15 pounds.**
- **If your parent works a lot of overtime or weekends, add 10 pounds.**
- **If the TV remote control is lost or broken, add 1 pound.**
- **If your parent often talks about being "broke" or having financial problems, add 15 pounds.**
- **If your parent talks about starting to feel old, add 10 pounds.**
- **If your parent has no time for regular exercise, add 10 pounds.**
- **If there's a pet in your household, add 2 pounds.**
- **If your parent does more than one job at church, add 10 pounds.**
- **If there's tension between your parent and you or your siblings, add 5 pounds.**
- **If your parent does most of the housework, add 5 pounds.**
- **If your parent does most of the cooking, add 5 pounds.**
- **If your parent is paying for college tuition, add 5 pounds.**

Feel free to add a couple of your own statements to the list.

Afterward, have group members total up their parents' "pressure pounds." Point out: **Some of your parents are living with some awfully big loads to carry. We don't often think about the pressures parents face. But those pressures are real—and they can have a serious effect on parents' lives.**

Be careful not to allow this to degenerate into a contest to see whose parent is the most frazzled. The reality here is that the parent with the most "pressure pounds" is *not* the winner! Stress isn't something to celebrate. Be sensitive to group members who are acknowledging major stresses in their parents' lives. These stresses often affect the kids as well.

STEP 3

Yes, Your Honor

(Needed: Chalkboard and chalk or newsprint and marker)

Say: **When we look at all the pressures our parents live with each day, it's a little easier to understand why God makes such a big deal about honoring our parents. In a number of places in the Bible, God makes His thoughts on the subject perfectly clear.**

Have someone read aloud Exodus 20:12. Then ask: **What does it mean to honor someone?** (It means to give that person respect, to do things for him or her, to show the person that he or she is valuable, to recognize his or her accomplishments or the things he or she does well, to put his or her interests ahead of ours, etc.)

Say: **When you guys were a little younger, honoring your parents was probably pretty easy. Your refrigerator doors were probably full of little signs and pictures you made at school that told your mom how great she was or that told your dad how much you loved him.**

Why does it sometimes seem harder to honor our parents as we get older? (As we get older, we begin to recognize some of their faults. It's also easier for us to be honest about our feelings when we're older.)

Then say: **By the same token, as we get older, the things we do to show others that we value and honor them are more mature and perhaps more meaningful.**

What are some things you can do to honor your parents now that you couldn't do when you were six or seven? (Talk to them about things that matter; get their advice on tough decisions you have to make; compliment them on things they do well; understand some of their pressures and encourage them or pray for them; etc.)

Say: **We'll come back to some of these practical ideas for honoring your mom or dad in a minute. But I thought you might be interested in knowing that honoring each other is a rule for the whole family, and not just kids. Turn in your Bibles to Colossians 3.**

Have someone read aloud verses 18-21. Then ask: **How can a wife honor her husband?** (By supporting his decisions, encouraging him, respecting his opinions, praising him, etc.) Try to avoid a long discussion on the true definition of "submission" here. But at least point out that submission doesn't mean being a "doormat" to be walked on.

OPTIONS

EXTRA ACTION

HEARD IT ALL BEFORE

LITTLE BIBLE BACKGROUND

MOSTLY GIRLS

MOSTLY GUYS

MEDIA

URBAN

How can a husband show honor to his wife? (By providing for her, encouraging her, respecting her opinions, praising her, etc.)

Say: **We've already talked about how kids need to honor their parents. But take a look at the last verse in the passage that was just read. How does a parent honor his or her children?** (By not embittering or discouraging them.)

Talk briefly about what it means to embitter or exasperate someone. Ask group members to name some things kids experience at home that are discouraging.

Say: **OK, so we all have a responsibility to honor one another. But how do we do that? In the verses just before the ones we read are some specific instructions for husbands, wives, parents, and even kids on how to honor one another. Let's take a look.**

Have someone read aloud Colossians 3:12-17. As the person reads, have the rest of the group members call out words in the passage that describe how we should treat our family members. Write the words on the board as they're named. Your list should include the following words: compassion, kindness, humility, gentleness, patience, forgive, love, peace, and thankful.

Ask: **If you and your family used these kinds of attitudes toward each other, what differences would it make in your family?** Get responses from as many group members as possible.

Then say: **Let's wrap up our discussion by looking at a passage from a letter Paul wrote to his friends in the city of Philippi. The passage is found in Philippians 2.**

Have someone read aloud verses 2-5. Comment briefly on the fact that these are the attitudes Jesus had and asks us to follow.

STEP
4

Putting It into Practice

(Needed: Seven signs from Step 1, marker, pencils, masking tape)

Say: **We've seen that honoring members of our families—
especially our parents—is something God commands us to
do. So, now what? What do we do with this information? Let's
try another exercise with the letter signs we used earlier.**

Turn over the seven signs you used in Step 1. As before, write one
of the letters of the word "P-A-R-E-N-T-S" on each sign. Then instruct
group members to write on the signs ideas for how they could show
honor to their parents. (Ideally, the ideas should start with the seven
letters on the signs; but, be flexible.)

Give group members a few minutes to work. When they're finished,
read aloud their suggestions. Use the following ideas to supplement
group members' responses.

P—Pick up after myself when I make a mess; pray for my parents.
A—Ask for permission before I do something; always call if I'm
   going to get in later than I'm supposed to.
R—Respect my parents' privacy; return things to where I found
   them.
E—Explain to my parents how much they mean to me; extend
   courtesy and politeness to them.
N—Never talk negatively about my parents to my friends; notice
   when my parents do something nice for me and thank them
   for it.
T—Talk to my parents nicely, rather than whining or yelling at them;
   take out the garbage, without having to be told to.
S—Say "I love you" more often; send flowers to my mom for no
   special reason.

This part of the exercise probably will be tougher for your group
members than the first part (in Step 1) was. Be prepared to help them
get started, but make sure to leave a lot of room for them to come
up with their own suggestions. Those are the ideas they'll feel some
ownership of.

Briefly review the list with your group members. Comment on a few
of the suggestions to help group members understand that honoring
parents involves more than just how we feel about them—it means
putting some things into action so parents actually feel honored.

OPTIONS

HEARD IT ALL BEFORE

LITTLE BIBLE BACKGROUND

MEDIA

SHORT MEETING TIME

JR. HIGH / HIGH SCHOOL COMBINED

SIXTH GRADE

MVP—My Valuable Parent

(Needed: Paper, pencils, copies of Repro Resource 3, markers)

O P T I O N S

Distribute paper and pencils. Then say: **Let's think of some practical ways we can start to honor our parents this week. Choose one action from the lists we've made on these sheets to work on this week. Try to choose an action that doesn't come naturally to you—one that would really show your parents that you're making an effort to honor them. Write the action on your piece of paper. Then make a commitment to follow through on that action throughout the week. Keep your piece of paper handy throughout the week as a reminder of your commitment.**

Distribute copies of "MVP Award" (Repro Resource 3) and markers. Explain to your group members that this award will serve as kind of a "primer" for their parents, to let them know that their kids are thinking about them and are taking specific actions to honor them. (Without this "primer," parents may be suspicious of their kids' motives—or they may faint dead away when their kids try to show them honor!)

Give group members a few minutes to work on their awards. They should write in their parents' names, as well as what their parents are being honored for ("For driving me to and from soccer practice every day and for never missing a game"). If there's time, group members might also decorate their awards accordingly.

Encourage group members to leave their awards in places where their parents will find them, rather than making a big deal out of the presentations.

Close the session in prayer, asking God to help your group members follow through on their commitments to honor their parents.

NOTES

THE "MOST VALUABLE PARENT(S)" TITLE

is awarded to

_____

This award is given in appreciation for

_____

_____

_____

_____

_____

NOTES

STEP 2

For this activity you'll need several cardboard boxes and large, heavy books. Have group members form pairs. Give each pair a cardboard box. (If possible, make sure all of the boxes are approximately the same size.) One at a time, have each pair bring its cardboard box to the front of the room, turn it upside down, and begin stacking books on top of it. The pair that stacks the most books on its box before the box collapses is the winner. Afterward, draw an analogy between the weight that was supported by the boxes and the "pressure pounds" that weigh on parents.

STEP 3

Have group members form pairs. Instruct each pair to come up with a brief roleplay demonstrating what might happen if a teenager tried to communicate with his or her parents in the same way he or she communicated with them when he or she was a kid (six or seven years old). For instance, one pair might have the teenager throwing a tantrum if he or she doesn't get his or her way. Another pair might have the teenager whining and talking like a baby. Another pair might have the teenager pouting after being reprimanded. Another pair might have the teenager clinging to his or her parent when he or she is being dropped off at school. One person in each pair will play the teenager; the other person will play the parent. Give the pairs a few minutes to prepare; then have them present their roleplays. Afterward, point out that we have the opportunity to communicate with our parents on a more adult level now. We also have the opportunities to honor them in ways we couldn't when we were six or seven.

STEP 1

Rather than having group members form teams to evaluate the words and phrases on the "P-A-R-E-N-T-S" sheet, evaluate them as a group. You will read each word or phrase aloud. If group members think it's complimentary, they should stand; if they think it's negative, they should sit on the floor; if they think it's neutral, they should squat—halfway between standing and sitting. Keep tally on the board of how many words or phrases are positive, how many are negative, and how many are neutral.

STEP 5

Take advantage of the size of your group by giving group members an opportunity to respond personally to each other's ideas. After each person chooses an action to honor his or her parents, have him or her share the idea with the rest of the group. Then have each of the rest of the group members offer a comment or piece of advice to the person concerning his or her idea. For instance, let's say someone chose "Explain to my parents how much they mean to me" as his or her action. One of the other group members might say, "Make sure not to give them the impression that you're being nice to them because you want something from them." Someone else might say, "Don't go overboard with your comments—just be honest." Someone else might say, "I tried that with my parents and this is what happened ..."

STEP 1

With a large group, you'll want to avoid having all of your group members crowded around the sheets at the same time trying to write. Instead, explain the activity while your group members are still in their seats and give them a few minutes to brainstorm what they'll write. Then have them line up single-file next to the first sheet. Give each person approximately 15 seconds to write his or her ideas on each sheet. After about 15 seconds he or she will move on to the next sheet. If you keep the line moving, you should be able to finish the activity in 5-10 minutes.

Step 2

As you read the list, write each item on the board. Then, after group members have totaled up their parents' "pressure pounds," have them form groups of four. In their groups they should discuss the following questions:

• **Which of these items on the board would you say is most stressful for your parent?**

• **Which of these items is most stressful for you?**

• **Which of these items is hardest for you to understand? In other words, which do you think shouldn't bother your parent as much as it does?**

• **Which of these items could you do something about?**

STEP 3

Many churches emphasize passages like Ephesians 6:1-3 and Colossians 3:20, which focus on children's responsibility to honor and obey their parents. Many churches also tend to downplay passages like Ephesians 6:4 and Colossians 3:21, which focus on parents' responsibility to their kids. So it might be an interesting change of pace for your group members to focus on Ephesians 6:4 and Colossians 3:21. Ask the following questions:

• **Do your parents ever "exasperate" you? If so, how do they do it?**

• **Do your parents ever make you feel bitter or discouraged? If so, how do they do it?**

• **How does the way your parents treat you affect the way you treat them?**

• **How do you wish your parents would treat you?**

• **How could you let your parents know how you feel?**

STEP 4

Because so little information is given about Jesus' youth, your group members who've "heard it all before" may think of Jesus only as a baby or as a man. Focus group members' attention on one of the rare Bible passages that talks about Jesus' childhood: Luke 2:41-52. Say: **It seems like Jesus may not have honored His parents in this passage. After all, they were worried because they couldn't find Him. And when they did find Him, He talked about having to be in His "Father's house." What do you think of His actions?** If no one mentions it, point out that God was Jesus' Father, and took priority in Jesus' life. Jesus wasn't being disrespectful to Mary and Joseph. He was just informing them of His priorities. Note that verse 51 says, "Then [Jesus] went down to Nazareth with [Mary and Joseph] and was obedient to them." This is the example of Jesus that we are to follow.

STEP 3

Some of your group members who aren't familiar with the commands of Scripture may reason, "Since my parents don't obey the command not to discourage or exasperate their kids, I don't have to obey the command to honor them." Point out that Colossians 3:21 and Exodus 20:12 are not "If … then" statements. We do not honor our parents only if they hold up their end of the bargain first. We have to honor them, no matter what. Encourage several group members to offer their opinions of this "honor no matter what" situation.

STEP 4

If your group members come from non-Christian households, they may be experiencing more severe parent problems than their peers who come from Christian households. Help group members see that the Bible covers all kinds of parent conflicts—Jacob deceiving and lying to his father Isaac (Genesis 27), Saul throwing a spear in anger at his son Jonathan (I Samuel 20), and the prodigal son taking his inheritance and leaving home (Luke 15), to name a few. Suggest that the fact that so many "modern-day" kinds of situations are covered in the Bible makes Scripture relevant for parent-teen relationships today.

STEP 2

Have someone read aloud Matthew 11:28. ("Come to me, all you who are weary and burdened, and I will give you rest.") Then, as a group, brainstorm a list of ways God can remove burdens from our parents' lives and give them rest. Write group members' suggestions on the board as they are named. If no one mentions it, suggest that one of the ways to remove burdens from parents' lives is to have their children honor and obey them. Point out to your group members that they could be part of God's plan to bring rest to their parents. Have a moment of silent prayer, thanking God for caring enough about us to give us rest when we're "weary and burdened."

STEP 5

Have group members pair up with someone they know fairly well. If not all of your group members know someone well in your group, have the partners take a few minutes to share some things about their parents with each other. Afterward each person should name one thing about his or her partner's parents that sounds good. (For instance, someone might say, "It's really cool that you and your dad both like baseball. I have a hard time getting my dad to watch a game with me.") Hearing their peers say good things about their parents may help your group members begin to see their parents in a different light.

STEP 3

Distribute paper and pencils. While you read aloud Colossians 3:12-17, each girl should make her own list of the words in the passage that describe how we should treat our family members. After you read aloud Philippians 2:2-5, group members should add at least one item or phrase from that passage to their lists.

STEP 5

Have your group members review the ideas they wrote on the "P-A-R-E-N-T-S" signs in Step 4. Instruct them to find any ideas that could be adapted as a group activity. Have your group members brainstorm together ways they can honor the parents of all the girls in the group. For instance, your group members might write a "round-robin" letter of appreciation or they might prepare and serve (or deliver) meals for the parents. When your group members have decided on a way to honor the parents as a group, help them do the planning to put their idea into action.

STEP 2

If some of your guys are into weightlifting, they may be more attuned to the "pressure pounds" analogy. Ask: **How much weight can you benchpress? How much can you squat? How much can you deadlift?** After you've gone through the "pressure pounds" list, ask: How much weight do you think you could carry around all day? Get responses from as many group members as possible. Then ask: **What kinds of effects do you think these "pressure pounds" have on parents who have to "carry them around" all day?** Encourage several group members to respond.

STEP 3

After you discuss Exodus 20:12, use the following questions to guide your discussion. (Be sensitive to kids whose parents are divorced, widowed, or unmarried as you discuss these questions.)

• **Is it easier for you to honor your mother or your father? Why?**

• **Is it easier for you to honor your parents verbally—by what you say—or physically—by what you do?**

• **Do your friends ever pressure you not to honor your parents? If so, how do they do that?**

• **Do you feel like your parents honor you? Do they treat you like a man or like a little kid? Explain.**

• **How does the way your parents treat you affect the way you treat them?**

STEP 1

Say: **Science and technology have perfected many procedures, industries, and gadgets. So what if they turned their attention to creating the perfect robotic parents? What would be the result? What kind of design and features would these parents have?** Have group members form teams of two or three. Distribute large sheets of paper, pencils, and markers to each team. Instruct the teams to come up with designs for the perfect robotic parents. For instance, the perfect robotic father might have a specially designed arm to throw footballs with perfect spirals and baseballs with incredible curves. He might also have an automatic teller machine on his hip to dispense money whenever his kids need it. The perfect robotic mother might have eyes all around her head so she can see everything her kids do. She might also have vacuums on the bottom of her feet so she can clean the floor while walking. When the teams are finished, have them explain their creations. Then point out that because our parents aren't perfect, we sometimes have trouble honoring them.

STEP 2

Ask for a couple volunteers to participate in a contest of strength and speed. Explain that the contestants will be competing to see who can pull people on a sheet of plastic from one part of the room to another in the shortest amount of time. Choose one member of the group to be pulled on the plastic for the first round. Time each contestant and write his or her results on the board. For the second round, add another person on the plastic to be pulled. Compare group members' times from the first round to the second round. Continue adding another person each round until your contestants are unable to pull. Then discuss how carrying around a lot of "pressure pounds" can affect a parent's "performance."

STEP 3

Record clips from several TV sitcoms featuring families. Among the shows you might record are reruns of *The Brady Bunch, Leave It to Beaver, My Three Sons, The Cosby Show, Roseanne, Home Improvement, Family Matters,* and *The Simpsons.* Try to record scenes that show kids interacting with their parents. Play back the clips for your group members and discuss which ones show kids honoring their parents and which ones show kids dishonoring their parents. Then discuss whether the media has any influence on the way we act toward our parents.

STEP 4

Bring in a video camera or tape recorder. Have your group members think of an everyday, normal thing they might say to their parents. (For instance, "Where's my sweater?") Record each group member saying his or her statement three different ways. First, he or she should say it happily or cheerfully. Second, he or she should say it angrily. Third, he or she should say it whiningly. Play back the recording for your group and point out that how we say something is as important as what we say.

STEP 1

Rather than taking the time to have group members come up to the signs and write, play a quick game. Have group members sit in a circle. You will give them a letter, and they will have to come up with a word or phrase (beginning with that letter) that describes something about parents. Group members will have five seconds to come up with a word or phrase. If a person fails to do so, he or she is out. Once everyone has had a turn, call out another letter, and repeat the process. (The letters you will use are P, A, R, E, N, T, S.) Continue the game until only one person remains. Afterward, discuss how many of the words and phrases named were positive, how many were negative, and how many were neutral.

STEP 4

If you didn't use the signs in Step 1, you'll need to make some adjustments in this step. Write the letters P, A, R, E, N, T, S on small slips of paper and put them in a container. Have group members draw a slip of paper and then come up with an idea—that begins with the letter they drew—of how to show honor to their parents. Give group members a few minutes to work; then have everyone share his or her response with the rest of the group. Write the responses on the board as they are named. Then have group members choose one idea from the board to work on with their parents.

STEP 2

Here are some additional "pressure pound" scenarios that may be reality for urban parents:

- **For each child selling or using drugs, add 20 pounds.**
- **If your parents are worried about your safety in the community, add 15 pounds.**
- **If any of your immediate family members** (brother, sister, parent) **were killed by gunfire or died unsuspectingly in the last year, add 40 pounds.**
- **If your parents have an unmarried daughter who is pregnant or an unmarried son who is a father, add 10 pounds.**

STEP 3

Some of your group members may have grown up in single-parent homes. One of their parents may have died when the child was young or ran from parental responsibility. As a result, some of your group members may not even know one of their parents. If that's the case with your group, have your young people brainstorm together ways to honor a parent they've never known. After considering some things that could be done, let them decide what they can do to improve their understanding and/or relationship with this missing parent. Help group members recognize that knowledge about a missing parent can lead to a better understanding of themselves.

STEP 4

To make the "P-A-R-E-N-T-S" activity a little more focused, separate your junior highers and high schoolers into two groups. Instruct your junior highers to focus on activities that have to do with curfew and jobs around the house. In other words, how can they honor their parents through their curfew and chores? (As much as possible, their suggestions should start with P, A, R, E, N, T, and S.) Use the following suggestions to supplement your junior highers' ideas: "Pick up the empty chip bags and soda cans when I finish eating in front of the TV"; "Always call home if I'm going to be late"; etc. Instruct your high schoolers to focus on activities that have to do with driving and friends. In other words, how can they honor their parents through their use of the car and by the company they keep? Use the following suggestions to supplement your high schoolers' ideas: "Put gas in the car when I'm finished with it"; "Turn around and walk out if I discover that people are drinking or taking drugs at a party I'm attending"; etc.

STEP 5

After your junior highers have chosen an action with which to show honor to their parents, have them share their ideas with the group. Then encourage your high schoolers to respond to those ideas—perhaps giving advice on what to do and what not to do in implementing the strategy, or relating experiences of when they tried similar actions with their parents. High schoolers should respond in a spirit of helpfulness; they should not belittle or make fun of your junior highers' ideas. The idea is to develop a "mentoring" relationship between your high schoolers and your junior highers.

STEP 2

Your sixth graders may not have a complete sense of the responsibility load of their parents—especially when it comes to the stresses of their parents' careers. So instead of going through the entire list of "pressure pound" scenarios with your group members, choose ten or so scenarios from the list that you think would be the most relevant (and recognizable) to them.

STEP 4

To stimulate your group members' thinking, brainstorm as a group a few general ways to show honor to parents. Then have your kids form seven teams. Assign each team one of the "P-A-R-E-N-T-S" signs. Instruct each team to come up with at least two ideas for honoring parents that begin with its assigned letter. If you don't have enough kids for seven teams, give two or more letters to each team.

Give the teams a few minutes to work; then have them share their ideas. After each team has shared, ask for additional ideas from the rest of the group.

DATE USED:

Approx. Time

STEP 1: *"P" Is for Parents* _____
- ❏ Small Group
- ❏ Large Group
- ❏ Extra Fun
- ❏ Short Meeting Time

Things needed:

STEP 2: *Pressure Pounds* _____
- ❏ Extra Action
- ❏ Large Group
- ❏ Fellowship & Worship
- ❏ Mostly Guys
- ❏ Extra Fun
- ❏ Urban
- ❏ Sixth Grade

Things needed:

STEP 3: *Yes, Your Honor* _____
- ❏ Extra Action
- ❏ Heard It All Before
- ❏ Little Bible Background
- ❏ Mostly Girls
- ❏ Mostly Guys
- ❏ Media
- ❏ Urban

Things needed:

STEP 4: *Putting It into Practice* _____
- ❏ Heard It All Before
- ❏ Little Bible Background
- ❏ Media
- ❏ Short Meeting Time
- ❏ Combined Junior High/High School
- ❏ Sixth Grade

Things needed:

STEP 5: *MVP—My Valuable Parent* _____
- ❏ Small Group
- ❏ Fellowship & Worship
- ❏ Mostly Girls
- ❏ Combined Junior High/High School

Things needed:

The Great Breakaway

YOUR GOALS FOR THIS SESSION:

Choose one or more

☐ To help kids recognize that they can help make their transition from childhood to adulthood easier by participating cooperatively in the process.

☐ To help kids understand that it's OK to want to establish an identity that is separate from their parents.

☐ To help kids decide to take on one specific responsibility in their families to indicate their willingness to act responsibly and earn a right of adulthood.

☐ Other:_____

_____

Your Bible Base:

Luke 15:11-20

STEP 1

Trading Places

(Needed: Two pieces of lumber)

Before the session, set out two 2" × 4" pieces of lumber. Each board should be between four and five feet long. Make sure there is enough room between the boards to let people move freely.

Ask for four volunteers—two pairs—to participate in a contest. Have the members of each pair stand on one of the boards, facing each other. The object of the game is for the members of each pair to change places on the board without falling off or touching the floor. The first pair to successfully change places wins.

To stir up your group members' imaginations and add some excitement and humor to the contest, you could have them pretend that the floor is shark-infested waters, an alligator pit, or a toxic-waste dump.

Give as many kids as possible a chance to compete, letting the winning pair stay on and having challengers try to outdo them. After all the challenges have been made, declare a winner.

Then ask: *What was the secret of success in this activity?* (Helping each other, cooperating, talking to each other, going slowly, etc.)

Say: **You guys are at a time in your lives when your position in the family is about to start changing. You're moving toward being an adult with all the rights, privileges, and responsibilities that come with growing up. It's a big change—and an important one. One of the things that needs to happen as you become an adult is that your relationship with your parents has to change. It's sort of like what you saw happening on the boards a few minutes ago.**

Point out that, like changing positions on the board, changing your relationship with your parents involves helping one another, talking to one another, cooperating with each other, and going slowly.

Growing Up in a Hurry

(Needed: Copies of Repro Resource 4, pencils)

Ask: **How many of you have ever wished you were grown up—that one day you would just suddenly become an adult and never be treated like a kid again?** Probably most of your group members have wished this at one time or another. Ask a couple of volunteers to explain their reasons for wanting to be an adult.

Distribute copies of "The Adventures of the Suddenly Grown Up" (Repro Resource 4) and pencils. Give group members a few minutes to read the story.

Then say: **Think about what Stan's life will be like now that he's grown up. What kinds of things will he be able to do now that he wasn't able to do before? What kinds of problems will he face now that he didn't have to face before?**

Have group members write or draw their ideas at the bottom of the sheet. Give them a few minutes to work; then have them share their responses with the rest of the group.

Group members might mention that, for Stan, growing up would mean being able to drive, being able to move out of his parents' house, being able to earn a lot of money, etc. They also might mention that growing up would mean more responsibility, having to get a job, having to pay bills, having to act "mature," etc.

Point out that becoming an adult is a process; it's a transition that takes time—perhaps as long as five or six years. It takes so much time because there's a lot of preparation that needs to be done. There are things we need to know, situations we have to experience, and wisdom we have to gain before we're ready for adulthood.

The Prodigal

OPTIONS

EXTRA ACTION

LARGE GROUP

HEARD IT ALL BEFORE

LITTLE BIBLE BACKGROUND

SIXTH GRADE

Say: **Jesus tells a story of a young man who decided to grow up very quickly. In the process, the young man made a lot of really dumb moves—and a couple of pretty smart moves. Jesus' story is found in Luke 15. I'll summarize it for you.**

Listen carefully as I read. Whenever you hear someone in the story making a bad move, shout "bad move" as loudly as you can. Whenever you hear someone in the story making a good move, shout out "good move."

A man had two sons (good move). **One day the younger son said to his father, "I want my share of your estate now instead of when you die"** (bad move). **His father agreed to divide his wealth between his sons** (bad move). **A few days later, the younger son packed all of his belongings and took a trip to a distant land** (bad move). **There he wasted all of his money on parties and prostitutes** (bad move).

About the time his money was gone, a great famine swept over all the land, and the younger son began to starve (bad move). **He persuaded a local farmer to hire him to feed his pigs** (good move). **The boy became so hungry that even the pods he was feeding the swine looked good to him. No one gave him anything.**

When he finally came to his senses (good move), **he said to himself, "At home, even the hired men have more than enough food to eat, and here I am dying of hunger! I will go home** (good move) **to my father and say, 'Father I have sinned against both heaven and you and I am no longer worthy to be called your son. Please take me on as a hired man'** (good move)." **So he returned home to his father** (good move). **While he was still a long distance away, his father saw him coming and was filled with loving pity** (good move). **The father ran and embraced his son and kissed him** (good move).

Have group members form teams of three or four. Distribute paper and pencils to each team. Instruct the teams to turn in their Bibles to the story you just summarized from Luke 15:11-20. Have them re-read the story. Every time they identify a "bad move" on the part of the younger son, they should write down a better choice he could have made. (For instance, rather than squandering his money on parties and prostitutes, he could have invested it, bought his own house with it, used it to start a business, etc.) Then the teams should describe how the Luke 15 story might have ended differently if the younger son had made better choices.

Give the teams a few minutes to work. When everyone is finished, have each team share its ideas.

Grown-Up Concentration

(Needed: Copies of Repro Resource 5, copies of Repro Resource 6)

Before the session, you'll need to cut apart copies of "Concentration Cards" (Repro Resource 5). You'll then need to attach those cards to copies of "Concentration" (Repro Resource 6). To do this, cut out the slots (indicated by dotted lines) on Repro Resource 6 and slide the "concentration cards" facedown into the slots to cover the rebus on Repro Resource 6.

Have group members form pairs. Distribute a covered copy of Repro Resource 6 to each pair. Explain that the facedown slips of paper are "privilege and responsibility" cards. These cards list a variety of benefits of growing up, as well as some responsibilities that come with being an adult. Point out that each privilege card has a corresponding responsibility card. For example, one privilege of growing up is having a driver's license and driving a car. The corresponding responsibility is to know and follow the rules of the road.

Explain that the members of each pair will be finding and matching these cards in a contest similar to the game "Concentration."

Players will take turns turning over two cards at a time. If a player finds a matching "privilege and responsibility" pair, he or she gets to remove those two cards and guess the rebus message underneath. If the player does not find a matching pair, he or she turns the cards back over and forfeits his or her turn. [NOTE: For easier identification, the privilege and responsibility cards are numbered. All group members have to do is match numbers on the cards.]

As the matching pairs are found, more and more of the rebus will be visible, making it easier for players to guess the message. The rebus message is "I'm not a kid anymore."

After all of the pairs have finished the exercise, say: **For every privilege associated with being an adult, there are some tough responsibilities that go along with it. Growing up is a** wonderful, exciting experience—but it also involves taking responsibility for our choices and earning the right to have the benefits or privileges that we look forward to.

Shock Their Socks Off!

Say: **Think of a responsibility you could take this week to show your parents that you're really serious about growing up. What could you do in your home or family that your parents wouldn't expect you to do in their wildest dreams— something so mature and grown up that it would shock their socks off?**

Find a partner—perhaps the person you played "Concentration" with earlier. Tell your partner what it is you plan to do this week to show your family that you really are serious about growing up. Then, if possible, check on your partner once or twice during the week to see how well he or she is doing.

Give the partners a minute or two to think of some ideas. If time permits, ask a couple of volunteers to share their ideas.

Point out to your group members that the surprise of their actions might be so great for their parents that their parents won't know how to respond right away. Emphasize that the real joy in this exercise is knowing that they are doing the mature thing, not that they are able to manipulate their parents into some new form of submission.

Close the session in prayer, asking God to help your group members in their continuing process of becoming a grown-up.

OPTIONS

HEARD IT ALL BEFORE

LITTLE BIBLE BACKGROUND

FELLOWSHIP & WORSHIP

EXTRA FUN

SIXTH GRADE

NOTES

The Adventures of the
SUDDENLY GROWN UP

Stan's fourteenth birthday party was OK—but it wasn't exactly what he wanted. There was plenty of cake and ice cream, and all his friends and family were there. But Stan wanted more.

When Paul, Stan's brother, turned seventeen, he and his friends were allowed to go to the drive-in (for a double feature)—and then, *afterward*, they went bowling for a couple hours. Paul didn't get in until *after 3:00 in the morning!*

Stan wanted to do the same kind of thing for his birthday. But his parents wouldn't let him. They said he was still too young to be staying out that late. Instead, Stan was allowed to rent a couple videos and have three of his friends stay overnight. Big deal.

When it came time for Stan to blow out the candles on his birthday cake and make a wish, he knew exactly what he'd wish for.

I wish I were a grown-up, Stan thought to himself as he blew out the candles. Ten seconds later, as his friends and family looked on in amazement, Stan's wish came true. He suddenly became a grown-up.

NOTES

Concentration Cards

1

As an adult, I have the privilege of having a driver's license and driving a car.

1

As an adult, I am responsible to know the rules of the road and live by them.

2

As an adult, I have the privilege of deciding what I want to eat and when to eat it.

2

As an adult, I have the responsibility of my health, and perhaps my family's.

3

As an adult, I have the privilege of deciding what to watch on TV and which movies to see.

3

As an adult, I am responsible to choose carefully the kinds of media messages I allow into my mind.

4

As an adult, I have the privilege of choosing what time I go to bed and how late I sleep.

4

As an adult, I am responsible to make good decisions about how I use my time.

5

As an adult, I have the privilege of picking my own friends and choosing whom to hang around with.

5

As an adult, I am responsible to know that the friends I pick will affect my life.

6

As an adult, I have the privilege of making my own decisions about drugs and alcohol.

6

As an adult, I am responsible for the harm I do myself or others while drinking or on drugs.

7

As an adult in college, I have the privilege of deciding whether or not to go to class.

7

As an adult in college, I am responsible for my grades and the money I spend on my classes.

8

As an adult, I have the privilege of earning as much money as I can.

8

As an adult, I am responsible to use my money wisely for bills, tithes, living expenses, etc.

Concentration

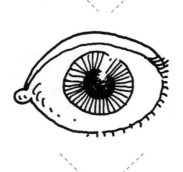 

A

Hi, Dad!

A+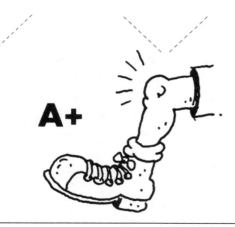

M+

STEP 1

Rather than having group members trade places on the boards, try a more active approach. Ask for three volunteers at a time to participate in a race. Two of the volunteers will be working as a team; the other will be working solo. Set down two sheets of newspaper. Explain that your contestants will be competing to see who can get from one end of the room to the other first—on the newspaper— without touching the floor or tearing the paper. The solo person probably will have to shuffle, scoot, and gyrate to move. The two contestants who are working together should decide which one will stand on the paper. That person may not touch the floor at all. However, his or her partner may. These two may move by having the person on the paper jump forward while his or her partner pulls the newspaper under him or her. If the two establish a regular pace, they should have an advantage over the person working solo.

Afterward, draw an analogy to the process of becoming an adult: It's easier when you work in cooperation with your parents, rather than trying to do it alone.

STEP 3

Ask for two volunteers to roleplay the story of the prodigal son while you read it. Assign one person to be the son and the other to be the father. The actors will speak and act according to what you read. You can have some fun with the fact that your actors won't know what they're supposed to do next (especially when you read, "He ran to his son, threw his arms around him and kissed him").

Rather than having group members form teams to discuss the story, replay the roleplay again. This time, however, when group members call out "bad move," the actors should freeze. Group members will then call out suggestions for better choices the characters could make. The actors must then say and do what the other group members suggest.

STEP 1

Have your group members line up single-file. If possible, put the two smallest people in the group at each end of the line. Each should be standing on a newspaper or some other object so that he or she is not "directly" touching the floor. Explain that the two people at the end of the line must trade places—without touching the floor and without moving the newspaper or object they're standing on. Group members will work together in accomplishing this goal. However, the other group members may not move from their single-file positions.

There are several ways to do this. The other group members may get down on all fours (remaining in their single-file positions) and allow the two end people to walk across them. The other group members may pick up the end people and "pass" them across. Or the people on the end could "jump" across, landing on the other group members' feet so that they don't touch the ground.

Afterward, discuss how the cooperation involved in the activity is similar to the cooperation needed between parents and kids as the kids become adults.

STEP 4

Rather than having kids pair up to play the "Concentration" game, play it as a group. However, you may want to "raise the stakes" a little. Each time a group member fails to match two cards, have him or her perform some kind of stunt in front of the group. Here are some ideas for stunts you might use:

• Do ten pushups while reciting the alphabet backwards.

• Whistle the theme to *Gilligan's Island* while standing on one leg.

• Lead the group in a cheer.

• Run around the room backward while you call out the names of everyone in the group.

• Tell your favorite (clean) joke in front of the group.

STEP 1

Have group members form teams of five. If possible, make sure that all teams have both big, strong people and small, light-weight people on them. Set up an obstacle course or racetrack in your meeting area. Explain that the teams will be competing to see which team can finish the course first—while carrying one of its members. Have each team choose one member (probably the smallest person on the team) to carry. The other teammates may hold the person over their heads, on their shoulders, by his or her arms and legs, or any other way they want. The only stipulation is that the person being carried may not touch the ground.

Have the teams line up behind a start/finish line. When you say go, they will run around the course as quickly as possible. If a team allows the person being carried to touch the floor at all, it must start over. Obviously, the more teams you have, the crazier the competition will be.

Afterward, point out that successfully navigating the course required cooperation. In the same way, successfully navigating the transition between childhood and adulthood requires cooperation between parents and kids.

STEP 3

To get group members more personally involved in this study, have them form teams of four. Distribute index cards and pencils to each team. Instruct each team to read Luke 15:11-20 and come up with a list of the top four "bad moves" made by the younger son in the story. Then have the teams list four better choices the younger son could have made, and describe how the story might have turned out differently if he'd made the better choices. Give the teams a few minutes to work. When they're finished, have each one share its responses with the rest of the group.

STEP 3

If your group members are overly familiar with the story of the prodigal son, use the story of Jacob and Isaac in Genesis 27 as your Bible study text. Have volunteers take turns reading aloud verses 1-41. Then, as a group, list the "bad moves" Jacob made in obtaining the blessing from his father. Afterward, go back through the story and have group members offer suggestions for better choices Jacob could have made to get Isaac's blessing—and how the story might have turned out differently if Jacob had made better choices.

Ask: **How do kids today deceive their parents to get what they want? How might these deceptions affect a person's relationship with his or her parents?**

STEP 5

Kids who've "heard it all before" may be able to recite from memory several *general* things they can do for their parents—"help out around the house," "tell my parents how much I appreciate them," "honor and obey my parents," etc.

To get beyond this nonspecific attitude, list on the board several specific things kids can do to demonstrate maturity to their parents. Have group members explain which ideas would and which ideas wouldn't work with their parents and why. Here are some ideas you might use:

• Offering to babysit your little brother or sister on Friday night rather than going out with your friends so your parents can have some "away" time alone.

• Buying your mother a "thank you" card in which you list twenty-five things you're thankful for about her.

• Refusing to argue, complain, or question the next time your parents tell you you can't do something you really want to do.

• Treating your whole family to ice cream with your allowance money.

• Giving up a whole Saturday to clean the house and work in the yard—without being asked.

STEP 3

If your group members are unfamiliar with the story of the prodigal son, you may want to give them a more complete understanding of its meaning and significance. You might say something like: **Not only does this story teach us some valuable lessons about making good decisions, it also gives us an idea of how God feels about us. The father in the story represents God; the younger son represents sinners. How do you think the father felt when his son decided to leave? How do you think God feels when He sees people sinning?** (Sad.)

Why didn't the father prevent his son from leaving? Why doesn't God prevent us from sinning? (We have free will; we are given the chance to choose to do right.)

How did the father react when the son repented and came home? How does God react when people ask for forgiveness from Him? (He welcomes us with open arms.)

STEP 5

You might want to wrap up the session by explaining the biblical principle of "reaping what you sow." Have volunteers read aloud Job 4:8 and Galatians 6:7. Ask: **How would you reword this principle in easier-to-understand terms?** ("What you dish out, you will get back." "If you act like a jerk, people will treat you like a jerk.")

How does this principle apply to the topic of our session—growing up? (If you act like a mature person around your parents, they will treat you like a mature person. If you act childishly, they will treat you like a child.)

If you have time, distribute index cards and pencils. Instruct group members to write out the text of Job 4:8 or Galatians 6:7 on their cards. Encourage them to keep the cards handy as reminders of the "reap what you sow" principle.

STEP 4

After the partners have completed the "Concentration" game, have them briefly share with each other an example of a set-back they've had in demonstrating their maturity to their parents. After each person has shared, his or her partner should offer words of encouragement and/or advice.

For instance, let's say one partner shares the following setback: "I threw a fit when my parents told me I couldn't go to the mall with my friends. I yelled and screamed and called them names. They said I was acting like a spoiled little kid. I think it'll take a long time before they think of me as being mature or grown up." His or her partner might offer the following words of advice: "If you apologize to them and let them know that you know how childish you were, they might respect your judgment and forget about the incident more easily."

STEP 5

Wrap up the session with a praise activity. Write the words "Thank You, God" vertically in big letters on the board. Then, as a group, brainstorm some benefits of maturing/becoming an adult that begin with each of the letters of "Thank You, God." Write the benefits on the board next to the appropriate letters. (For instance, "T" might be "Talking on the phone with my friends as long as I want"; "H" might be "Having my own car"; etc.) When group members have named at least one benefit for each letter, have them form a circle for closing prayer. Instruct each person to choose one of the benefits on the board and say a sentence prayer, thanking God for it.

MOSTLY GIRLS

STEP 2

After distributing copies of "The Adventures of the Suddenly Grown Up" (Repro Resource 4), instruct the girls to change the name of the character on the sheet from Stan to Sandra (or some other feminine name of their choosing). Also instruct them to change some of the details of the story to make it more applicable to the female character. For instance, rather than being envious of Paul's seventeenth birthday party with his friends, the main character of one of your girls' stories may be envious of her sister's date with her boyfriend on her seventeenth birthday.

STEP 4

Provide some blank index cards for a second round of "Grown-Up Concentration." Have your group members work in teams of three or four, writing additional privilege and responsibility cards that include other things that appeal to them about being an adult. After the cards are finished, collect and shuffle them. Spread them out on the floor, and have your group members take turns choosing two cards at a time, trying to find a match. You may want to award a prize to the person who finds the most matching cards.

MOSTLY GUYS

STEP 1

Guys might be more comfortable trying to knock each other off the board than they would be trying to work together on it. So you may need to alter the activity a bit. Give each contestant a foam rubber bat. Have the contestants face each other on the board. When you say go, the contestants will try to knock each other off the board using only the foam rubber bats. (Contestants may not touch each other at all.) The first person to fall off the board—or even touch the floor—loses. If you have time, you may want to make this a tournament, with the winners advancing to the next round until you have a champion ("the chairman of the board"?).

Afterward, point out that when kids begin to mature and take their first steps toward adulthood, it can cause some mighty clashes between them and their parents—if the situation is not handled correctly.

STEP 4

Use the following questions to focus on some of the specific family responsibilities guys may face in the future.

• **Imagine that you're an adult, with a family and a good job. You work hard forty hours a week. But when you get your paycheck, almost all the money goes toward paying bills, buying diapers and formula for your kid, and paying for car repairs on your mini-van. How do you think you would feel about spending your hard-earned money this way?**

• **Imagine that your son got caught doing something wrong at school. The school principal calls you in for a conference. How would you handle the situation?**

• **Imagine that you're invited to play on your church's Saturday-morning softball team. Unfortunately, your wife works on Saturdays and you have to stay home with the kids—so you can't play. How do you think you'd feel?**

EXTRA FUN

STEP 2

Have group members form two to four teams (depending on the size of your group) for a "growing up" relay. Have the teams line up at one end of the room. When you say go, the first person in each line will crawl (like a baby) to the other end of the room and back. Then the second person in line will do the same thing. When all of the team members are finished crawling, the first person in line will then "toddle" (like a toddler)—by taking two steps and falling down, taking two steps and falling down—to the other end of the room and back. When all the team members are finished toddling, the first person will run (like a teenager/adult) to the other end of the room and back. When all the team members are finished running, the first person in line will walk slowly (like an elderly person)—heel-to-toe, heel-to-toe—to the other end of the room and back. The first team to complete all four legs of the relay wins.

STEP 5

As you wrap up the session, play a quick game to reinforce the idea of "shocking parents' socks off." Have group members form two teams. Instruct the teams to line up at one end of the room for a relay race. Place two paper bags (one for each team) at the other end of the room. When you say go, the first person in each line will remove his or her shoes, run to the other end of the room, and remove his or her socks. After dropping the socks in the team bag, the person will run back to the team and tag the next person in line. That person will then repeat the process. However, the next person in line may not begin to remove his or her shoes until he or she is tagged. Award a prize to the team that finishes first. [NOTE: You may need to bring some extra socks to the session for sockless group members.]

STEP 1

Have group members form teams of two or three. Distribute several magazines, catalogs, and newspapers to each team. Instruct the members of each team to look through the material and find pictures of people that resemble what they think each other will look like as adults. Encourage them to be sensitive as they select pictures (i.e., don't choose pictures of fat, ugly, or grotesque people). Afterward, have the team members discuss what they think each other will be like as adults.

STEP 2

Instead of using Repro Resource 4, rent a video of the movie *Big*, starring Tom Hanks. Show several clips from the movie. (You'll need to preview them first to check for offensive language and suggestive situations.) Among the scenes you might want to show are the one in which the young boy makes a wish that he was grown up; the one in which he wakes up the next morning to find he is grown up; the one in which he spends the night alone in a run-down, scary hotel; the one in which he's discovered playing in a toystore by the owner of the toy company and given a new position in the company; and the one in which he returns home, a young boy again.

Afterward, discuss the clips, using the following questions.

• **Would you be willing to give up your teenage years to have the kind of life Josh had as a grown-up? Why or why not?**

• **What kinds of things was Josh unprepared for as an adult? Do you think you would be any better prepared for these situations than Josh was?**

• **What kinds of things do you think you need to know before you become an adult?**

STEP 2

Rather than distributing copies of Repro Resource 4 to your group members and waiting for them to fill it out, simply read aloud the story on the sheet. Then ask the following questions:

• **How do you think Stan's life will change now that he's grown up?**

• **What kinds of things will he be able to do now that he probably wasn't able to do as a kid?**

• **What kinds of problems will he face now that he probably didn't have to face as a kid?**

• **Has anyone ever told you that you were "trying to grow up too fast"? What did the person mean by that?**

• **Do you think it's possible to grow up too fast? Explain.**

STEP 4

You may not have time to wait for each pair of group members to complete the game and solve the puzzle. Instead, you may want to have just one copy of Repro Resources 5 and 6 for all of your group members to use. Tape the "Concentration" game to the wall and have group members form a line in front of it. One at a time, each group member will have a chance to choose two cards. If the cards match, the person gets to keep the cards, attempt to solve the puzzle underneath, and choose two more cards. If the cards don't match, the person must go to the end of the line and wait for his or her next turn. Award a small prize to each person who finds matching pairs of cards and a grand prize to the person who correctly solves the puzzle.

STEP 1

If you don't have the lumber required for the opening activity, use masking tape instead. Tape two slim, rectangular strips on the floor (each approximately five inches wide and five feet long). You'll also need to appoint two "floor judges" to observe the pairs and determine whether any part of the contestants' feet touch the floor outside the taped boundaries. Those whose feet touch the floor outside the boundary will be disqualified.

STEP 2

Some of your group members may have been forced by circumstances to "grow up in a hurry." Address this possibility with the following questions.

• **How many of you would say you've already taken on adult roles in your family? What are those roles?** (Some of your group members may be responsible for taking care of younger siblings or for shopping and housecleaning.)

• **Why do you have those roles in your family?** (Some group members may come from families in which both parents work long hours. Other group members may come from families in which one parent is absent. Still other group members may have parents who are unwilling or incapable [perhaps due to alcoholism or drug addiction] of taking care of their kids.)

• **Are there any benefits to growing up in a hurry? What are some of the drawbacks?**

STEP 2

Separate your junior highers and high schoolers into two groups. Have the junior high group answer this question: **What are three things you're looking forward to when you become an adult?** (Among the things group members might mention are getting a driver's license, buying a car, getting a job, getting married, having kids, getting out of school, making a lot of money, etc.)

Have the high school group answer this question: **What are three things about being a kid that you miss now or probably will miss when you get older?** (Among the things group members might mention are having someone cook and clean for you, not having to make "big" decisions, being able to play with friends without having to be "cool" or self-conscious, feeling safe with and protected by your parents at home, not having to worry about paying bills, etc.)

Getting two different perspectives may help your group members form a more complete picture of the ups and downs of growing up.

STEP 4

After the "Concentration" game, distribute the "privilege" cards among your junior highers and the "responsibility" cards among your high schoolers. Have the person with privilege card #1 stand up, read it aloud, and then tell why he or she is excited about having that privilege in the future. (For instance, someone might say, "I'm excited about having a driver's license and driving a car because I'll be able to go where I want, when I want.") Then have the person with responsibility card #1 stand up, read it aloud, and tell why that responsibility is important. (For instance, someone might say, "Following the rules of the road is important because if you ignore them just once, you could ruin your life or someone else's.") Continue until all of the privilege and responsibility cards have been read.

STEP 3

Instead of having your sixth graders re-read all of Luke 15:11-20 to find the "bad moves," assign the teams only a few of the verses. Instruct half of the teams to read verses 11-14 and write down better choices for the actions described in those verses. Have the other teams read verses 15-17 and write down better choices for the actions described in those verses. Give the teams a few minutes to work. When they're finished, have them share what they've written. Then discuss as a group how the story might have been different if the characters had made some of the choices suggested by your group members.

STEP 5

Before having kids pair up, discuss as a group some things that parents (rather than kids) would view as a step toward maturity. Ask: **Can you name some things that are important to your parents and would show them you're ready to take on more responsibility? What things do your parents say are stressful to them? Do they want more help around the house? Start noticing what your parents think is important and do something about it.**

DATE USED:

Approx. Time

STEP 1: *Trading Places* _____
- ❏ Extra Action
- ❏ Small Group
- ❏ Large Group
- ❏ Mostly Guys
- ❏ Media
- ❏ Urban

Things needed:

STEP 2: *Growing Up in a Hurry* _____
- ❏ Extra Fun
- ❏ Mostly Girls
- ❏ Media
- ❏ Short Meeting Time
- ❏ Urban
- ❏ Combined Junior High/High School

Things needed:

STEP 3: *The Prodigal* _____
- ❏ Extra Action
- ❏ Large Group
- ❏ Heard It All Before
- ❏ Little Bible Background
- ❏ Sixth Grade

Things needed:

STEP 4: *Grown-Up Concentration* _____
- ❏ Small Group
- ❏ Fellowship & Worship
- ❏ Mostly Girls
- ❏ Mostly Guys
- ❏ Short Meeting Time
- ❏ Combined Junior High/High School

Things needed:

STEP 5: *Shock Their Socks Off!* _____
- ❏ Heard It All Before
- ❏ Little Bible Background
- ❏ Fellowship & Worship
- ❏ Extra Fun
- ❏ Sixth Grade

Things needed:

Who's the Boss?

YOUR GOALS FOR THIS SESSION:
Choose one or more

☐ To help kids recognize that most rules make sense when you stop to think about them.

☐ To help kids understand how one member of a family, operating by his or her own rules, can disrupt the entire family.

☐ To help kids identify the reasons behind some of the specific rules in their families and recommit themselves to obedience.

☐ Other:_____
_____

Your Bible Base:

Exodus 20:1-17
Proverbs 6:20-22
Ephesians 6:1-3

Checkered Competition

(Needed: Cut-apart copies of Repro Resource 7, buttons)

Before the session, you'll need to cut apart copies of "Championship Checkers" (Repro Resource 7). Make sure you keep the two sections at the bottom of the sheet ("Official Rules for Checkers" and "New-and-Improved Official Rules for Checkers") separate.

As group members arrive, have them form pairs. Distribute a checkerboard from Repro Resource 7 and several buttons (which will serve as checkers) to each pair. [NOTE: You'll need thirty-two buttons for each pair. If possible, give each pair sixteen buttons of one color and sixteen buttons of another color.] Then give one person in each pair the "Official Rules for Checkers" section and give the other person the "New-and-Improved Official Rules for Checkers" section.

Announce that you're going to have a checkers tournament, and that the rules for the tournament are written on the slips of paper you just handed out. Group members must follow the rules when playing.

Have group members begin playing. It shouldn't be long before you start hearing complaints and accusations of cheating. If someone comes to you with a complaint, simply say: **Both of you have your rules— just finish your game.**

No matter how strongly some group members object to the rules, encourage the pairs to complete the games. As they are finishing up, throw one more curve into the process by explaining that there's one rule you forgot to announce: The person with the *fewest* number of buttons left wins the game.

Afterward, point out that the purpose of this exercise was to show how playing by your own set of rules can lead to frustration and chaos.

Say: **The topic of our session today is rules. We are surrounded by rules every day—rules of the road, rules at school, rules of the sports we play, and, of course, the rules our parents give us to live by at home. Today we're going to focus on home rules—the laws you live by at your house.**

Probably few, if any, of you were happy with the way our checkers tournament went. Unfortunately, when everyone plays by his or her own rules, no one can really have a good time. The same can be said for rules at home. When one person in a family thinks he or she can live by his or her own rules, it can be frustrating for everyone else.

STEP 2

My Family's Six Commandments

(Needed: Copies of Repro Resource 8, index cards, pencils)

Ask your group members some of the following general questions about rules at home. Encourage most of your group members to respond to each question.

Who makes up the rules at your house?

Do the same rules apply to all the members of your family? In other words, do mom and dad live by the same rules that the kids live by? What about older or younger siblings?

What's a rule in your house that's changed since you've gotten older? For instance, have your bedtime, chores, or curfew changed?

Distribute copies of "Family Commandments" (Repro Resource 8) and pencils. Have group members write down three "thou shalt" and three "thou shalt not" rules from their families. ("Thou shalt" rules might include something like "Thou shalt take out the garbage on Thursday night." "Thou shalt not" rules might include something like "Thou shalt not get in after 11 p.m. on Saturday night.")

Give group members a few minutes to work. When they're finished, have them compare rules with the people sitting around them.

Distribute two index cards to each group member. Then say:

Sometimes it's tough to understand all the rules our parents think are so great. Look again at the rules you wrote down. Are there any that make no sense at all to you? If possible, choose one "Thou shalt" rule and one "Thou shalt not" rule that you have a hard time understanding the reasons for. Write these rules on your index cards. We'll look at them later to see if we can make some sense out of them.

Have group members write the two rules on separate index cards. Then collect the cards and save them for later.

OPTIONS

SMALL GROUP

LARGE GROUP

MOSTLY GUYS

MEDIA

SHORT MEETING TIME

SIXTH GRADE

God's Top Ten Rules

(Needed: Copies of Repro Resource 8, chalkboard and chalk or newsprint and marker)

Say: **Perhaps we can get a better understanding of rules by looking at the "top ten" rules God set down for His children.**

Have group members turn in their Bibles to the Ten Commandments passage in Exodus 20. Read aloud verses 1 and 2. Then have group members take turns reading aloud the following passages, as indicated: verse 3; verses 4-6; verse 7; verses 8-11; verse 12; verse 13; verse 14; verse 15; verse 16; and verse 17.

After all the commandments have been read, read aloud verse 18. Then say: **It sounds like the people of Israel were getting a fairly serious message. Imagine a mountain shaking, with smoke and lightning all around, and invisible trumpets blasting. (And you thought your parents were dramatic when they laid down their rules!)**

God obviously wanted to get the people's attention. That must mean the stuff He was saying was pretty important.

Refer group members back to the rules they wrote down on Repro Resource 8. Have them choose from their lists one or two rules that they consider "good," "reasonable," or "useful." Ask volunteers to call out some of the rules they chose. Write the rules on the board as they are named.

Afterward, go through the list of rules, asking of each one: **What makes this a good rule?** You may get a variety of answers, but chances are they will boil down to two criteria.

A good rule does one of two things:

(1) It keeps you from getting hurt, treated unfairly, or ripped off.

(2) It insures that you get something you need.

Say: **We could say that a good rule either protects you or provides for you. Let's look at the top ten rules God gave us in the Bible. Just to make sure everybody understands these rules let me rephrase them in easier-to-understand terms.**

Paraphrase each commandment so that group members understand the concepts clearly. For instance, "You shall have no other gods before me" is simply a command to worship only the one true God. Committing adultery is having a sexual relationship with someone you're not married to. Giving false testimony is telling a lie about someone.

On the board, write the following two headings: "Protects" and "Provides." Then ask: **Which of the Ten Commandments would you say are designed to protect people?** (Commandments like "You shall not murder," "You shall not commit adultery," "You shall not steal," "You shall not give false testimony," and "You shall not covet" are pretty obviously designed to protect people. Commandments like "You shall have no other gods before me," "You shall not make for yourself an idol, "You shall not misuse the name of the Lord," and "Honor your father and your mother" protect people from the *consequences* of these actions.)

Which of these commandments is designed to provide, or make sure people get what they need? ("Remember the Sabbath day by keeping it holy" could be an example of this. Part of keeping the sabbath is resting. Resting on the sabbath gives us the refreshment and energizing we need to face the rest of the week.)

Avoid getting into a long discussion about the pros and cons of the Ten Commandments. That's not the point of the activity. You're simply trying to show your group members that good rules have good reasons behind them.

Say: **Of course God's rules are good; after all, God is perfect. But our parents aren't perfect. What does that say about their rules?** Get a few responses.

Have someone read aloud Proverbs 6:20-22. Ask a few volunteers to comment on the passage. Emphasize the importance God's Word places on parental rules.

Then say: **We've seen how God gives us rules that protect us or give us what we need, and we've seen how a father's rules can do the same for his kids. But what about the rules at your house?**

STEP 4

To Obey the Impossible Rule

(Needed: Index cards from Step 2)

OPTIONS

Have group members form teams of two or three. Bring out the index cards you collected in Step 2 and distribute them among the teams.

Explain: **Earlier you wrote down some hard-to-understand rules from your family. Let's take a look at these rules again—this time keeping in mind the two purposes for good rules. A good rule is one that either *protects* us from something or *provides* something for us.**

Instruct the teams to read their assigned rules and try to figure out the reasons behind each rule. Are the rules designed to protect? Are they designed to provide? Or are there really no good explanations for them?

Give the teams a few minutes to work. Then have each team read a couple of its assigned rules and share its conclusions. It may be helpful to some of your group members to hear their peers spotting the logic in some of their parents' rules.

Afterward, ask: **What can we do about unreasonable rules—those rules that aren't really designed to protect or provide?** Be sensitive here. Some of your group members may really be struggling with unreasonable rules at home. Encourage them to respectfully ask their parents to help them understand these rules. Also encourage them to be open to their parents' explanations and think through what it means to be responsible for a family's protection and provision. Putting themselves in their parents' place may help them accept seemingly unreasonable (and unchangeable) rules.

STEP 5

Obeying Parents = Obeying God

Say: **One of the rules in God's "top ten list" in Exodus 20 had to do with honoring our parents. Ephesians 6:1-3 tells us that the best way to honor our parents is to obey them.** Have someone read aloud the passage.

Then say: **God must think that obeying our parents is a pretty important rule. He put it in there with the other nine biggies. That means when we obey our parents and respect the rules they put down for us, we are actually obeying God.**

Close the session with a time of silent prayer. Encourage group members to tell God how they honestly feel about the rules in their families. You might encourage them to start their prayers with a statement like "Dear Lord, sometimes I feel like my whole life is controlled by rules" or "Heavenly Father, You gave me parents who seem so strict compared to my friends' parents. Help me to respect and obey them even when ..."

Offer to meet privately after the session with any group member who wants talk about unfair rules in his or her family.

OPTIONS

FELLOWSHIP & WORSHIP

MOSTLY GIRLS

URBAN

CHAMPIONSHIP
CHECKERS

OFFICIAL RULES FOR CHECKERS
You may move your checkers diagonally one square at a time. When you are next to (on a diagonal) your opponent's checkers, you may "capture" them by jumping over them with your checkers. Failure to obey these rules means you automatically lose the game. Have fun!

NEW-AND-IMPROVED OFFICIAL RULES FOR CHECKERS
Do *not* show your opponent these rules!
The old rules for checkers were boring, so we changed them. Don't worry about only moving diagonally. Move any direction you want—one square at a time. However, on every other turn, you can move to any square on the board. And, by the way, you don't need to jump *over* a checker to capture it. You can jump right on top of it to clear it off the board. Have fun!

FAMILY
Commandments

STEP 1

Have group members form two teams to play volleyball. (Kickball or dodgeball would also work, depending on your group members' preferences.) Tape a string or piece of rope between two walls to serve as a net. You could also use tape to mark the out-of-bounds lines. Explain the rules very carefully to your group members. You'll serve as referee for the game. At first, be extremely nit-picking in calling violations. Watch for double hits, carries, illegal serves, close out-of-bounds calls, etc. If possible, make a call on every volley. When group members complain, go to the opposite extreme in your refereeing: don't call anything. If the ball hits out of bounds, count the point. If a person throws the ball over the net, count the point. If the ball rolls under the net, count the point. When group members complain again, discuss as a group the importance of good rules—in competition, as well as in life.

STEP 4

Have group members form two teams. One team will line up against a wall; the other team will line up against the opposite wall. On one of the other walls, you'll need to put a container labeled "Good Rules"; on the wall opposite of it, put a container labeled "Bad Rules." You'll stand in the middle of the room with the index cards you collected in Step 2. (Use half of the cards for each team.)

When you say go, the first person in line for one team will run to you and grab an index card from your hand. He or she will read aloud the rule written on the card and decide whether the rule is good or bad. Then the person will run to the appropriate container, drop the card in, and run back to his or her team. Continue until you run out of cards for that team. Then have the other team take its turn. Time each team, and award a prize to the winners. Afterward, ask group members to explain their reasoning in determining whether a rule is good or bad.

STEP 2

If your group is small, it's likely that your group members know each other fairly well. In that case, they may be comfortable sharing more specific, personal information with each other. Use the following questions to address some of the specific rules in your group members' families.

• **What is your curfew on school nights? What is your curfew on weekends? For those of you who have older brothers or sisters, is their curfew any different from yours? What about younger brothers or sisters?**

• **What is your bedtime on school nights? What is your bedtime on weekends? Are your older siblings allowed to stay up later than you are? Do your younger siblings have to go to bed before you?**

• **What jobs and chores are you responsible for around the house? What jobs and chores are your older siblings responsible for? What about your younger siblings?**

Some of your group members may feel better about their parents' rules if they discover that other kids face the same kinds of rules. However, be sensitive to kids whose parents are obviously much stricter than other parents.

STEP 4

If your group is small enough, you won't need to have group members form teams to discuss their families' hard-to-understand rules (which group members wrote on index cards in Step 2). Instead you can discuss them together as a group. Read each rule aloud. Then have your group members vote as to whether they think the rule is good or bad. (Remind them that good rules usually either *protect* us from something or *provide* something for us.) After group members have voted, ask a couple of them to explain their reasoning. If you have differing opinions about a rule, encourage a brief debate.

STEP 2

If you have a large group, it might be difficult to have most of your group members respond to the questions about their families' rules. To make this section more personally involving, have group members form teams of three. One person on each team will share with the others about his or her family's rules concerning bedtime—what time he or she has to go to bed on school nights and weekends, what time his or her older and younger siblings have to go to bed, etc. Another person will share with the others about his or her family's rules concerning jobs and chores around the house—who's responsible for what and what happens if jobs don't get done. The other person will share about his or her family's rules concerning curfew—what time he or she has to be home on school nights and weekends, what time his or her older and younger siblings have to be home, etc.

STEP 3

Skip the part of the session in which group members call out the rules they wrote down on Repro Resource 8. After you've discussed the Ten Commandments and explained the criteria for a "good" rule (one that either protects you from something or provides something for you), have group members reassemble into the teams of three they formed earlier (if you used the "Large Group" option in Step 2). Have the members of each team look at the rules they wrote down on Repro Resource 8 and decide together which rules are "good," based on the criteria from the session. Then have them brainstorm what might happen if they were to disobey these good rules.

STEP 3

For those of your group members who are more familiar with the Ten Commandments than Charlton Heston, you'll need a fresh approach. Try having them "rank" the commandments from 1 to 10, based on how important they think each one is. Distribute index cards and pencils. Have group members decide which commandment is most important, which is second-most important, and so on. Give group members a few minutes to work. When everyone is finished, have each person share his or her list. Pay particular attention to where each person ranks "Honor your father and your mother." Ask several volunteers to explain why they ranked it as they did. Afterward, point out that all of the commandments carry equal weight—none is more important than the others.

STEP 4

Probably most of the lessons and sermons your group members have heard on the Ten Commandments have focused on the importance of *obeying* the commandments. So you may want to try a different approach: focusing on the results of not obeying them. Write each of the Ten Commandments on the board. Then, as a group, brainstorm possible results of not obeying each commandment. (For instance, not obeying Commandment #6, "You shall not murder," might result in being sent to prison or executed. Not obeying Commandment #9, "You shall not give false testimony against your neighbor," might result in losing friends.) Pay particular attention to group members' responses for Commandment #5, "Honor your father and your mother." You may want to refer back to these possible results in Step 4, as you discuss the importance of obeying parental rules

STEP 3

If your group members aren't familiar with the Bible, you may need to reword some of the Ten Commandments to help group members understand them better. (For instance, "have no other gods before me" means not allowing anything to become more important to us than God.) Use some of the following questions to guide your discussion of each commandment.

• **What percentage of the people in our country would you say obey this commandment?**

• **What is the result in our society of people disobeying this commandment?**

• **How would our society be different if everyone obeyed this commandment all the time?**

Pay particular attention to group members' responses concerning the "Honor your father and your mother" commandment.

STEP 4

In abusive homes, certain "rules" may result in physical or emotional harm for kids. Group members who are facing such situations—and who have little Bible background—may misunderstand your emphasis on obedience. They may conclude that obeying their parents involves suffering abuse, and resign themselves to their fate. Or they may decide that you're so "out of touch" with their situation that they can't come to you with their serious problems at home. Emphasize that obeying parents does *not* include suffering abuse. Have each group member write his or her name on an index card. Then ask: **Are you having serious problems with physical or emotional abuse at home? Do your parents have rules that put you in danger, rather than protecting or providing for you? If so, write yes on this card. If not, write no.** Explain that you will meet privately with anyone who writes yes on the card, and that you will do whatever is necessary to help him or her.

STEP 3

Write some of the following Scripture passages on the board—Deuteronomy 6:5-9; 7:9-11; 8:1; 12:32; 30:16; Joshua 22:5; Proverbs 13:13; Joel 2:11; John 14:15, 21; 15:14; Ephesians 6:1-3; 1 John 3:24. (All of the passages have to do with obeying God's commands.) Have group members form teams. Instruct each team to come up with a song or chorus that uses the words of one or more of these passages and the tune of a well-known song. (Teams might use tunes from hymns, well-known choruses, or even pop songs.) Give the teams a few minutes to prepare; then have each one perform its composition. To make the presentations more interesting and fun, you might want to distribute kazoos and other toy instruments for the teams to use.

STEP 5

As you wrap up the session, have group members form pairs. (It would be good if group members paired up with a friend or someone they know fairly well.) Have group members share *honestly* with their partners how they feel about the rules in their families. If one of your group members is completely fed up with the rules in his or her house, he or she should say so without worrying about what his or her partner will think. After both partners have shared, they should pray for each other's situations.

STEP 3

After Proverbs 6:20-22 is read, have group members form teams. Assign each team one or more of the phrases from this passage. Instruct the teams to reword or paraphrase their phrases in a way that would be appropriate for today. For example, in verse 21, "Bind them upon your heart forever" could be reworded to say, "Write them down and memorize them so you will always remember them." After the teams have completed their paraphrases, ask them to read the new versions to the rest of the group.

STEP 5

After Ephesians 6:1-3 has been read, discuss as a group our choices in obeying God's rules. Ask: **Does God say that we are to obey our parents only if they are ideal parents? What should you do if your parents aren't obeying God's rules themselves? Does this give you the freedom to choose not to obey them? Why or why not?**

STEP 1

Most of your guys probably are more interested in basketball than in checkers. So, to more effectively demonstrate the idea of unfair rules, substitute a game of "Pig" (using paper wads and a wastebasket) for the checkers tournament. Give each person a paper wad; then assign the order in which your group members will shoot. In "Pig," if a person makes a shot, the next person must make a shot from the exact same spot. If he misses, he receives a letter (P-I-G). When a person gets three letters, he's out of the game. Play the first round according to the "real" rules; then, add some of your own. Here are some suggestions you might use:

• When a person makes a shot and the next person makes the same shot, give a letter to the first person.

• When a person receives his first letter, tell him that he's out—because you need to "speed up the game."

• When a person makes a shot and the next person makes the same shot, give a letter to the second person—because his shot didn't have the exact same angle as the first person's.

• If a person misses a shot, give a letter to the next person if he doesn't miss his shot in the exact same way.

Afterward, discuss the importance of having "fair" rules.

STEP 2

As you discuss the specific rules of your group members' families, focus on gender-related rules. Ask: **Are there any rules in your family that seem to "pick on you" specifically because you're a guy? Are there jobs around the house that you have to do that your sisters don't have to do? If so, how do you feel about that? Are there jobs your sisters have to do that you don't have to do? If so, how do you feel about that? Would you trade jobs or rules with your sisters if you could? Explain.**

STEP 1

Open the session with a game of "Follow the Rules." Have your group members form two teams for a relay race. Arrange the teams in two lines at one end of the room. Then explain the rules of the contest and give the teams the signal to start. Your explanation of the rules of the contest is the key to the activity. You'll need to come up with a ridiculous number of rules. As needed, use some of the following suggestions to supplement your own ideas. (You might want to write the rules on the board so group members can refer to them during the contest.)

• Both of your feet may not touch the floor at the same time during the race.
• Your right heel may not touch the floor at all during the race.
• One of your shoelaces must be tied in a double-knot before you race.
• After every third step you take, you must turn and look at me.
• If your shirt has any green in it at all, you must run backward during the race.

Afterward, discuss as a group how having a lot of rules can ruin a person's fun. Ask volunteers to say whether they think they have too many rules to follow at home.

STEP 3

Have group members form teams. Instruct each team to write a brief skit, demonstrating what an evening newscast might be like in a society that didn't have the Ten Commandments. In such a society, things like murder, theft, and adultery wouldn't be illegal, or even looked down on. This would make for an interesting newscast. For instance, the anchorperson might report on the murder of an elderly person in his home, and then go live to a correspondent on the scene—for a real-estate report on the suddenly vacant home. And because adultery would probably be widespread, the Hollywood gossip reporter might report on famous couples who allegedly *aren't* having affairs. Use this activity to lead into a discussion on the importance of rules.

STEP 2

You'll need to find a recording of the classic Coasters' song, "Yakety Yak." Play the song for your group members. Then have them form teams of three or four. Instruct the teams to rewrite the lyrics of the song so that they reflect the rules a young person today faces. Among the lines group members may rewrite are the following.

• "Take out the papers and the trash—or you don't get no spending cash."

• "Just finish cleaning up your room; let's see that dust fly with that broom."

• "Get all that garbage out of sight—or you don't go out Friday night."

• "You just put on your coat and hat, and walk yourself to the laundromat; and when you finish doing that, bring in the dog and put out the cat."

When all the teams are finished, have each one share (perhaps in song form) its new lyrics.

STEP 3

You'll need to bring in several newspapers and magazines. You'll also need to have scissors, tape, and paper available. Instruct group members to look through the magazines and newspapers to find pictures that represent their parents' rules. For instance, if someone thinks his or her parents' rules are extremely strict and well-enforced, he or she might cut out pictures of police officers or army drill sergeants. Have each group member form a collage with his or her pictures by taping them on a piece of paper. When everyone is finished, have each person display and explain his or her collage to the rest of the group.

STEP 1

If you're short on time, you may not want to wait for the pairs to finish their "checkers championship." Instead, lead your group members in a game of "Simon Says"—with a twist. Before the game you'll need to choose two or three group members to whom you'll show special favor. Explain to these kids (privately, apart from the others) that they don't have to follow the rules in the game. They don't have to wait for you to say "Simon Says" before they make a move—in fact, they don't even have to do what you say when you say, "Simon says." During the game, other group members may complain or try to get away with not following the rules—but don't allow them to. If they don't follow the rules, they're out. Continue the game until only your pre-chosen group members are left. Use the activity to lead into a discussion of the importance of fair rules.

STEP 2

Rather than distributing copies of Repro Resource 8 and waiting for group members to fill them out, discuss the topic of family rules as a group. Ask two or three volunteers to talk about "the one rule at their house that affects them the most every day," and explain why the rule affects them so. For instance, someone might say, "Having to do the dishes after dinner before I can watch TV affects me the most, because there are so many dishes that I usually end up missing my favorite shows." After your volunteers have shared, distribute index cards and have each group member write down two rules in his or her family that make no sense to him or her. Collect the cards and save them for later in the session (see Step 4).

STEP 3

Have your group members come up with a list of ten commandments (or rules) they believe both children and parents should respect at all times—rules that should not change as children get older. Explain that the purpose of the list is to provide a never-changing basis for parent-child rule making and obedience. Afterward, have your group members decide how they could make this list available to their parents—perhaps through a newsletter, the church bulletin, or some other promotional means.

STEP 5

Wrap up the session with the following comments: **One definition of the biblical word "honor" that is often overlooked is "to esteem." Esteeming our parents means not neglecting the God-given responsibility to care for and present our parents with great respect, because of the sacrifices they made for us. Honoring our parents does not suggest that parents are never wrong—or that we have to obey them in extreme or abusive situations. Honoring our parents means doing our best to treat them with the respect they are due for caring enough to raise us—even if they weren't always perfect parents. It also means that when they're too old to provide or care for themselves anymore, we have a responsibility to care for them, to give them esteem and personal honor.** Discuss some ways kids can esteem their parents.

STEP 1

As much as possible, pair up junior highers with high schoolers for the "championship checkers" tournament. Make sure you give the "New-and-Improved Official Rules for Checkers" slips (from Repro Resource 7) to the high schooler in each pair. When the junior highers begin to complain about their partners' cheating, tell them to be quiet and finish their games. Afterward, give junior highers a chance to vent their frustrations. Use the activity to lead into a discussion of who has the most rules: older or younger siblings. Give both your high schoolers and junior highers a chance to comment on the "fairness" of different rules for different siblings.

STEP 4

Ask a couple of high school volunteers to stand up and tell the group about a time when they didn't obey one of their parents' rules—and what happened as a result. If possible, have your volunteers focus on the theme of finding out too late that the rules they failed to obey were meant to protect them. The benefits of this simple exercise may be two-fold: (1) hearing a high schooler talk about the importance of obeying rules may mean more to your junior highers than hearing you talk about it; (2) giving your high schoolers a chance to "share their wisdom" with junior highers may give them more of a sense of responsibility and importance in your group.

STEP 2

Before distributing copies of "Family Commandments" (Repro Resource 8), briefly discuss as a group the word *rule*. Use the following questions to guide your discussion.

• **What does the word *rule* mean?**

• **What are some other words that might mean the same thing?** (Law, requirement, guideline, etc.)

• **What are some places other than your home where you are guided by rules?**

• **What would happen if there were no rules anywhere?**

STEP 4

Instead of distributing the index cards from Step 2 and having group members work in teams, do this activity as an entire group. Write each rule on the board as you read it aloud. Then have group members suggest possible reasons for the rules. After reading and discussing several of the rules, ask group members to suggest ways to modify them to make them "fairer" or easier to obey.

DATE USED:

Approx. Time

STEP 1: *Checkered Competition* _____
❑ Extra Action
❑ Mostly Guys
❑ Extra Fun
❑ Short Meeting Time
❑ Combined Junior High/High School
Things needed:

STEP 2: *My Family's Six Commandments* _____
❑ Small Group
❑ Large Group
❑ Mostly Guys
❑ Media
❑ Short Meeting Time
❑ Sixth Grade
Things needed:

STEP 3: *God's Top Ten Rules* _____
❑ Large Group
❑ Heard It All Before
❑ Little Bible Background
❑ Fellowship & Worship
❑ Mostly Girls
❑ Extra Fun
❑ Media
❑ Urban
Things needed:

STEP 4: *To Obey the Impossible Rule* _____
❑ Extra Action
❑ Small Group
❑ Heard It All Before
❑ Little Bible Background
❑ Combined Junior High/High School
❑ Sixth Grade
Things needed:

STEP 5: *Obeying Parents = Obeying God* _____
❑ Fellowship & Worship
❑ Mostly Girls
❑ Urban
Things needed:

Operation Family Storm

YOUR GOALS FOR THIS SESSION:

Choose one or more

☐ To help kids recognize that even the best of families have conflicts from time to time.

☐ To help kids understand that family conflict can lead to family growth if the conflict is handled correctly.

☐ To help kids identify some specific, God-honoring steps they can take to help resolve conflict in their families.

☐ Other:_____

_____

Your Bible Base:

Romans 12:10-21
James 4:1-3

STEP 1

Family Blowups

(Needed: Copies of Repro Resource 9, pencils, scissors, blindfold, inflated balloons, straight pins)

OPTIONS

EXTRA ACTION

SMALL GROUP

LARGE GROUP

LITTLE BIBLE BACKGROUND

MOSTLY GUYS

EXTRA FUN

MEDIA

SHORT MEETING TIME

URBAN

Open the session with the following comments: **We're going to have to change our plans today. Last night I found out that the session we were supposed to study today is on family conflict. Family conflict—can you believe it?! Why would we need a session on family conflict? After all, most of us come from pretty good families, so we don't have to worry about conflict—right?** Probably most of your group members will strongly disagree. If they do, pretend to be surprised.

Ask: **Are you telling me you guys have conflict in your families?** (Yes!) **Well, then I guess we won't have to change our plans today.**

So group members don't feel abnormal for admitting to conflict in their families, assure them that *all* families have conflicts.

Have group members form teams of two or three. Distribute copies of "Family Land Mines" (Repro Resource 9) and pencils to each team.

Say: **Sometimes family life can seem a little like war. Even though most of the time we really do care about our family members, it seems that we get into the biggest blowups over the silliest little things. The sheets I'm giving you have some innocent-looking little disks on them. Actually, they're deadly land mines waiting to explode in your family.** [NOTE: You may need to explain to your group members that land mines are booby-trap explosive devices that are usually buried in the ground. When someone or something passes over the top of a land mine, it explodes, causing massive injury and destruction.]

The scrambled letters you see on top of the mine go into the blanks below. Each of the land mines on your sheet will spell out something that causes "explosions" among family members.

Have the teams compete to see who can unscramble the letters and identify the areas of conflict first. The first team to correctly identify all eight areas of conflict is the winner. Announce that the winning team will be given a "special privilege" later in the session.

Give the teams a few minutes to work. When they're finished, go through the answers one at a time. The correct answers are as follows:

(1) curfew; (2) friends; (3) chores; (4) music; (5) clothes; (6) telephone; (7) homework; (8) allowance.

Cut up two copies of Repro Resource 9 so that you have sixteen individual "land mines." Scatter the land mines on the floor in an open area of the room. Ask for two or three volunteers to attempt to negotiate the "mine field" while blindfolded. Let the volunteers look at the arrangement of the mines before you blindfold them.

To add some excitement to the proceedings, distribute several inflated balloons and straight pins to the members of the winning team from the earlier activity. These group members will follow your blind-folded volunteers through the mine field. Whenever a volunteer steps on a mine, they will pop a balloon. [NOTE: For safety's sake, make sure the balloons aren't popped near people's ears or faces.]

Afterward, say: **Think about the last blowup you had in your family over one of these issues. Which one was it? What happened?** Encourage several group members to share honestly. However, don't allow the discussion to degenerate into a gripe session. Keep in mind some of the stories your group members share. You may want to substitute them for some of the case studies and examples used later in the session.

Two Sides to Every Story

Ask: **What does the expression "There are two sides to every story" mean?** (When two people are involved in an incident or conflict, each of them will have a unique perspective on the event. If you listen to only one person's version of the events, you miss out on the whole story.)

Point out that family conflicts often occur when one person fails or refuses to see the point of view of another person.

Say: **Let's look at some examples of family confrontations and find out how not seeing another person's point of view can lead to conflict.** Note that the case studies are based on some of the "family land mines" from Repro Resource 9.

- **Susan has a lot of friends at school. Unfortunately, they're not the kind of friends her parents would like her to have. Susan's friends do a little drinking on weekends, and their idea of right and wrong is quite a bit different**

OPTIONS

LARGE GROUP

MOSTLY GIRLS

MOSTLY GUYS

URBAN

JR. HIGH / HIGH SCHOOL COMBINED

SIXTH GRADE

from what Susan's parents believe to be true. Susan's friends are loyal, they like her, and they're really fun to be around. However, Susan's parents have told her she cannot spend time with them.

How might not seeing both sides of the story lead to conflict in this situation? (If Susan's parents don't see Susan's side of the story, they might not recognize some of the good points of her friends. If Susan doesn't see her parents' side of the story, she might not recognize the dangers of spending too much time with her friends.)

- **The rule at Stephanie's house is that no personal phone call can be more than ten minutes long. Her parents have explained to her that when she is with her friends all day long, there's no need to be tying up the family phone for long periods of time in the evening. They've thought about the rule carefully, and to them it makes all the sense in the world. However, to Stephanie it makes no sense at all.**

How might not seeing both sides of the story lead to conflict in this situation? (If Stephanie's parents don't see Stephanie's side of the story, they might not understand how important evening phone calls are for staying in the "information loop" in junior high. If Stephanie doesn't see her parents' side of the story, she might not understand the importance of keeping the phone lines open in the evening.)

- **"Your bed wasn't made, the trash wasn't taken out, and the dog wasn't fed. Get used to the house because that's where you'll be staying all weekend. You're grounded." Josh knew his dad was right about the jobs not being done. But Josh had a good reason for not doing his chores—at least, to him it was a good reason.**

How might not seeing both sides of the story lead to conflict in this situation? (If Josh's dad doesn't see Josh's side of the story, he might not discover that Josh had a legitimate excuse for not doing his chores. If Josh doesn't see his dad's side of the story, he might underestimate the importance of completing his chores.)

- **Lionel's dad is lying in bed staring at the ceiling. His mom is nervously pacing the floor. It's 12:15 and Lionel is nowhere to be found. His curfew is 11:00, and the rule is that if he's going to be late, he must call to say why. His mom is imagining the worst—she's sure there's been a horrible accident. His dad is just plain ticked off.**

How might not seeing both sides of the story lead to conflict in this situation? (If Lionel's parents don't see Lionel's side of the story, they might not discover that he was absolutely unable to call them. If Lionel doesn't see his parents' side of the story, he might not understand how much he upset them.)

STEP 3

Conflict Causes

(Needed: Chalkboard and chalk or newsprint and marker, paper, pencils)

Say: **Families have had conflicts and misunderstandings ever since there have been families. Can you think of some families in the Bible that had conflicts?** (The conflict between Cain and his brother Abel resulted in Cain killing Abel. The conflict between Joseph and his brothers resulted in Joseph being sold into slavery by his brothers. Even Jesus experienced conflict with His parents when He was separated from them at the feast in Jerusalem.)

Write the following statement on the board: "The best families are those in which there is never any conflict." Have group members tell you whether they agree or disagree with the statement.

Then ask: **What causes conflicts in a family?** Chances are group members will mention specific incidents like "My brother comes into my room and takes my stuff without asking" or "My dad changes the channel on the TV to the news when I'm watching a show," etc. Help group members get beyond these specific incidents and into the underlying attitudes like lack of respect for privacy or selfishness.

Point out that a similar question is asked and answered in the Bible. Have someone read aloud James 4:1-3. Then ask: **According to this passage, what causes conflicts?** (Selfishness—people demanding things and doing whatever is necessary to get their own way.)

Say: **Think about the last big blowup you had with your parents. Did selfishness play a role in the conflict? Explain.** If group members are hesitant to talk about their own family conflicts, discuss what role selfishness played in the conflict case studies in Step 2.

Point out that not only does the Bible identify causes for family conflict, it also offers suggestions on how to avoid and resolve conflict.

Have group members form pairs. Distribute paper and pencils to each pair. Instruct the pairs to read Romans 12:10-21 and list at least eight practical suggestions found in the passage for avoiding or resolving conflict.

Give the pairs a few minutes to work; then have them share and explain their responses. For instance, if someone suggests "Be devoted to one another," ask what "being devoted" means. Write the responses on the board as they are named.

OPTIONS

HEARD IT ALL BEFORE

LITTLE BIBLE BACKGROUND

FELLOWSHIP & WORSHIP

MOSTLY GIRLS

MEDIA

SHORT MEETING TIME

JR. HIGH / HIGH SCHOOL COMBINED

SIXTH GRADE

Use the following responses to supplement the pairs' answers:
- Be devoted to one another (vs. 10).
- Honor one another above yourselves (vs. 10).
- Be joyful (vs. 12).
- Be patient (vs. 12).
- Share with people in need (vs. 13).
- Practice hospitality (vs. 13).
- Do not be proud (vs. 16).
- Do not be conceited (vs. 16).
- Do not repay evil for evil (vs. 17).
- Do what is right (vs. 17).
- Do not take revenge (vs. 19).

You Say You Want a Resolution

(Needed: Copies of Repro Resource 10, pencils)

Distribute copies of "Solving Conflict Problems" (Repro Resource 10) and pencils. Instruct group members to fill out the top half of the sheet. Explain that the report card is for their eyes only—no one else will see it. Its purpose is to help them evaluate how they're doing in some important conflict areas.

When group members are finished filling out the report card, have them review their answers. Ask them to consider what they could do in these areas to lessen the conflict in their families. For instance, are there any "Never" responses they could improve on? Are there any "Always" responses they could work on eliminating?

Give group members a few minutes to pray silently, committing themselves to working on one area this week—perhaps to be a better listener or to control the expression of their emotions.

As you wrap up the session, refer group members to the bottom half of Repro Resource 10. Point out that these are six steps they could use in resolving family conflicts. Briefly go through the six steps. Encourage group members to discuss the principles on the sheet with their parents.

Close the session in prayer, asking God to help your group members follow through on the commitments they made for resolving conflict in their families.

NOTES

FAMILY LAND MINES

1

ACME   LAND   MINES
E   R   C
Guaranteed to cause family explosions.
_ **U** _ **F** _ **W**

2

ACME   LAND   MINES
R   D   N
Guaranteed to cause family explosions.
F _ **I** _ **E** _ _ **S**

3

ACME   LAND   MINES
E   R   H
Guaranteed to cause family explosions.
C _ _ **O** _ _ **S**

4

ACME   LAND   MINES
M   C   S
Guaranteed to cause family explosions.
_ **U** _ **I** _ _

5

ACME   LAND   MINES
T C E O
Guaranteed to cause family explosions.
_ **L** _ _ **H** _ **S**

6

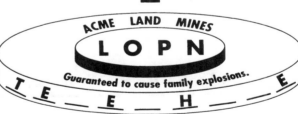

ACME   LAND   MINES
L O P N
Guaranteed to cause family explosions.
T _ **E** _ **E** _ **H** _ _ **E**

7

ACME   LAND   MINES
E M K O H
Guaranteed to cause family explosions.
_ _ **O** _ _ **W** _ **R** _ _

8

ACME   LAND   MINES
E W N L
Guaranteed to cause family explosions.
A _ **L** **O** _ **A** _ **C** _ _

Solving Conflict Problems

	Always	Sometimes	Never
I find it easy to say I'm sorry.			
I find it easy to forgive others.			
I'm a good listener.			
I start arguments or fights for no reason.			
When I feel hurt, I give people the "silent treatment."			
I express my emotions whenever and however I want to.			
I feel sad when I have an unresolved conflict with someone.			

Six STEPS to Solving Conflict

1. Understand that all families have conflict.

2. *Make sure you understand both sides of the story. Ask questions if you don't.*

3. **Be willing to take responsibility for your part in the conflict.**

4. Work together at listing all the possible solutions.

5. *Decide on a solution and work at it together.*

6. *Be willing to forgive or ask for forgiveness if necessary.*

EXTRA ACTION

STEP 1

Distribute index cards and pencils. Instruct group members to come up with a list of conflict-causing situations in families. The situations may be as general ("arguments about privacy") or as specific ("My dad barged into my room while I was writing in my diary and read what I was writing") as group members desire. After a few minutes, collect the lists. Then give each person a balloon. You will read aloud the group members' lists. Every time you call out a conflict-causing situation, each group member will blow one deep breath into his or her balloon, and then hold it carefully so that no air escapes. When you read the next conflict-causing situation, he or she will blow another deep breath into the balloon. The first person to pop his or her balloon (by wind power alone) wins. Afterward, discuss how conflict-causing situations, if not handled properly, can lead to "explosions" in families.

STEP 4

Ask for three pairs of volunteers. You will give one person in each pair an assignment for the pair to complete. He or she may not tell his or her partner what the assignment is. (Assignments could involve anything from stacking a pile of books in a certain way to cutting out certain letters from a newspaper to form a message.) The members of one pair may not talk to each other at all. They may communicate only through gestures. The members of another pair must wear Walkmans (with the volume turned way up) or earplugs. They may communicate only by yelling. The members of the third pair may communicate with each other normally—so obviously it will be easier for them to complete their assignment than it will be for the other two pairs. Afterward, draw a parallel to family communication: It's a lot easier to resolve conflict with your family members if you're communicating normally than if you're not talking at all or if you're yelling at each other.

SMALL GROUP

STEP 1

With a small group, you have the luxury of being able to personalize the topic of family conflicts. Have group members form pairs. Instruct each person to share with his or her partner a conflict he or she had with his or her parents recently. Each pair should then choose one of the two conflicts to act out in front of the whole group. The person in the pair who actually experienced the conflict should play himself or herself; the other person should play the parent with whom the conflict occurred. After each pair performs, ask the rest of the group members to share about similar conflicts they've had with their parents.

STEP 4

If your group is small and close-knit, they may be willing to share their "grades" from Repro Resource 10. If so, go through the seven statements one at a time, and have each group member share his or her grade for that statement. By doing so, you will help group members see that they are not alone in their problems with parents—that others have similar problems. If you have time, you may want to have group members who score low on the same statements get together to discuss ways to improve in those areas.

LARGE GROUP

STEP 1

Have group members complete Repro Resource 9 individually. When finished, have them form teams of five or six. Instruct teams to spread out as far away from each other as possible. Each team will cut apart one copy of Repro Resource 9, set up a "mini-mine field," and have its members attempt to step through it while blindfolded (see the description in Step 1). However, team members won't pop balloons when someone steps on a mine. Instead, they will briefly share examples of how the topic of the mine that was stepped on can cause real-life conflicts.

STEP 2

Have group members form six teams. Assign each team a case study (including the two given below). Instruct the teams to discuss their case studies and answer this question: **How might not seeing both sides of the story lead to conflict in this situation?**

Here are the additional case studies.

• On Friday nights, Kendra is not allowed to go out until her homework is done. Usually that's not a problem. Either Kendra doesn't make plans for Friday night or she finishes her homework in study hall. This Friday, however, is the big pool party at Marti's house. And because of a school assembly Friday afternoon, Kendra couldn't get her history report done in study hall.

• Lisa hates the way her mom makes her dress. Her jeans are too baggy, her skirts are too long, and her sweaters don't do a thing for her. When Lisa complains, her mom usually has one of two responses: (1) "I don't want you looking 'sleazy'"; or (2) "I can't afford the clothes you want to wear."

Encourage each group member to participate in his or her team's discussion. Afterward, have each team share its responses.

STEP 3

Phrases like "Honor one another" and "Be joyful" probably hold very little meaning for kids who've heard them hundreds of times before. To address this problem, have group members brainstorm very specific, modern-day examples of the commands found in Romans 12:10-21. For instance, for "Be joyful," someone might say, "Be in a good mood in the morning when your mom tries to talk to you during breakfast." Or, for "Practice hospitality," someone might say, "Invite the new kid at school to sit with you at lunch—even though your friends think he's weird and it could cost you your 'status.'" If your group members aren't specific enough with their examples, don't hesitate to tell them and have them try again.

STEP 4

Group members who've "heard it all before" are probably used to hearing what *they* need to do (obey their parents, honor their parents, respect their parents, etc.) to bring conflict resolution to their families. As you wrap up this session, give them an opportunity to share what they'd like their parents to do to resolve conflicts. For instance, someone might say, "I wish my dad would *listen* to me when I talk, instead of trying to find something wrong with everything I say." After several group members have shared, pray as a group for family-conflict resolution efforts from both sides—kids *and* parents.

STEP 1

Kids with little Bible/church background may be reluctant to admit that they have conflict in their families, for fear of being thought of as "unspiritual." Set them at ease at the beginning of the session by sharing some conflicts you had with your parents when you were younger. Also be prepared to explain how you resolved those conflicts and what your relationship with your parents is like now. If possible, bring in some other adults from the church to share about the conflicts they had with their parents. Your goal is to help group members see that conflict between parents and kids is normal—and solvable.

STEP 3

Briefly summarize the stories of Cain and Abel (Gen. 4:1-12), Jacob and Esau (Gen. 27), and Joseph and his brothers (Gen. 37: 39—47). Afterward, use the following questions as necessary to guide your discussion of the passages.

• **Why did Cain kill his brother?**

• **Has jealousy ever caused conflict between you and one of your family members? If so, what happened? How was it resolved?**

• **What was the cause of the conflict between Jacob and Esau?**

• **Have you ever been tricked by one of your family members? How did it make you feel? What did you do about it?**

• **How did God use the conflict between Joseph and his brothers to accomplish good?**

• **How might God use the conflict between you and your family members to accomplish good?**

STEP 3

Point out that not only does God give us guidelines in His Word for resolving conflict, He also comforts us and gives us strength in the midst of conflict. To help your group members celebrate this fact, lead them in singing the hymn, "Great Is Thy Faithfulness." Focus specifically on the third stanza: "Pardon for sin and a peace that endureth, thine own dear presence to cheer and to guide; strength for today and bright hope for tomorrow, blessings all mine, with ten thousand beside."

STEP 4

Rather than having group members pray silently about their "always" and "never" statements on Repro Resource 10, give them an opportunity to share their needs with another group member in a time of fellowship. Have group members pair up (with someone they feel comfortable talking to, if possible). Instruct each person to share with his or her partner one "always" or "never" statement he or she would like to work on in the coming week. After each person has shared, have the partners pray together, asking God to help them follow through on their commitments in the coming week.

STEP 2

Divide the girls into two teams for the discussion of the case studies. After talking about seeing both sides of the story, ask the members of Team 1 to put themselves in the place of the kids in the case study. Ask the members of Team 2 to put themselves in the place of the parents involved. Have the teams discuss the emotions their characters are probably experiencing. Then have the teams come together to talk about what might happen *next* in each case study to help resolve the conflict.

STEP 3

Have your group members form pairs. Instruct each pair to read Romans 12:10-21 and make a list of the practical suggestions found in the passage. Then ask the pairs to mark three suggestions on their lists that might be the most helpful in resolving the conflicts they face most often. Have the pairs read aloud the three suggestions they marked. List the suggestions on the board as they are named. Then, as a group, choose three items from the board and brainstorm some specific examples of ways a person (specifically a girl) could put those suggestions into practice.

STEP 1

Use the following questions to get your guys talking about conflict and how they handle it.

How do you usually resolve a disagreement or conflict with …
- **one of your friends?**
- **one of your enemies?**
- **your brother?**
- **your sister?**
- **your father?**
- **your mother?**

Encourage group members to share honestly. Afterward, discuss why they resolve conflicts differently with different people.

STEP 2

If your group is made up primarily of guys, the first two case studies (involving Susan and Stephanie) may not be applicable. You may want to use the following two case studies as substitutes.

- **Jeff made the basketball team at school. This is his big chance to be popular. The guys on the team—and the cheerleaders—seem to like Jeff. They invite him to their parties. The problem is that Jeff's parents don't like Jeff's new friends. They say these friends are "too wild"—just because some of them swear and drink a little, and because some of the girls dress a little provocatively. Jeff's parents have forbidden him from hanging around with these new friends outside of school.**

- **One day while Damon's mother was cleaning Damon's room, she noticed one of his heavy metal CDs lying open on his desk. Curious, she read some of the lyrics on the disk—and nearly had a heart attack. She couldn't believe what the songs were saying! Before Damon got home from school, his mother had thrown out all of his heavy metal disks. Now he's not allowed to buy a disk without his parents' permission.**

STEP 1

Open the session with a game of "Cup Conflict." Have group members form two teams. Give each team a paper cup, some kind of pedestal or stand (if nothing else is available, a chair would be OK), and several sheets of scrap paper. Each team will place its cup on the pedestal or stand. (Once the game has started, no one may touch the cups at all.) The object of the game is for each team to knock over the other team's cup with paper wads. The paper wads will also serve as "deadly missiles." If a person is hit with a paper wad, he or she is immediately out of the game. As more and more people are put out of the game, strategy for defending your team's cup and attacking your opponent's cup becomes more important. Use the activity as a lead-in to the topic of today's session: conflict.

STEP 4

To wrap up this session—and your *Parent Pains* study—invite your group members' parents to join your group for a celebration. Bring in some refreshments (and perhaps even some decorations if you're feeling particularly festive). Organize some games in which parents and their kids can compete together. You'll probably want to include both physical games (like three-legged races) and mental contests (like trivia quizzes). The goal of the activity is for kids and parents to have a good time together. [NOTE: You may want to have some extra adults available to team up with kids whose parents couldn't make it to the meeting.]

STEP 1

Before the session, you'll need to record several video clips of boxing matches, wrestling matches, fistfights in movies and TV shows, arguments and screaming matches in movies and TV shows, battle scenes from war movies, etc. Have this video playing when your group members arrive. To begin the meeting, have a contest to see who can guess the session topic (family conflict) based on the clues given in the video. Afterward, discuss how family conflict is like and unlike the various kinds of conflict shown in the video.

STEP 3

Before the session, you'll need to record several adults (including some of your group members' parents) saying different things that may or may not cause conflict with kids. If possible, have some of the adults use different tones of voice and phrasings in saying essentially the same thing. For instance, one of them might say, "Your room is a pigsty! Get in there and clean it up now!" in a harsh, angry voice. Another might say, "How many times have I told you to clean your room? Why doesn't anyone in this house listen to me?" in a whiny, self-pitying voice. Still another might say, "Would you please clean up your room tonight? We've got company coming tomorrow and I'd like to show off your room" in an even, reasonable voice. Play the recording for your group members, and have them explain which voices/statements might provoke them to conflict and why.

STEP 1

When group members are done filling out Repro Resource 9, quickly go through the answers. Then, as a group, brainstorm for each "family land mine" one example of a family conflict having to do with that topic. For instance, for "curfew" someone might say, "My dad grounded me for a week because I was fifteen minutes late getting home from a basketball game. I told him it was because my watch was slow, but he didn't believe me." Skip the activity in which group members try to negotiate the "mine field" while blindfolded. Go directly to the case studies in Step 2.

STEP 3

If you're short on time, skip the discussion of family conflicts in the Bible. Instead, focus on the conflict in your group members' families. Ask: **What are the top three things that cause conflict in your family?** Group members may respond with something as general as "bad moods" or something as specific as "My mom doesn't like the clothes I wear." Both answers are OK. Encourage as many group members as possible to respond (even if they can name only one or two causes). Then skip the James 4:1-3 passage and go straight to the discussion of Romans 12:10-21.

STEP 1

You might want to change the opening statement of the session to make it more applicable to the urban family situation. You might say something like the following: **We're going to have to change our plans today. Last night I found out the session we were supposed to study is on family conflict— can you believe it? I keep hearing reports on TV and all throughout the media that the urban family is all messed up. I don't know if it's true. Maybe it is! Do you think it's true?** After your discussion, continue with the rest of the activity as planned.

STEP 2

The following two situations may be more applicable to an urban setting.

• **Jaleel and his three younger brothers share two beds in the same room. Because his family does not have much money, this has always been the case. But Jaleel is thirteen now and wants his own space to invite friends over. He's mad at his parents because they remind him there is no other room for him to move to. This isn't a good enough explanation for him. How might not seeing both sides of this story lead to conflict?**

• **Shadonda's mother works two jobs to keep a roof over her family's heads. As a result, Shadonda rarely sees her mother anymore. Her mother's asleep in the morning and working at night. Shadonda wants to talk to her mother about some things that are going on in her life, but her mother never seems to have the time. Shadonda feels neglected and robbed of her mother. Her mother keeps promising Shadonda that they will talk, but she never seems to find the time. How might not seeing both sides of this story lead to conflict?**

STEP 2

If possible, pair up three junior highers with three high schoolers for a roleplay activity. (Make sure you choose people who feel comfortable performing in front of a group.) Assign each pair a conflict-causing topic such as curfew, allowance, music, clothes, etc. Give each pair a few minutes to come up with a roleplay demonstrating an argument between a parent and a kid, based on the pair's assigned topic. The high schooler should play the parent in the roleplay; the junior higher should play the kid. After the members of each pair perform their roleplays, they should explain to the group why they think their characters were right in the conflict. Use this activity to lead into a discussion of the statement, "There are two sides to every story."

STEP 3

Distribute index cards and pencils to your junior highers. Instruct each one to write down a conflict he or she is having or has had with his or her parents. Your junior highers should not, however, write their names on the cards. When they're finished, collect the cards. Ask your high schoolers to come to the front of the room to serve as a panel of "experts" in family conflict. Read each "conflict card" aloud. Then have your high school "experts" come up with a solution for the conflict or advice for handling it correctly—based on their own experiences. Not only will this give your junior highers an opportunity to sound off about the conflicts they're facing at home, it will also give your high schoolers an opportunity to serve as mentors to your junior highers.

STEP 2

Before the session, you'll need to write each of the case studies and its accompanying question on a separate sheet of paper. (Do not write the suggested answers on the sheet.) Have group members form four teams. Assign each team one of the situations. Instruct the members of each team to discuss their assigned situation and answer the question. Give the teams a few minutes to work. Then have each team read its situation and present its conclusions.

STEP 3

For the activity on avoiding or resolving conflict, have your sixth graders work in teams of three or four. Instruct half of the teams to read Romans 12:10-15 and list at least four practical suggestions. Instruct the other half of the teams to read Romans 12:16-21 and list at least four practical suggestions. Give the teams a few minutes to work. Then have the teams take turns sharing their ideas, with each team sharing one suggestion at a time.

DATE USED:

Approx. Time

STEP 1: *Family Blowups* _____
- ❏ Extra Action
- ❏ Small Group
- ❏ Large Group
- ❏ Little Bible Background
- ❏ Mostly Guys
- ❏ Extra Fun
- ❏ Media
- ❏ Short Meeting Time
- ❏ Urban

Things needed:

STEP 2: *Two Sides to Every Story* _____
- ❏ Large Group
- ❏ Mostly Girls
- ❏ Mostly Guys
- ❏ Urban
- ❏ Combined Junior High/High School
- ❏ Sixth Grade

Things needed:

STEP 3: *Conflict Causes* _____
- ❏ Heard It All Before
- ❏ Little Bible Background
- ❏ Fellowship & Worship
- ❏ Mostly Girls
- ❏ Media
- ❏ Short Meeting Time
- ❏ Combined Junior High/High School
- ❏ Sixth Grade

Things needed:

STEP 4: *You Say You Want a Resolution* _____
- ❏ Extra Action
- ❏ Small Group
- ❏ Heard It All Before
- ❏ Fellowship & Worship
- ❏ Extra Fun

Things needed:

NOTES

Unit Two: Extreme Friendship

Friendship, Fellowship, and Shipwrecked Relationships

Talking to Young Teens About Friendship

by Duffy Robbins

The long shadows dancing in the trees around our campfire were swaying to the familiar tune,
"Friends are friends forever if the Lord's the Lord of them, and a
friend cannot say never 'cause the welcome will not end. Though it's
hard to let them go, in the Father's hands we know that a lifetime's
not to long (sniff, sniff, wipe tears away) . . . to live as friends."
("*Friends,*" Michael W. Smith)

It was one of those magic camp night moments when the kids were holding hands, staring into the fire, and feeling the warmth of being together in the presence of God's Spirit. I thought to myself, "Thank you, Lord. Thank you for the way you're working among these kids; thank you for giving my students this taste of genuine fellowship . . . and thank you that they didn't decide to sing 'Pass It On!'"

It wasn't cynicism that ushered me to my next thought; it was the realism that comes with over two decades of youth ministry. Glancing around at the golden, glowing faces I thought, "If only we could make this moment last . . . at least until we all finish the bus ride home tomorrow!"

We're one in Spirit...but I'm number one in real life.

I can't really condemn the kids for the struggles they have in maintaining healthy relationships. Building community is tough. Authentic friendship is hard work. "Extreme Friendship" is extremely difficult. You don't have to be a teenager to relate to the words of the old hymn:

"To dwell above with saints we love, O that will be glory!
But to dwell below with the saints we know, that's another story."

And yet, this is our mandate, and one of the primary ways by which we can prove to the watching world that we are followers of the Lord Jesus. There certainly was nothing neat, easy, and clean about Jesus' act of servanthood that night in the upper room when He took a towel in hand and began to wash the feet of His disciples. When He had finished washing from their feet the last coat of dust and camel dung from the streets of downtown Jerusalem, He made it very clear what the stakes of obedience are:

"You call me 'Teacher' and 'Lord' and rightly so, for that is what I am. Now that I, your Lord and Teacher, have washed your feet, you also should wash one another's feet. I have set you an example that you should do as I have done for you. . . . A new command I give you: Love one another. As I have loved you, so you must love one another. By this all men will know that you are my disciples, if you love one another" (John 13:13-15, 34-35).

Going to Extremes

Your mission with this curriculum on "Extreme Friendship" is to help students count the cost of that kind of authentic love. "Extreme Friendship" is designed to help you and your students explore the challenges, difficulties, and practical realities of loving as Jesus loved, and learn what it really means to be friends ". . . if the Lord's the Lord of them" (*"Friends,"* Michael W. Smith).

Why is this so hard? What is it about who we are and the culture in which we live that makes Extreme Friendship so extremely tough? No doubt, there are lots of factors that make intimacy and genuine friendship such a stranger to us, but let me suggest three that are especially at work in the world of your junior high students.

• *They don't know what friendship means.* Your junior highers are growing up in a world in which commitment has been drained of any real meaning. Marriage vows that promised to love and cherish "till death do us part" are bulldozed out of the way because the promise-makers decided "it just wasn't working out." Professional athletes switch teams at the drop of a hat, or more accurately, at the drop of a larger paycheck. The old concept of a neighborhood as a place of community and shared responsibility has been replaced by a sterile geographical term describing the temporary stopping place of families on the move who occupy a certain property until the next transfer comes along. In short, commitment means, "I am committed to you until I am no longer committed to you."

It's in this cold, arid relational climate that kids are trying to forge friendships and understand commitment. No wonder that most kids define friendship in terms of what another person will do for them: "A friend is someone who will lie for you (when you need an alibi), buy for you (if you're underage), and pry for you (when you want to find out if he/she will go out with you)." The "towel concept" seems kind of extreme in that culture.

• *They don't know what friendship looks like.* Remember, these are kids who have learned about friendship by watching a TV show called "Friends" where several incredibly beautiful people work through all kinds of problems in just under 30 minutes—with non-stop laughs in the process! Even when they tune in to MTV to see the "Real World," where they get to watch real people who live real lives wrestle with real issues, it probably doesn't dawn on them that the entire premise of the show is completely unreal. How many teenagers and 20-somethings do you know who are given $50,000 by some TV producers to start their own business, and offered a fully furnished waterfront home in Miami while they work through "real life" worries?

The good news is the gallery is not bare. God has given us a number of vivid, deeply touching portraits of true friendship in His Word. There is Nathan, the friend who cared enough to confront David (2 Sam. 12). And Aquila and Priscilla, the fabric merchants from Corinth, who probably offered financial support to their friend Paul the Apostle and traveled with him on his missionary journey to Ephesus (Acts 18:18). Or what about Barnabas, the "Son of Encouragement," always ready with an act of kindness, who was committed enough to his young friend John Mark not to give up on him when others did (Acts 15:36ff)? And who could not be moved by the tapestry of

David and Jonathan, two men whose lives are interwoven in remarkable and even tragic ways? Of course, Jesus is the ultimate model God has given us to show what friendship looks like. And that's what this book is all about. It asks the critical question, "What kind of friend would Jesus be?"

Many junior highers believe that Jesus was a really nice guy who walked around telling people "It'll be all right" and "I'll be there for you." The truth is, Jesus was an Extreme Friend. He wasn't just nice. He put friendship into action.

You'll find quickly that none of the lessons in this book are new. Service. Encouragement. Forgiveness. Accountability. Introducing our friends to Jesus. They don't represent some trendy new twist on friendship. They are foundational lessons that teach the basic friendship skills most junior highers still need to master. When junior highers meet a God who serves them, who forgives them, and who believes in them, they'll meet a mind-blowing God. They will certainly become better friends to each other when they build their own friendship with Jesus.

• *They don't know how friendship works.* One of the especially helpful aspects of this curriculum is that it encourages students to take those baby steps of practical obedience. It is not enough to walk wide-mouthed and open-eyed through the gallery of biblical friendship. God calls us to take up the brush and begin to paint these relationships into our own lives. That means we must emphasize the "how-to" of friendship.

Duffy Robbins is Chairman of the Department of Youth Ministry at Eastern College in St. Davids, Pennsylvania. He is also a well-known conference speaker, seminar leader, and author.

The images on these two pages are designed to help you promote this course within your church and community. Feel free to photocopy anything here and adapt it to fit your publicity needs. The stuff on this page could be used as a flier that you send or hand out to kids—or as a bulletin insert. The stuff on the next page could be used to add visual interest to newsletters, calendars, bulletin boards, or other promotions. Be creative and have fun!

Are You Ready For
Extreme Friendship?

You've heard of extreme sports like bungee jumping and luge running.
But what is *Extreme Friendship?*
It's not just being nice. It's more than saying, "I'll be there for you."
It's all about being the kind of self-sacrificing, life-laying-down
friend-in-action that JESUS is to us. Are you ready for this?

Who:

When:

Where:

Questions? Call:

Unit Two: Extreme Friendship

Life's short. Cheer hard.
Be a **Bleacher Friend.**

Will you **forgive?**

Get off the couch. Get into
somebody's life. Be a **Foxhole Friend.**

You can make a difference. You can introduce your friends
to Jesus. You can step up and be a **Stretcher Friend.**

Friends don't let friendships die
quietly. Will you be a
Second-Chance Friend?

Extreme Friends

YOUR GOALS FOR THIS SESSION:
Choose one or more

☐ To help students get an overview of what kind of friend Jesus was on earth—He put friendship into action.

☐ To help students understand a mind-blowing idea about service: Jesus served others instead of demanding to be served.

☐ To challenge students to be Extreme Friends—friends who put friendship into action by serving others like Jesus did..

☐ Other:_____
_____

Your Bible Base:

Mark 6:30-44
Mark 7:31-37
Luke 6:17-26
Luke 10:25-37
Luke 10:38-42
John 11:1-44

STEP 1

Name that Foot

(Needed: posterboard and tape (or window curtains, mural paper, or chalkboard on wheels and bedding sheets), paper, pencils, CD player and CD)

OPTIONS

Before the session make a large "mystery curtain" (about 8' x 5') by taping posterboard together or use other supplies listed above.

Recruit adult or student volunteers to hold the curtain in place between the doorway to your room and the place where your group will sit. Pass out paper and pencils. Choose six volunteers to be "mystery guests." Escort them out of the room and tell them to take their shoes and socks off. Have them re-enter the room completely hidden from the rest of the group by the mystery curtain—except for their bare feet. The rest of the group members write down their guesses as to which foot belongs to which mystery student. Consider having upbeat music playing in the background. Anyone who correctly guesses the identity of all six feet earns a dirty sock as a prize. That's nothing to sniff at! If you have time, repeat the game with six more mystery guests.

A good way to transition from a fun activity to the heart of the lesson is to throw out a "quick question" students can discuss with one or two people next to them. Ask: **In this game, we found out how well you know each other—well, at least how well you know each other's big toes. Do you think knowing someone well is *the* key to having a good friendship? If not, what *do* you think is the key to a good friendship?**

STEP 2

Friendship Collages

(Needed: old magazines, newspapers, scissors, glue, markers, posterboard, tape)

Divide into small teams (optimal size four to six students) and give each team a piece of posterboard and other collage supplies.

Discuss: **What kinds of things do you do with your friends? What makes your friendships great?** Explain that instead of just talking about their friendships, your students will have a chance to *show* what their friendships are all about. Give them 10 minutes to cut out and paste together as many words, pictures, and symbols they can find that show: 1) what kinds of things they do with their friends, and 2) what makes their friendships great. Then let one person from each team explain the collages. Tape all the collages to a wall in your room. You will refer to them in Step 3.

How many of you are satisfied with mediocre or just OK friendships? How many of you want friendships that are great like the ones described by your collages?

If you really want great friendships, where do you go to learn more about great friendship? Who do you look to as a model of great friendship?

If you really want great friendships in your life, you'll study the greatest friend of all time. And that's exactly what we're going to do in this series. Jesus Christ is the world's all-time greatest friend. He can teach us some mind-blowing things about friendship. He can show us how to go beyond mediocre, OK friendship so we can build Extreme Friendships.

Teacher Tip: Making collages can be a successful activity for many junior high groups if you keep a couple things in mind: First, be sure to provide magazines that students will enjoy thumbing through (like *Sports Illustrated* for guys and *Brio* or similar magazines for girls). Add a competition element. For example, you might throw out the challenge: **Who can fill up their posterboard with the most pictures?** Finally, give each team a small enough piece of posterboard that it's a realistic goal to cover up all the empty space in the time allotted.

OPTIONS

SMALL GROUP

LARGE GROUP

MOSTLY GIRLS

MOSTLY GUYS

EXTRA FUN

MEDIA

SHORT MEETING TIME

URBAN

JR. HIGH / HIGH SCHOOL COMBINED

SIXTH GRADE

Jesus Collages

(Needed: Bibles, collage supplies (from Step 2), white board, marker)

List the following Bible passages on white board ahead of time: Mark 6:30-44; Mark 7:31-37; Luke 6:17-26; Luke 10:38-42; and John 11:1-44. These are the passages students will study to get an overview of the kind of friend Jesus was. Pass out new sheets of posterboard. If students need to replenish their supply of collage materials (magazines, newspapers, markers, scissors, glue) pass these supplies out too.

Have students stay in the small groups from Step 2. Ask each group to use a Bible to read the verses you've listed on the board and answer two questions for each verse: 1) What words best describe the kind of friend Jesus was? and 2) What pictures come to mind when you think of how Jesus treated others? Each group should make a second collage based on their answers by writing down words, drawing pictures, or clipping words and pictures out of magazines and newspapers. Give students 10 minutes to complete the new collages.

Hang the new "Jesus collages" on a wall next to the "friendship collages" students made in Step 2. Discuss:

What kinds of words and pictures did you use to describe Jesus' friendship with others? Why?

What *kind* of people did Jesus befriend?

Did Jesus just talk about being a great friend to people in need? Or did He put His friendship into action? How did He put His friendship into action? Supplement students' answers by saying something like: **Jesus was an Extreme Friend— He didn't just say "I'll be there for you." He wasn't just "nice" to His friends. He put His friendship into action by *serving* others.**

If Jesus was an Extreme Friend, what kind of friends do you think we should be?

How to be an Extreme Friend

(Needed: cut-out copies of Repro Resource 1, paper, pens)

Ahead of time, cut a copy of "What's a Friend to Do?" (Repro Resource 1) into five pieces along the dotted lines. (If you have more than 30 students, you will need to cut apart more than one copy of Repro Resource 1.)

Introduce the parable of the Good Samaritan by saying something like: **Jesus told a story that can help us apply the extreme idea about service in the real world.**

As a group, read Luke 10:25-37. If your students have trouble relating to the context of the story, you might also try reading this modern paraphrase:

A man was hitchhiking from Chicago to Detroit when some guys jumped him, stole his wallet, beat him up, and left him lying by the side of the road. A pastor drove by and saw him, but the pastor was busy rehearsing his sermon and kept on going. Then a businesswoman drove by, but she was late for a meeting and quickly changed lanes to pass him. Finally, a beat up Chevy pulled to a stop. A poorly dressed man with dirty fingernails, messy hair, and an odd smell got out and put the man in his car. He took him to the nearby Hilton, ordered room service, and made sure the hotel doctor took care of him. The man spent every dime he had to take care of the stranger.

How does this modern paraphrase help you better understand the story of the Good Samaritan?

What do you think Jesus wants us to learn from the story of the Good Samaritan?

What does this story teach us about being Extreme Friends?

Supplement students' answers with the following info as needed: **Unlike the two other people in the story, the Good Samaritan saw someone in need and he said, "Whatever it takes, I'm going to put this person first and serve him." He was an Extreme Friend because he served others just like Jesus did.**

Form small groups of four to six students. Give each group one of the cut-out pieces of Repro Resource 1, a blank sheet of paper, and pens. Ask each group to look at its card from the resource sheet

O P T I O N S

EXTRA **ACTION**

HEARD IT ALL BEFORE

LITTLE BIBLE BACKGROUND

MOSTLY GUYS

URBAN

JR.HIGH HIGH SCHOOL **COMBINED**

and think about this question: **What would it look like to be an Extreme Friend in this situation?** Tell the groups to write down as many ways they can think of to serve someone in that scenario. After five or six minutes ask each group to read its final list out loud. Write down all the ideas on a white board. Make sure to congratulate your students on the creativity of ideas they have shared.

Say something like: **Now we have a clear picture of what it would look like to be Extreme Friends in the real world. You can see that none of these ideas is easy, but they're all worth it. Are you up for the challenge? Will you choose to be an Extreme Friend?**

STEP 5

Putting Service into Action

(Needed: list of "Extreme Friendship" ideas from Step 4, pens, transportation —optional)

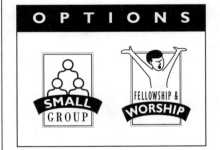

OPTIONS

SMALL GROUP

FELLOWSHIP & WORSHIP

Let's not just talk about being Extreme Friends. Let's get out and do it. Explain that students have 10 minutes to walk around with a partner and look for ways to be an Extreme Friend somewhere right outside your meeting place. Give them a few ideas, such as being an Extreme Friend to the gardener by pulling weeds in specific places around the church, or to the custodian by picking up some trash, or to a single parent trying to walk his or her children to their Sunday school class.

When students return, discuss: **How did you put friendship into action? How did it feel?**

It's usually easier to be Extreme Friends here at church rather than out in the real world but let's think about the rest of the week. Of all of the ideas we listed earlier, which idea sticks out to you as the best way you can put friendship into action this next week?

Explain that if students would like to commit to putting service into action this week by doing one of the ideas on the list on the board made in Step 4, they should come forward and put their initials next to that idea. If a student has another idea that hasn't been mentioned yet, he or she can write that idea down, then put his or her own initials next to it. Give your students a few minutes to complete this task. You may want to lead the way by placing your own initials next to an idea.

After your students have finished, close in prayer. Pray that God will strengthen each person to be an Extreme Friend this week.

Teacher Tip: The "Service Tour" directions above work best for Sunday school classes. But if you're meeting at another time or place, you can modify the directions as needed. Or you might arrange some kind of service opportunity your group can do right where you are. For example, you might cook a meal for a needy family (give small groups of students responsibility for preparing different parts of the meal). Consider your time and other limitations and be creative!

What's a Friend to Do?

Extreme Friendship

WHAT YOU SAY
IN CLASS TO A FRIEND

WHAT YOU SAY
AFTER SCHOOL TO A FRIEND

Extreme Friendship

Extreme Friendship

WHAT YOU DO
WITH A FRIEND
ON THE WEEKEND

WHAT YOU DO
WITH A FRIEND WHEN
YOU'RE AT HER OR HIS HOME

Extreme Friendship

Extreme Friendship

WHAT YOU DO
WITH A FRIEND DURING
LUNCH AT SCHOOL

NOTES

STEP 1

To introduce the concept of Extreme Friendship, put the following words on slips of paper: bungee jumping, mountain biking, snowboarding, rock climbing, friendship. Divide into teams of four to six students and give each team modeling clay or dough. Each team should choose a "modeler." Pick the first clue and show it to each modeler. The team that first shouts out the clue being modeled wins one point. (No words or gestures allowed.) Discuss: **What did all of the clues have in common?** (They are "extreme" activities.) **Do you think "friendship" belongs with the rest of the clues? Why or why not? When is friendship "extreme"?** Say: **Extreme Friendship is being a friend like Jesus. Jesus is the ultimate modeler of Extreme Friendship. He always lived on the edge and pushed the status quo. What kind of friendship do you model?**

STEP 4

After discussing the parable of the Good Samaritan, use this activity to add more action to the brainstorming of service ideas: Divide into equal teams of four to six. Have teams circle up; give each team a tennis ball. Read the first scenario on Repro Resource 1. When you say go, one person on each team names one way he or she can put friendship into action in that scenario. That student throws the ball to another in the circle, who names a different answer, and so on. See how fast teams can get. Repeat with as many scenarios as you have time for.

STEP 1

"Name that Foot" requires six mystery guests. Instead, have students tell two true and one false statements about themselves. Others must guess which is the lie.

STEPS 2/3

In a small group, making collages may not produce enough ideas for an effective discussion. Instead, bring in a wide variety of odd and normal objects to represent different aspects of friendship. As a group make a human collage representing a "good friend" by posing, adding props, and making up additional signs and symbols to place on one volunteer. Be creative—a wrench in his hand might represent that a good friend "fixes" problems; a ring on his finger might represent that a good friend is committed. After reading the Scripture passages, make a second human collage to represent the kind of friend Jesus was. You might include props like: a hammer (He built into His friends), torn clothes (He made Himself a lowly servant), a wooden cross (to represent His death).

STEP 5

Instead of using the service tour idea, you have a great opportunity with a small group to arrange a service project ahead of time. You might arrange to drive your students off-site and serve in a soup kitchen or help with a project like Habitat for Humanity. The best projects will involve enough sacrifice to challenge students and enough service for them to experience some of the rewards of befriending and serving people in need. If you can't arrange the project ahead of time, you might spend a few minutes planning a project for a different meeting time.

STEP 1

In a large group, your students may not even know each other's names, much less their feet! Instead of playing "Name that Foot," have your students pair up with and face one friend. They should take a minute to notice their partner's hair, clothes, and other physical characteristics. Then pairs should stand back to back and students should change three things about themselves (unbutton a button, tousle their hair, untie a shoe, and so on). Finally, have the pairs face each other again and try to identify the changes.

STEPS 2/3

The collages described in Steps 2 and 3 could be difficult for large groups—we're talking a lot of magazines and glue! Instead, divide into groups of six to eight and have each group brainstorm a list of words and phrases. Write these down on posterboard or newsprint in lieu of magazine pictures. In Step 2, the words should describe students' friendships. In Step 3, the words should describe Jesus' friendships. You might make it a contest each time to see which group can create the longest list or the list that contains the most ideas not found on other groups' lists.

STEP 3

Many well-meaning church groups practice "sloppy agape"—they put too much emphasis on being "nice" but they don't put friendships into action. If this is reflected in your students collages from Step 2, point it out. Discuss: **Friends say stuff like "I'll be there for you" and "It'll be alright" all the time. What do these phrases mean?** If students are honest they may admit those phrases are just "nice" things friends say but don't often relate to action. Instead of making more collages, have each group perform a skit that shows what its Scripture passage might have looked like if Jesus was just "nice." For example, the Mark 6:30-44 group might show Jesus, instead of feeding the crowd, simply saying, "I'm sorry you're hungry. But it's OK. I'm here for you." After each presentation, read what Jesus really did. Brainstorm words to define Extreme Friendship (sacrifice, service, etc.)

STEP 4

Even groups that have "heard it all" will probably still respond to seeing it in action. Invite two old and "extreme" friends to tell stories to your group. Encourage the friends to talk honestly and openly. As they talk about a difficult friendship issue, kids will wake up and listen closely. Some potential follow-up questions include: **What's the most you ever sacrificed for your friend? Have there been any tough times? How did your friendship survive? How hard was it to forgive?**

STEP 3

Help students understand Jesus wasn't just a great friend a long time ago—He is a great friend today. Follow the directions for Step 3, then discuss: **How can Jesus provide for our needs today? In what ways can Jesus heal us? How does Jesus serve us? How does He comfort us?** Be prepared to discuss specific experiences of your own. For example, try not to just say, "Jesus answered my prayers"; give details like "I was praying for a way to pay my rent and I got an unexpected refund check in the mail."

STEP 4

Students with little Bible background may need help making the jump from "Jesus is a good friend" to "We should be good friends like Jesus." Recruit spiritually mature high school students or adults to give one- or two-minute testimonies about why and how they try to be good friends to others because Jesus is such a good friend to them. They should detail their motives (thankfulness to Jesus, wanting to obey Scripture, etc.) and the specific ways they try to be Extreme Friends. Once you've made this introduction, use Step 4 as directed.

STEP 3

After completing Step 3 you might use one or more of these ideas to help students reflect on and praise Jesus for the friend He is to us:

• Write thank you letters to Jesus.

• Read John 13:1-9. Discuss that this was one more story of Jesus putting friendship into action with service, and wash each student's feet with water and a wash rag.

• Read "The Ragman" by Walter Wangerin, Jr. (*Ragman and Other Cries of Faith,* Harper & Row, 1984) or another story that helps illuminate the extreme idea that Jesus serves us.

• Sing worship songs you are familiar with that celebrate Jesus' friendship with us or his servant's attitude toward us.

STEP 5

The idea for an extended prayer time will help students close the meeting with an upward focus. Divide into groups of three. Help students get in a quiet mood by turning the lights down and singing several praise songs. As you finish singing, ask students to close their eyes. Read Proverbs 17:17a to them: "A friend loves at all times . . ." If you want, challenge students to memorize the verse. Then ask students to take a minute and pray for the others in their group. Students should pray that God will give them courage and opportunities to put specific friendship ideas into action.

MOSTLY GIRLS

STEP 1

Girls love looking at things that identify themselves and their friends. Identifying baby pictures might be more fun for a group of mostly girls than the "Name that Foot" game. Tell students ahead of time to bring their baby pictures in. Mix up the baby pictures and tape them to a large piece of cardboard or to a wall. Assign each photo a number. Distribute index cards and ask students to list the number of each photo on their card followed by the name of the girl they believe each photo shows. Reveal the true identities and see who got the most answers right. Discuss: **What similarities do you see in the baby photos and in each other as you are now?** Say: **Every one of you has a Friend who not only knows exactly what you looked like as a baby, He actually knew you before you were born! Jesus knows you inside and out. You may know that He wants to be your best friend. In this series we'll also learn He wants to teach you how to be good friends to others.**

STEP 2

Friendship is a strong value for many girls; a value they love to share and celebrate. Follow the directions for Step 2 with this variation: Have each girl make her own friendship collage as a gift she can give later to one of her friends. Pass out a small piece of posterboard to each student. Put collage supplies in a place where students can share. Tell girls to cut and paste words, pictures, and symbols that represent the specific friendship they choose. Give each student a chance to display her collage. Use the concluding comments as written in Step 2.

MOSTLY GUYS

STEP 1

Guys will eat up any tie-in you can make to "extreme" activities before talking about Extreme Friendship. consider these ideas:

• **Extreme Video:** Watch a clip from an extreme sports video (e.g., *Angel's Cliff* or any other video by Warren Miller).

• **Extreme Diving:** Lay a couple of gym mats or mattresses down. See who can make the most "extreme" dive.

• **Extreme Athlete Contest:** Decide who the "Most Extreme Athlete " is by holding a combination of contests, including pushups, foot races, weightlifting, etc.

STEPS 2/3

Instead of asking students to make collages of their friendships, ask them to design the "Ultimate Guy" or "Most Extreme Guy" posters. Discuss: **How does the Ultimate Guy treat his friends? Is it "extreme" or "uncool" to serve others? Why? What would happen if you sacrificed for and served your friends?** Then follow Step 3 as directed and compare the Ultimate Guy posters to the Jesus collages. Ask guys if they want to change any part of their posters to reflect the kind of Ultimate Guy Jesus is.

STEPS 4/5

Find a challenging hill to climb or trail to hike and take your group there. Make each student start the hike carrying something heavy, like a huge rock. When the guys get tired, take as many of their rocks as possible and carry them up the rest of the way. At the end of the trail explain that's what Extreme Friendship is—it's not just saying nice things, it's jumping in and sacrificing so your friend is better off. Challenge students to read and memorize Galatians 6:2.

EXTRA FUN

STEP 1

Introduce the friendship series with a variety of games and fun activities such as these:

• **Famous Friends:** Have teams list pairs of famous friends—real or fictitious. Award prizes to the team with the most.

• **Do I Know You?:** This is kind of a "Newlywed Game" for friends. Have kids pair up, then send one half or every pair out of the room. Ask questions of the remaining friends. Then bring the others back in and check answers.

• **Draw a Friend:** Give groups of four large sheets of butcher paper and markers. Have them draw a life-sized "perfect friend."

• **Friendship Food:** Serve snacks (candy, cookies, chips, etc.) Have kids choose a snack and describe why that item is like friendship (e.g.,"This cookie is like friendship because going through heat made it better").

STEPS 2/3

Divide into about four teams (optimal size: four or five students each). Display a collection of odd props, like a toilet plunger, a stapler, a Frisbee, a box, a radio, a rope, and a teddy bear. Be creative and choose an odd assortment. Explain to the teams that they'll have five minutes to create a commercial that reflects what a good friendship is like. The only rules are that it has to be 30 seconds or less, has to be about friendship, and must use all the props. (The props can be used to *represent* something else, however.) After several minutes, have the teams perform their commercials. Repeat this activity for Step 3, asking the teams to put together commercials that reflect the friendship characteristics of Jesus.

STEP 1

Make arrangements ahead of time with a parent to film a student's room but don't let the student know. Keep the segment short. Record clips of you being greeted by a parent, pictures of the student on the wall, and an in-depth look at various parts of the student's room. Cue the video and say: **How well do we really know our friends? Let's take an in-depth look at one student's private world. See if anything surprises you about how [he or she] *really* lives.** For an ongoing gag, film a different student's room each week.

STEP 2

Arrange for students to bring in songs that contain messages about friendship. Even secular music can help you contrast Jesus' ideas about friendship with the world's. Give each student a chance to play part of the song, explain what the message about friendship is, and tell what they like or dislike about the message. Be prepared to point out any differences from Jesus' views on friendships.

STEP 1

Instead of waiting for all students to arrive, as students enter have them pair up and tell each other about one important friend. (Also, remember that if you're *really* short on time and your group doesn't need to be "warmed up," you can usually skip Step 1 altogether without missing any of the "meat" of the lesson.)

STEP 2

Prepare students ahead of time to bring in photos of themselves with their friends in a variety of activities. Instead of having students take the time to cut pictures out of magazines, make one "friendship collage" using the pictures students brought in. Modify the discussion in Step 2 as needed.

STEP 3

Instead of making "Jesus collages," read each Bible story one at at time. Have volunteers act out the actions of their assigned characters. Then compare Jesus' friendships to students' friendships as directed in Step 3.

STEP 4

Brainstorm one list of ways students can serve others. (Needed: newsprint, marker.)

STEP 5

Skip the tour around the church. Return to the collages or posters made in Step 2. Let students decorate the old collages by drawing new pictures with markers or crayons that symbolize what they will do to serve others in the coming week. (Needed collages from Step 2.)

STEP 1

If your group members find exposing their feet awkward, modify the Name that Foot directions slightly: Cut a space in the mystery curtain for noses and have the group guess who those belong to. (This also works with thumbs and mouths!) (Needed: mystery curtain from Step 1)

STEPS 2/3

To make the friendship collage applicable to the cultural images experienced by city teens, bring in magazines like: *Emerge, Right On, Vibe, Bronze Thrills, Braids and Beauty, Ebony, Essence, Black Enterprise, Jive, The Source, Jet, Hype Hair, YSB, Free 4080, Upscale, Black Hair, Heart & Soul, Black Beat,* and any others you know of.

STEP 4

Instead of the paraphrase included in the main lesson, read this urban version of Luke 10:25-37: Two days before Christmas, Hector Fernandez missed the last bus home by seconds and had to walk 10 miles. He was stopped by three gang members who accused him of being on the wrong side of town, beat him, and left him there bleeding. They also took all his cash—the Christmas bonus Hector needed to buy gifts for his family. A pastor looking to help the homeless drove by. "Hello, do you need a sandwich or a cup of coffee?" Hector said, "I'm hurt! I need an ambulance!" But the pastor just threw him a sandwich and drove on. Next a jogger ran by. Hector tried to motion that he was hurt. The jogger, startled, crossed the street and kept going. Finally, a police car pulled up. This officer attended to Hector, took him immediately to the best hospital in town, paid the hospital bill at his own expense, and raised enough money to buy gifts for Hector's whole family for Christmas.

STEPS 2/3

If some of the high school students in your group would find the collage activities "cheesy," try this creative discussion starter. Fill up a "Friendship Box" with random items, some that have to do with friendship (friendship bracelet, phone, pictures of friends, etc.) and some where the connection is not so obvious (toilet plunger, lava lamp, baseball, anything else wacky enough to get your student's attention). Each student or pair of students must choose an item from the box and give a two- to five-sentence mini-message on friendship based on that item. For example, a student might pick the phone and give a message about how good communication is an important part of friendship. For Step 3, students should use the same objects to give mini-messages about what Jesus thinks about friendship.

STEP 4

This activity might work better with high schoolers in the group because their answers will help inspire your junior highers. Divide into groups of four or five, each a mixture of some junior and senior high students. Tell students to imagine what kinds of headlines and newspaper stories might be written about their group if they were to become Extreme Friends like Jesus. They might come up with headlines like "Youth Group Impacts Campus" and specific stories about how teens serve others at their school by providing for those who have needs for food or clothes, spending time with less popular students, etc. Pass out a large sheet of newsprint and markers for each group to record its answers and share them with the rest of the group.

STEP 2

Sixth graders are concrete thinkers. This memory game is a fun, concrete way to begin defining friendship. Sit in a circle (or divide into circles of 10-15 students each if you have a large group). for the first round, start the game by saying, "An ideal friend is thoughtful." Point to your head. As you continue to your left, each player then repeats the words and actions of those before them and then adds a new word and a new action. This continues until all but one player has made a mistake and dropped out of the game. Before moving on, make a list of all the words or phrases players used to describe an ideal friend. Record these on newsprint or white board. If you have time, start another round with "A terrible friend is..."

STEP 3

Write the following headings on newsprint or white board: "Normal" and "Extreme." Divide into five teams and give each team a pen and paper. Assign each team one of the five Scripture passages listed. Teams should write down four words to describe how Jesus treated His friends in their passage. Discuss: **How did Jesus treat his friends? Was he just a normal friend or did He ever do anything extreme?** Have students list their four words under either the "Normal" or "Extreme" headings. Most words, like serving helping, and caring, belong under "Extreme."

DATE USED:

Approx. Time

STEP 1: *Name that Foot* _____
- ❑ Extra Action
- ❑ Small Group
- ❑ Large Group
- ❑ Mostly Girls
- ❑ Mostly Guys
- ❑ Extra Fun
- ❑ Media
- ❑ Short Meeting Time

Things needed:

STEP 2: *Friendship Collages* _____
- ❑ Small Group*
- ❑ Large Group*
- ❑ Mostly Girls
- ❑ Mostly Guys*
- ❑ Extra Fun*
- ❑ Media
- ❑ Short Meeting Time
- ❑ Urban*
- ❑ Combined Junior High/High School*
- ❑ Sixth Grade

Things needed:

STEP 3: *Jesus Collages* _____
- ❑ Heard It All Before
- ❑ Little Bible Background
- ❑ Fellowship & Worship
- ❑ Short Meeting Time
- ❑ Sixth Grade

Things needed:

STEP 4: *How to be an Extreme...* _____
- ❑ Extra Action
- ❑ Heard It All Before
- ❑ Little Bible Background
- ❑ Mostly Guys*
- ❑ Urban
- ❑ Combined Junior High/High School

Things needed:

STEP 5: *Putting Service into Action* _____
- ❑ Small Group
- ❑ Fellowship & Worship

Things needed:

* combined steps

Bleacher Friends

YOUR GOALS FOR THIS SESSION:

Choose one or more

☐ To help students learn how Jesus valued a bleeding woman others labeled "unvaluable."

☐ To help students discover a mind-blowing truth about value: In Jesus' eyes, even the unvalued are invaluable.

☐ To help students become Bleacher Friends—friends who "cheer on" and value people like Jesus did.

☐ Other:_____
_____

Your Bible Base:

Mark 5:21-34

Marshmallow Mash

(Needed: several bags of large marshmallows; rope, tape, or cones)

Divide your room into four equal areas using tape, rope, or cones. It would be helpful but not necessary to move chairs and tables out of the way. Then divide your group into four teams. For best results, divide according to natural affinity groups, such as school, gender, or grade level. Assign each team one of the four areas.

When you say go, have teams try to throw any marshmallows out of their team area and into another team's area. When you call stop, the team with the least marshmallows in its area wins. Make a big deal of congratulating the members of the winning team. Treat them like they're more important than members of the losing team.

Have students discuss the following questions with one or two people next to them: **Do you think winners are more valuable than losers? Why or why not? If not, why is winning such a big deal? And why is it that one of the worst things you can call somebody is a "loser"?**

Teacher Tip: Many competitive junior high students will still fall for the age-old trick of making a contest out of cleaning up. If your group will go for it, challenge teams to see which can pick up all of its marshmallows first. For added fun, tell students they can only use their feet.

The Price Is Right

(Needed: pen and paper, sticky notes (substitute cardboard or posterboard, scissors and tape), marker, magazine pictures of both current celebrities and people considered "outcasts," and approximately seven household and food items, such as garbage bags, laundry detergent, candles, cookies, cake mix, etc.)

Ahead of time, remove the price tags from each household and food item, but keep a list of the correct prices. For each item, make a new price tag that is 10 cents either higher or lower than the actual price. Price tags can be as simple as a sticky note, or more elaborate tags cut out of cardboard or posterboard. Use a marker to write the new price on the price tag. For the second part of this activity you'll need to clip a handful of pictures of celebrities out of magazines. Try to choose some that are popular with your group and others that are in the "out" crowd. Also clip out pictures of "unvalued" people: the homeless, elderly, poor, etc.

Introduce the game by saying something like: **How many of you have seen "The Price is Right" game show? Who wants to "come on down" and be a contestant?**

Choose seven volunteers. Show one student at a time a household or food item and the incorrect price. Ask the contestant to guess whether the item is higher or lower in value than the price tag displayed. Encourage the contestants to involve the audience as much as possible by asking other group members to shout out advice. If the contestant answers correctly, let him or her keep the item. Do this until you have used all seven items.

The second part of the game uses the same principles but involves your entire group. Display two magazine pictures of celebrities. Ask: **If these pictures had a price tag on them, which would be higher and which would be lower in value in the eyes of our culture? Why?** Your students will likely answer that question based on physical attractiveness or recent accomplishments. You might let students vote by applause to determine the more valuable. Do this with several pairs of pictures. Toward the end the game, match the most popular celebrities up against each other and come up with an MVP (Most Valuable Person). Finally, display some pictures of people the culture considers "unvaluable," match them up against some of the most popular celebrities, and ask students to vote by applause for whom they think is more valuable.

Who is more valuable at your school: popular people or unpopular people? How do you know? What are some ways people in your school show that they value popular people more than unpopular people? (Ask these same types of questions about the athletes, well-dressed students, and other categories of "valued" students at their schools and in their spheres of influence.)

Besides the things we've talked about, at your school what other factors determine whether someone's valuable or not?

How does this method of determining someone's value affect our friendships? (Sometimes there's a price tag put on friendships. If you're not cool enough, you can't be friends with cool people. If you don't have enough value, you can't hang out with people that are valued.)

A lot of people who think like this fall into the Value Trap. They get trapped into thinking that some of their friends have value and some don't. They are nicer to and more interested in people who are popular or smart or good looking. Do you ever think like this? Do your friendships ever fall into the Value Trap?

Teacher Tip: Sometimes students will deny that the Value Trap exists in their circle of friends, especially those students who want to please you by giving the right "church" answers. One of the best ways to get students to talk about the Value Trap, though, is to ask them to talk about times when *they* felt "unvalued." You might try to prepare one or two students ahead of time to tell stories about how they were treated meanly and unfairly by peers. One honest story may open the floodgates to many more of your students' stories.

STEP
3

Ultimate Affirmation

(Needed: cut-out copies of Repro Resource 2, Bibles)

Prepare a large amount of "Funny Money" by copying Repro Resource 2 on green paper and cutting it into separate bills. Also, prepare students to play the parts of the woman and the four Value Judges in the scene described below.

What would Jesus say about the Value Trap?

Explain that Jesus was confronted by the Value Trap several times during His life. Read Mark 5:21-28 aloud.

Ask the student playing the part of the woman to come to the front of the room with four $10, "Funny Money" bills. One by one, have the Value Judges come in front of her and make a pronouncement. For example, the first judge should pronounce, "She is a woman!" Stop to ask the audience: **Does the fact that she is a woman make her more valuable, less valuable, or neither?** Let students shout out answers. Regardless of what the audience says, have the first Value Judge pronounce, "Unvaluable!" and take a $10 bill away. Do the same thing for the other three judges who should pronounce, respectively: "She is bleeding!"; "She is unable to be healed by doctors"; and "She can't have any contact with other people." Each Value Judge should end by talking $10 away from the girl until she's left with no money. Refer back to the story of the bleeding woman in Mark 5:21-28 and explain that in the culture she lived in, being a woman with incurable bleeding would have made her a social outcast. She would have had virtually no value in her culture.

Read Mark 5:29-34. Help students see the significance of Jesus' action by saying something like: **Jesus looked at a woman who many people labeled "unvaluable," and He affirmed her value in front of everyone there. Jesus proved that she was valuable and gave her something that could never be taken from her.** As dramatically as you can, hand the student playing the part of the woman a stack of $10 bills to represent the value Jesus gave to her.

Imagine you are the woman in the story we just read. If Jesus affirmed your value right in front of everyone, how would you feel?

Why do you think Jesus treated this woman the way He did? Was there something special about her?

If you wanted to be seen as valuable in Jesus' eyes, what would you have to do? Supplement students' responses by saying something like: **Here is the key: You can't do** *anything* **that will make you any more valued in Jesus' eyes. Jesus already values you more than you can possibly know. Jesus puts no price tags on His friendships!**

But many people don't think of Jesus as a friend. They think that Jesus is just waiting to condemn us for the things we do. Explain that the Bible tells us that Jesus doesn't condemn those that believe in Him. Even though we are all sinners, Jesus never values us any less. Instead, Jesus' great love for us gives us value that no one can ever take away.

In Jesus' eyes, even the unvalued become invaluable. If Jesus has no price tags on His friendships—if He values everyone no matter how smart or good-looking or popular he or she is—how we should treat *our* **friends?**

STEP 4

How to Be Bleacher Friends

(Needed: three copies of Repro Resource 3, pens, index cards)

About a week ahead of time, prepare three students to each read one of the monologues from "Feeling Unvalued" (Repro Resource 3). Give them copies of the resource so they can practice.

If you were the woman who was healed by Jesus you would have felt very special. Jesus cheered her on when no one else would. Jesus was a "Bleacher Friend" to the bleeding woman. Have you ever had a Bleacher Friend? Bleacher Friends sit in the bleachers of our life and cheer us on. They encourage us. And they show us and tell us how valuable we are. Has anyone ever been a Bleacher Friend to you? Tell us about it. Let as many students share as you have time for.

You live in a world stuck in the Value Trap. Wouldn't it be a mind-blowing thing if we all decided to break out of the trap and be Bleacher Friends to the people in our lives? What if we decided to be like Jesus and value the unvalued? Have the three students you've prepared read their monologues. While students listen, tell them to think about: **What would Jesus do if He knew these people? How would Jesus show that He values them?**

OPTIONS

LARGE GROUP

LITTLE BIBLE BACKGROUND

SHORT MEETING TIME

JR. HIGH / HIGH SCHOOL COMBINED

SIXTH GRADE

Pass out pens and index cards and tell students to write an encouraging note on their cards to one of the three unvalued people. When students finish writing, they should get up and give their index cards to the appropriate actor.

Do you think these teens would feel valued by these letters? Why or why not?

Besides writing letters, what else could we do to value these three people?

What kinds of people are unvalued at your school? How can you be Bleacher Friends to them?

Teacher Tip: You may have some students who won't go along with the concept of being "Bleacher Friends." Some students may ignore your directions and write harsh and discouraging statements on the cards they give to the actors. (Such can be life in junior high, unfortunately.) This doesn't mean the activity has failed. Since the cards will be anonymous, you have a great opportunity to use the statements as an example of the Value Trap.

STEP 5

Putting Value into Action

(Needed: copies of Repro Resource 4)

If possible, have students sit on stairs. The stairs will work as temporary bleachers from which students can cheer each other on. If that's not possible, arrange chairs in a semi-circle.

Ask for a volunteer to stand up in front of the rest of the group. Each time a student stands up, lead the rest of the students in loud, rowdy, and encouraging cheers, as if you were cheering on a sports team or a musician at a concert. Discuss what it feels like to be "cheered on." Tell students to remember how much they like to be cheered on and encourage them to remember to cheer on others.

Finally, pass out copies of "I Value You! (Repro Resource 4). Encourage students to take it home, fill it out, and send it to someone they want to value. Close in prayer, asking God to help your group become Bleacher Friends.

OPTIONS

EXTRA ACTION

SMALL GROUP

HEARD IT ALL BEFORE

FELLOWSHIP & WORSHIP

MOSTLY GUYS

MEDIA

SHORT MEETING TIME

Funny Money

Photocopy this sheet on green paper and cut these bills apart.

NOTES

Feeling Unvalued

Try to put yourself into the shoes of these students as you read their thoughts and feelings aloud.

Student #1: Clothes Carol

I hate my mom's job. I mean, I guess being a secretary is an OK job, but she sure doesn't make much money. All through elementary school I wore my older sister's hand-me-downs. None of the other kids could tell, though. My sister had pretty good taste then, and her clothes looked pretty good on me.

But now my mom *still* doesn't make much money, and most of the clothes that I wear are *still* my older sister's hand-me-downs. Now the other kids can tell. They make fun of me, even my best friend Robyn. She told me yesterday as we were getting dressed after P.E., "Carol, your clothes are pretty much out of it. You look kinda dorky." I don't think she really meant to hurt my feelings, but that afternoon when I got home from school, I went to my bedroom and cried.

Student #2: New Girl Nancy

"You'll make tons of friends," my dad told me when we moved from my old house to my new house. "You'll love your new school," he said. Well, I don't have any friends and I don't like my new school. Everyone ignores me. It's like I don't even exist. I feel invisible. I tried to be nice the first few days, but what difference does it make? Everyone has his or her own group of friends.

No one seems interested in inviting me to join them. I sit alone at lunch, and I walk home alone after school. I just wish I could go back to my old friends and my old school.

Student #3: Failing Frank

I don't even want to see my report card. I know that I'm going to fail my math class this year. I'm not good at math. Too many numbers. Too much homework. I even tried to study harder, but I still didn't understand it. What's the point of studying if I fail anyway? I tried to go after school and get some help from my teacher. That helped a little, but not enough. My parents are going to kill me if I fail math.

I Value You!

You are **IMPORTANT** to God.

And you are **IMPORTANT** to me.

Here are some things that I value about you:

_____

_____

_____

_____

_____

_____

_____

_____

_____

_____

_____

_____

_____

_____

_____

_____

_____

_____

_____

STEPS 1/2

Spread out junk items (newspapers, paper plates, cardboard boxes, etc.) Divide into teams of 7-10. Each team member must make it to the other side of the room by stepping only on the junk. If a student touches the floor, he or she must go back to the start. On each team: blindfold two students, tie up the legs of two, tie up the arms of two, and plug the ears of one. Tell students the key to this activity is valuing each student so that some strong students will have to carry some leg-tied students, etc. Most teams will need about 20 minutes. (Large groups can run two or more courses at the same time.) Ask questions that help teens draw their own conclusions. **Were you tempted at times to feel some teammates were less valuable then others? What did you learn about teamwork? What did you learn about valuing others?** Explain the "Value Trap" concept (see Step 2) and discuss questions like: **What did this game teach us about the Value Trap?**

STEP 5

Many students *mean* to express value to one another but they never get around to it. Make a "round tuit" for each student by tying the ends of a 3-foot rope together. Scatter several round tuits on the ground and have each student stand in one. Tell half the group to move clockwise and the other group to move counterclockwise and step in as many "round tuits" as time allows. If someone else is in the "round tuit" they step in, they must tell that person an "I value you because. . . ." statement before moving on. Close by telling students how much you value them.

STEPS 1/2

You can help your small group experience what it's like to be unvalued before you talk about valuing others. Arrange to take your group to a grocery store. Assign each group member a family role: parent(s), adolescent(s), grandparent(s), baby. Give your group five dollars (or a five dollar limit) and explain the five dollars must buy food for the whole family for a week. Give students 15-20 minutes to buy the food (or make a list of food items to buy). Discuss what they chose and why, then ask: **If you weren't pretending to be a struggling family and I gave you $5, what *would* you have bought? Was it frustrating to have such a limited budget? How would you feel if you had to live on that budget all the time? Do you ever think about people who actually have to live on $5 per week?** Discuss the "Value Trap." Explain that our culture sees some people—for example people who don't have a lot of money—as less valuable than others. If you had your students buy the food, donate the food to a needy family or shelter.

STEP 5

This affirmation activity works best in a small group where students know each other well. Bring in a large ball of yarn. Gather teens in a circle. Throw the ball to one student and make an "I value you because. . . ." statement to that student. That student should then hold on to the yarn, throw the ball to a different person, and say something affirming about him or her, and so on. Make sure no one is left out or feels unvalued by the time you're done.

STEP 3

First, divide into groups (girls vs. guys, Central Middle School vs. North Middle School) and play a modified version of "Win, Lose, or Draw." Ahead of time, write the following terms on slips of paper: "skinny," "poor," and "unpopular." Give each team $500 in Funny Money (Resource 2) to start with and put markers and a flip-chart or large piece of newsprint in front of each team. Have one representative come forward from each team. Show the representatives the first clue and have them try to draw it while their team guesses. To demonstrate that each of these clues is something that makes someone less valuable in your students' culture, take $100 *away* from the team that gets the clue right first. Get new students to draw for each clue. Continue with these new clues: "woman" and "bleeding." Explain how these things made the woman in the Bible story less valued in her culture. Then continue with Step 3 as written.

STEP 4

In a large group, it might be impractical to read all the ideas from your students' index cards. Huddle up in groups of six to eight. Pass out one copy of Repro Resource 4, blank paper, and pencils to each group. Ask: **What would Jesus do if these unvalued people were His friends?** Then have students write detailed stories of how someone like themselves could be a Bleacher Friend to the unvalued teens.

STEP 3

Students who have heard "Jesus loves and values everyone" all their lives will benefit from this fresh approach. Think about something you (or someone you know) owns that is extremely expensive or valuable (maybe even priceless) that you could bring to your group. Sound risky? It has to be to make the point. For example, one youth worker did this activity with borrowed Super Bowl and airplane tickets. Another showed a diamond that was an irreplaceable family heirloom. One brought currency in an amount students had never seen before. Show and describe the items to the group and explain why they are so valuable to you. During your "show and tell" have an adult come in the room with a small child (preferably one your students know). Have the adult ask about what you're doing. Explain the priceless items, then offer to exchange them for the child. After having a little fun pretending to barter over price ("Come on, the kid is 95% water!"), have the adult turn down the offer and leave. Say: **Obviously, the child is worth more than these priceless items. She's really priceless! That's how Jesus views people: it doesn't matter who or what we have done, He values us for who we are.**

STEP 5

Since students have "heard it all before," challenge them to start living it out. Pass out bright-colored construction paper, scissors and markers and tell students to make "coupons" to give to the friends in their life they want to value. Coupons could be for anything from: "one free ice cream on me" to "one-time room cleaning."

STEP 3

Help students with little Bible background get exposure to more than just one story about how Jesus valued others. Read the following passages: Matthew 9:9-13 (Jesus valued the lowly tax collector, Matthew); Mark 5:25-34 (Jesus valued a bleeding woman); and John 8:1-11 (Jesus valued an adulteress). If you have time, expand the "Value Judges" skit to include Matthew and the adulteress. Or, divide into three groups, assign each group a passage, and ask groups to act out their passages. Discuss: **How do you think these people felt when Jesus valued them? How do you think they responded to Jesus?** Use the end of Step 3 in the main lesson.

STEP 4

Set a wooden cross at the front of the room. Discuss: **When we know what great lengths Jesus has gone to value us, how can we respond to Him?** Help students understand how to respond to Christ by detailing how you made Jesus your Leader and Forgiver and how you try to value others because Jesus valued you. Tell students if they want to respond to Christ they can write one of two responses on the backs of their Funny Money (cut-out copies of Repro Resource 2 students should still have from Step 3). First, they might write a letter to Jesus telling Him they want to make Him their Leader and Forgiver. Or, if they have already made that decision, they might write specific ways they can value others, one way on each bill. Have students lay their money at the foot of the cross.

STEP 3

Pass out copies of Resource 4. Tell students to reflect on how much Jesus values them. Have students complete Repro Resource 4 by writing out what they think Jesus might write to them. Choose a few volunteers to share their letters. Then ask students to write letters to Jesus on the back of the resource thanking Jesus for His great love. Ask: **How should we respond to the way Jesus values us?** Lead students in a response time by singing worship songs you're familiar with that celebrate how Jesus values us. Explain that one of the ways students can respond to Jesus is by being Bleacher Friends to other unvalued people. Pass out pens and paper and challenge students to write down the names of one or two people they can be a Bleacher Friend to in the coming week.

STEP 5

For a different ending to the lesson, have students hold hands in a circle and turn the lights in your room down low. Play a meaningful song that celebrates friendship. Next, encourage students to pray out loud as they thank God for their friendships in the group. Make sure no students are left out.

MOSTLY GIRLS

STEP 2

This activity will capitalize on girls' love for makeovers. Bring in make up and costume accessories. Get permission from one of the students ahead of time and give her a makeover. Call your volunteer to the front of the room and explain to the class that they have 10 minutes to give her a complete makeover. (If you have a large group, you might choose more than one volunteer and divide into makeover teams.) Discuss: **Does she look prettier now? Does she have more value now because she looks prettier? Why or why not? Would most girls at your school think you were more valuable if you were prettier? Do you think Jesus would think you were more valuable if you were prettier? Why or why not? What do you think makes you more valuable to Jesus?**

STEP 3

Use the "Value Judges Skit" from the main lesson. Then discuss how much Jesus values each of us today. Say: **We often think we have to look a certain way, wear the best labels, or spend a specific amount of time on ourselves before we have value. That's not true! Jesus values us just the way we are, no matter what we look like, no matter what the rest of the world thinks of us.** If possible, have various Valentine's Day cards to show the students. Explain that we use valentines to show how much we love and value someone. Pass out paper, glue, scissors, and other materials for making valentines. Then have girls make a valentine to themselves as Jesus might have written it.

MOSTLY GUYS

STEP 1

Guys this age learn best from concrete images and strong object lessons. What if you took your group to a YMCA gym, a local football or soccer field, or some other place where you can all actually sit in some bleachers? Decide on a physical challenge that is difficult but not impossible for your guys. For example, you might have them do 20 push-ups, or you might have them sit back to back, link elbows and require them to stand up without touching the ground. Choose a few volunteers for the challenge. Instruct the rest of the guys NOT to cheer. Then do this a second time with different guys, but this time instruct everyone to encourage and cheer on the volunteers. Refer back to this game when you discuss how important it is to have and be Bleacher Friends who cheer one another on. If possible, continue the rest of the lesson with students sitting on the bleachers.

STEP 5

Step 5 can be particularly effective while sitting in a set of actual bleachers. Have guys come down from the bleachers one at a time. When down in front, have each guy share an area of his life where he is facing a challenge or is lacking confidence. Tell the rest of the group to bombard him from the bleachers with encouragement, support, and value. If a particular guy is not ready to share a struggle from his life, that's fine. Just have him stand there and let the group encourage him in whatever way they want. This activity will help your guys feel what it's like to have friends in the bleachers. They won't forget that feeling.

EXTRA FUN

STEP 1

Play up the marshmallow theme in Step 1 by using some of the games below. Be sure to end with "Marshmallow Mash," as written in the main lesson to help you transition to Step 2. Try:
• **In Your Face:** Thread string through marshmallows covered with chocolate syrup and dangle them in a doorway or from a pole. Have students race to eat the marshmallows with hands behind backs.
• **Chubby Bunny:** Each round, give contestants one more marshmallow to shove in their mouths (no chewing allowed!), and have them try to say "Chubby Bunny." They're out when they're not audible or when they spit out their mouthful. Hint: have a trash can nearby—*very* nearby!
• **Marshketball:** Yup, it's basketball with marshmallows. Use trash cans for baskets. Play with multiple teams and marshmallows if you have a large group (optimal team size: four or five). No dribbling; you can only take two steps if you have a marshmallow.
• **Marshmallow Sculpture:** Provide lots of marshmallows and toothpicks. Ask teams of three or four to make sculptures.

STEP 3

Decide ahead of time what the main points are of the Bible study. Discuss these as a group. Then send kids out in teams to find things that will represent the points. If you have lots of time, take your kids to a grocery store or drug store with $4 per team, and ask them to buy things that will represent the points. If you've got less time (or less $!), send them out in and around your church (or wherever your group meets) with instructions to find things wherever they can. Have the groups share their findings.

STEP 1

The song "Treasure of You" by Stephen Curtis Chapman (on the *Heaven in the Real World* CD) will help students understand how much Jesus values them. Use Step 3, then have someone stand and read Matthew 13: 44-46. When done, ask students to think about whether or not they could actually sell everything they have to follow Christ. As they think about this, play "Treasure of You." If possible, put the lyrics on an overhead and call students' attention to them. When the song is done, confess that you also find it difficult to sell everything to follow Jesus. But then say: **I'm going to read the passage again, but this time I want you to think about the story in a different manner. This time, the treasure is not diamonds or jewels, but it's you that's really the treasure.** Read the passage again. **You see, we are the treasure that Jesus found—and He sold everything He had to buy us. That's how much He values us; He was willing to give it all up for you and me when He died on the cross.**

STEP 5

Mr. Holland's Opus is a powerful movie about the life of a giving orchestra teacher. Cue the scene at the end where Mr. Holland (Richard Dreyfuss) is given a surprise concert by his former students. Show how Mr. Holland basks in the applause of his friends and family. Discuss: **How did Mr. Holland feel at that moment? How did his friends feel? Have you ever helped encourage and thank a friend? How did he or she feel? Who can you think of right now who needs to be cheered for his or her friendship? What can you do to cheer him or her on?**

STEP 1

Instead of playing "Marshmallow Mash," scatter various coins around the room and when all students arrive, have them race to see who can gather the most points (in total value of money gathered). If you don't have a lot of spare change, this can also work with "Funny Money," which you can make by copying Repro Resource 2 on different colored paper. Discuss that assigning different values to different kinds of money is OK, but we sometimes fall into a trap of doing the same thing with people—we think some people have more value than others.

STEP 2

Instead of playing "The Price Is Right," read pairs of items and people and ask students to stand on one wall if they think the first item is more valuable or the other wall if they think the second item is more valuable.
For starters: **What's more valuable ... A family car or a family photo album? A close relative or your best friend? A trophy you earned or an expensive piece of jewelry someone gave you? Brad Pitt or Wesley Snipes? A young teen or a senior citizen?** Use this activity to introduce the Value Trap.

STEP 4

Skip Resource 3 and brainstorm as a class how you might encourage unvalued people.

STEP 5

Skip the "Bleacher Cheers" activity. Instead, pass out copies of Repro Resource 4 and encourage students to finish it and mail it to a friend.

STEP 2

In the inner city, racism is a daily reality. This activity will educate teens on the terrible nature of racism which values individuals by skin color. Play "The Race is Right" like "The Price is Right," except each time compare black objects with white objects. Set it up so the white object always has more financial value than the black object. This works best if a few trials are absurd, e.g., a white cupcake vs. a black television. Before long some will realize that the pricing values are in favor of the white items. Before moving on, show some pictures of faces from different ethnicities and let students decide for themselves which face is more valuable. If they already understand that in actuality neither face is more valuable, great! Discuss: **Can color really tell us anything about value?** (No.) **Can one's race or ethnic group tell us anything about a person's value to the world?** (No.) Explain the Value Trap in detail and discuss other ways besides racism people fall into the trap.

STEP 3

After reading the story of the bleeding woman, read one more story, that of the African, Simon of Cyrene (a country in North Africa), who during Jesus' march to Golgotha helped bear the weight of the cross with Jesus on the Via Dolorosa (see Matthew 27:32, Mark 15:21, and Luke 23:26). To those teens whose cultural self-image is harmed by racism, discussing how Jesus valued Simon just as much as He did the bleeding woman will help restore an image of ethnic value.

STEP 1

Play any game that will produce a team or individual champion—from football or volleyball to "Bible baseball." Treat the members of the winning team as if they are more valuable than the losers by giving them special privileges and saying especially encouraging things to them. Then discuss: **Is this team really more valuable because it won the game? If not, what really makes someone valuable or not valuable? Do you think people ever get caught up in valuing "winners" more than "losers"? What are some other ways people fall into the "Value Trap" of treating some people like they're more important than others?**

STEP 4

Instead of using the case studies on Resource 4, let your group create its own. Begin by explaining that Driving Dan just got his driver's license, but because he arrived home past his curfew and forgot to fill the car up with gas, his dad and step-mom are about ready to ground him. Ask for a volunteer to share one sentence describing how Driving Dan feels or what he thinks. That volunteer then gets to pick another student who adds a second sentence by building on the thoughts and emotions of the first sentence, and so on until you have 10 sentences. Ask students to think of creative ways they could be a Bleacher Friend and encourage Driving Dan even if he gets grounded. Repeat the process with "New Girl Nancy" by explaining that she has just moved to your neighborhood and although she was popular in her old school, she is having trouble meeting people and often eats lunch alone.

STEP 1

The learning process will be strengthened for your sixth graders if the theme of encouragement is reinforced through-out the session. Ask for two or three volunteers from each team to be a cheering squad for their team during the Marshmallow Mash. Ask them to cheer with words that are encouraging and uplifting. Give cheerleaders their own marshmallows to juggle—and to throw at the other teams.

STEP 4

Most sixth graders welcome the challenge of working toward a significant goal. Put several sign-up sheets around the room. Have all students sign one sheet with either something they want the others to pray for or one thing they are thankful for. Pass out paper to each student and have him or her copy from the sign-up sheets the names and prayer requests (or thankful things) of at least six other students. Encourage students to choose names of new friends. Be sure every student is on at least two prayer lists. **When you pray for someone every day for 30 days, you soon realize not only how important that person is to God, but also that he or she is becoming even more important to you. You become interested in how God is answering prayer for that person.** Tell students that you will ask about their prayers each week. Suggest that they post their prayer list somewhere where they will see it each day—on the bathroom mirror, on the refrigerator, on their locker, next to their bed, etc.

DATE USED:

Approx. Time

STEP 1: *Marshmallow Mash* _____
- ❑ Extra Action*
- ❑ Small Group*
- ❑ Mostly Guys
- ❑ Extra Fun
- ❑ Media
- ❑ Short Meeting Time
- ❑ Combined Junior High/High School
- ❑ Sixth Grade

Things needed:

STEP 2: *The Price Is Right* _____
- ❑ Mostly Girls
- ❑ Short Meeting Time
- ❑ Urban

Things needed:

STEP 3: *Ultimate Affirmation* _____
- ❑ Large Group
- ❑ Heard It All Before
- ❑ Little Bible Background
- ❑ Fellowship & Worship
- ❑ Mostly Girls
- ❑ Extra Fun
- ❑ Urban

Things needed:

STEP 4: *How to Be Bleacher...* _____
- ❑ Large Group
- ❑ Little Bible Background
- ❑ Short Meeting Time
- ❑ Combined Junior High/High School
- ❑ Sixth Grade

Things needed:

STEP 5: *Putting Value into Action* _____
- ❑ Extra Action
- ❑ Small Group
- ❑ Heard It All Before
- ❑ Fellowship & Worship
- ❑ Mostly Guys
- ❑ Media
- ❑ Short Meeting Time

Things needed:

* two combined steps

Second-Chance Friends

YOUR GOALS FOR THIS SESSION:
Choose one or more

☐ To help students learn that Jesus forgave Peter's big mistake.

☐ To help students understand a mind-blowing idea about forgiveness: Jesus gives all of us more chances than we deserve.

☐ To challenge students to become Second-Chance Friends—friends that forgive people like Jesus did.

☐ Other:_____

_____

Your Bible Base:

Mark 14:27-31
Mark 14:43-50
Mark 14:66-72
Mark 15:16-72
Luke 23:32-43
John 21:1-19

Unhand Me!

OPTIONS

(Needed: rope—one 2-foot piece for each student (or towels, rubber bands, or hair ties), gum)

Divide into two teams by age, gender, or at random, and "handcuff" the teams together. To do this, give each student a piece of rope. Students should tie one end of the rope to one of their own wrists and the other end of the rope to the closest wrist of the person next to them. You will probably have to walk around the room and help tie the students' wrists together. The end result is that each team becomes a line of people whose adjoining hands are tied together.

Give each student a piece of gum. Each team member must unwrap, chew, and blow a bubble with the gum. The first team done wins. This is much harder than it seems because it requires students to work together.

The first team to do 20 relatively normal-looking jumping jacks, wins. This one is certain to produce hilarious results.

NOTE: Don't let students untie the ropes just yet. It's important to let them experience the feeling of being "handcuffed" throughout the lesson.

Teacher Tip: If you can't find enough rope, give each student a towel. Students should grab one end of one towel with their left hands, then with their right hands grab the open end of the towel held by the person on their right. If any student lets go during one of the challenges above, his or her team must start over.

STEP 2

The Friendship Graveyard

(Needed: copies of Repro Resource 5, pens or pencils, tape)

OPTIONS

LITTLE BIBLE BACKGROUND

EXTRA FUN

MEDIA

URBAN

JR.HIGH HIGH SCHOOL COMBINED

Have students discuss the following questions with one or two people next to them: **Just now, you experienced a little bit of what it's like to feel handcuffed. And while we may not know what it's like to be truly handcuffed, there are things that handcuff our friendships, too—things that bind our friendships and keep them from growing. Not forgiving is like that. We like to hold grudges and stay angry at our friends, but we never realize that not only does this handcuff us, it slowly (or not so slowly) kills our friendships.**

Think for a moment about the friendships that have died in your life. I'm not talking about friendships where one person physically moves away or moves on to another school, job, or stage of life. I'm talking about situations when a good friendship goes bad because one mistake or source of conflict was never dealt with. Ask students to think of a friendship that was handcuffed and eventually died.

Pass out pens and copies of "Friendship Tombstone" (Repro Resource 5). Instruct students to complete the resource with a short summary of why one friendship from their past ended up in the Friendship Graveyard. This will be difficult for students to do while they're tied up, but not impossible if they work together. After three or four minutes, collect the friendship tombstones and tape them to one of your walls.

We've created quite a Friendship Graveyard here. What might have saved these friendships, or brought them back to life? What would have given them a second chance? It's pretty simple actually. No matter how much a friend has hurt us, or no matter how much we have hurt a friend, there *is* something that can bring a friendship back to life. It's forgiveness. Imagine how different this wall would look if forgiveness could bring these friendships back to life.

STEP 3

The Great Debate

OPTIONS

(Needed: paper, pens, white board or newsprint, marker, copies of Repro Resource 5, scissors or knife)

Explain: **Jesus is our model for what makes a good friendship. If we want to know how to survive the Friendship Graveyard, we need look no further than how Jesus dealt with forgiveness.** Read the following Scripture passages aloud and ask students to come up with a one-sentence summary statement of each passage. Sample summary statements are included in parentheses below. Record answers on white board or newsprint.

- Mark 14:27-31 (Jesus predicted Peter's denial).
- Mark 14:43-50 (Jesus was arrested and all the disciples—including Peter—abandoned Jesus).
- Mark 14:66-72 (Peter denied Jesus three times, then wept about it).
- Mark 15:16-32 (Jesus was mocked and crucified).

Tell students to imagine the scene after Jesus' resurrection when Jesus met with Peter again. Ask: **If you were Jesus, would you still be angry with Peter for deserting you while you hung on the cross?** Set up a debate to decide whether or not Jesus should forgive Peter. Students should still be in two teams tied together at the wrists. Make one team the "YES" team (defending the position that Jesus SHOULD forgive Peter) and the other the "NO" team (arguing that Jesus SHOULD NOT forgive Peter). Explain that each team should make a list of all the arguments that support its side. Explain that even if students don't necessarily agree with the position that they've been assigned, as good debaters their job is to come up with the best possible arguments anyway. If possible, ask adults to help the students to determine and refine their best arguments. Then let the teams express their opinions in a standard debate format: one representative from the YES team tells why Jesus should forgive, then a representative from the NO team gives a rebuttal, and so on. Read what Jesus did in John 21:1-19.

What did Jesus mean when He said, "Feed my sheep"? (Jesus had trained Peter to be a leader of the forthcoming church. Jesus was telling Peter to go and do what he had been trained for—to shepherd Jesus' "sheep"—the people who would decide to follow Jesus. Essentially, Jesus was saying, "I'm not going to hold a grudge against you. I forgive you and I'll give you a second chance.")

Do you think forgiveness was hard or easy for Jesus? Why?

What can we learn about overcoming the Friendship Graveyard from the way Jesus forgave Peter?

Jesus put up with people mocking Him, spitting on Him, calling Him names. He endured hanging on the cross, the most brutal way to die in the society in which He lived. And in the meantime, He had to suffer while His best friends on earth deserted Him. Jesus had every right to be flaming mad. Instead, Jesus did something incredible. He forgave Peter. He let Peter know that they would still be friends and partners in ministry. Did you know that same forgiveness extends to you and to me? Isn't that a mind-blowing idea? Untie or cut loose half of students' wrists so that students end up tied to one partner, instead of to a whole team. **If Jesus forgave us like that, how could we NOT forgive others?**

Optional: Help students *experience* the idea that the forgiveness Jesus gave Peter extends to them as well. Pass out additional copies of "Friendship Tombstone" (Repro Resource 5). Have students write down just one wrong thing they've done at some point in their past. (Again, this will be difficult but not impossible while they are tied at the wrists.) Explain that even if students had lived a perfect life except for the one thing on their tombstones, that one thing would still be enough to send their friendship with Jesus to the "graveyard." Tell students to close their eyes and imagine how full their tombstones would be if they wrote down *everything* they ever did wrong. Tell students that the sins they are thinking about are the reason Jesus died on the cross. While students keep their eyes closed, try to describe some of the things Jesus might have been thinking about as He hung on the cross. Make it as personal as you can for the students—Jesus may have thought about them and their sins. As you speak, walk around and tear up each of the "Tombstone" resources.

STEP 4

How to Be a Second-Chance Friend

(Needed: pens, slips of paper, white board (or newsprint), marker, scissors or a knife to cut the rope off of students' wrists)

Write out about six situations that your students would find hard to forgive, each on its own slip of paper. For example:

• My friend told a lie about me to impress some popular kids.
• My friend borrowed $10 from me and never paid it back.
• My friend ruined my favorite CD that I loaned him (or her).
• My little brother is a pest and a pain.

Give each slip of paper to one student.

The students who have the slips of paper should take turns reading the situations listed on those sheets. For each situation, two or three other people should call back with negative consequences for not forgiving a friend in that situation. For example, students might call back: You'll stay angry; you won't want to see your friend at school; you won't want to sit next to her in class. Make a list of all the negative consequences students come up with for not forgiving. Put this on a white board or newsprint.

Direct students' attention to the list and say: **This is quite a list. Wouldn't it be good to be free of all of this?** Hold up one students' free hand and say: **We've been cut free from *our* mistakes by what Jesus did for us. Why would we want to stay handcuffed with our other hand because we don't want to forgive others? When we don't forgive other people, our handcuffs are our bitterness and anger toward the people who have wronged us. Saying "I forgive you" cuts us free from these consequences.** Go around the room and untie or cut loose the ropes that tie pairs of students together.

What you've just experienced is how it feels to be a Second-Chance friend. Second-Chance friends are friends that forgive others whether or not it seems "fair" at the time. They give up their grudges, like Jesus did. It's often hard to forgive our friends. Are you willing to be a friend like Jesus?

STEP 5

Putting Forgiveness into Action

(Needed: copies of Repro Resource 6, pens)

Pass out pens and copies of "I Forgive You" (Repro Resource 6). Challenge students to write a letter expressing forgiveness of someone they have bitterness toward. Introduce the letter-writing activity by saying something like: **Many of us have been carrying around the weight of unforgiveness for years. Maybe a friend hurt our feelings or a teacher blamed us for something we didn't do. What seems fair at first is not to forgive that person. But if you choose not to forgive, you end up in handcuffs. Today is your chance to be a Second-Chance Friend and move on in freedom. If you're ready, write a letter on the resource sheet to a person you need to forgive. It's up to you whether or not you ever give this letter to the person. What is most important is that you sincerely forgive the other person in your own heart.**

After students finish writing their letters, refer back to the Friendship Graveyard on your wall (from Step 2). Give students a chance to pull the tombstones off the wall if they are ready to forgive the person who took the friendship to the graveyard in the first place. Give students the option of doing this silently. But some students will be ready to talk about their commitments. Encourage them to explain what friendship they're committing to forgive and what step they will take toward restoring the friendship.

Close in prayer, thanking Jesus for the way He forgives us which allows us to forgive our friends.

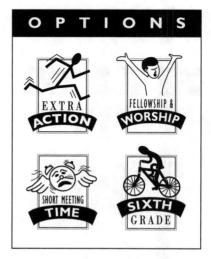

OPTIONS

EXTRA ACTION

FELLOWSHIP & WORSHIP

SHORT MEETING TIME

SIXTH GRADE

Friendship Tombstone

Rest in Peace

This friendship died because:

NOTES

I Forgive You

I don't want to handcuff our friendship anymore.
I FORGIVE YOU. Here's what I need to say to you:

_____

_____

_____

_____

_____

_____

_____

_____

_____

_____

_____

_____

_____

_____

_____

_____

_____

_____

NOTES

STEPS 1/2

Divide into teams of four to six students. Give each team an egg, a piece of newspaper, two straws, and three inches of masking tape. Tell teams to create a protective structure around the egg so that the egg can survive a fall from the top of an eight-foot ladder without cracking. This is an impossible challenge. Use provoking questions to engage students' feelings when they fail: **Did anyone feel angry toward a teammate? Why? What does it feel like to fail? What does it feel like when other people fail us? What should you do when you experience failure?** Give teams a second chance—this time with more materials: one egg, a whole newspaper, six straws, and 12 inches of masking tape. Students should be able to create enough protection around the egg so it can survive the fall. Continue to discuss: **How did you feel when you were given a second chance? Do we need second chances in life? When? If we all need second chances, why is it so hard for us to give people who hurt us second chances?**

STEP 5

Pass out copies of Repro Resource 6 and have students write letters to someone they need to forgive. Have students drop the letters from the top of a ladder to a "drop zone." To make the drop zone: Use rope or tape to mark off four concentric circles on a small tarp or blanket. Ask for volunteers to share about what they wrote.

STEPS 1/2

In a small group, it's easier to arrange to meet in an off-site location. Take advantage of this and begin with a tour of a local jail or correctional facility. Many facilities will be happy to comply. Be sure to inform parents of your plans. Finish your meeting in a conference room or lobby. Discuss: **Can criminals be forgiven? Can a mass murderer like Charles Manson or the Unabomber be forgiven? Do some people deserve forgiveness but others don't? How do you know when someone deserves forgiveness? Have any of you ever experienced undeserved forgiveness? How did it feel? Can God forgive criminals? Why would He?**

STEP 3

If the debate would not work for your small group, read the Scripture together and discuss whether or not Peter deserved Jesus' forgiveness. Help students see that none of us really deserves Jesus' forgiveness—He's holy and we are sinners. Use the optional activity at the end of Step 3 to reinforce this idea.

STEP 4

In a small group, you have an opportunity for deeper discussion. Try to bring in a pair of real handcuffs. (Toy cuffs will also work.) Sit in a circle, hold the cuffs, and (without mentioning names) talk about a person in your life who has been hard to forgive; tell how not forgiving the person has made you feel "handcuffed." Then pass the cuffs around the circle and encourage each person to share a similar story (but don't force anyone). Ask follow-up questions like: **What makes it hard to forgive? After today are you willing to forgive?**

STEP 1

In a large group, it might be difficult to handcuff all your students. Instead, you can create energy and momentum by dividing into teams according to schools or gender. Choose three members per team for each of the bubble gum and jumping jack challenges and tie the wrists of the contestants for each team together. Encourage the "audience" to cheer for the respective team representatives. Consider giving a prize (like a bag of candy to share) to the winning team.

STEP 4

To stimulate discussion, prepare two or three students to give testimonies about how God has created in them a more forgiving heart. For best results, interview the students. This gives you a little more control in helping guide students to hit the important points of their stories. It's also a less intimidating format for students who may not be comfortable speaking to a large group. Use questions like: **What was it like before you had a forgiving heart? Did you ever feel "handcuffed" because you weren't willing to forgive others? When did you come to understand Jesus' unconditional forgiveness for you? Did it become easier to forgive others then? Why? What's one example of someone you forgave recently? What did that feel like?** After the interviews, break down into small groups and use the first activity in Step 4.

STEP 1

To start the meeting, explain that you're a little frustrated because of a slight traffic "incident" on your way in. Arrange for a police officer to enter your room, act as if he or she recognizes you, then handcuff you and read your rights. Explain that it was all just a gag. But prepare the officer to refuse to release you. Instead, continue to talk to the students and explain to them how difficult it is to express yourself with your hands cuffed. Refer back to this when you talk throughout the lesson about how holding grudges "handcuffs" our friendships. You might be amazed how many police officers enjoy playing along to make a point. It might help to persuade an officer on the idea if you invite him or her to give a five-minute talk on law enforcement, who gets handcuffed, whether it's fun to arrest youth workers, etc. Oh, and be sure to tell the senior pastor about your plans.

STEP 3

Your group may take Jesus' forgiveness for granted. Instead of debating whether Jesus should forgive Peter, research the story of a real-life, hardened criminal, and send a summary of the story to your students in the week ahead of time. Include the question: **Should Jesus forgive him?** (This has the added benefit of promoting your meeting.) Use the same debate format described in the lesson. After the debate, read Luke 2:39-43 and 1 John 1:9. Make the point that the hardened criminal doesn't deserve Jesus' forgiveness, but Jesus certainly *would* forgive him. Then explain that God doesn't rank sins and all of us are just as sinful as the murderer you debated—we all fall short of God's glory (Romans 3:9-18). Use the optional activity to reinforce this.

STEP 2

It may be important for your group to first focus on the question, "Will Jesus forgive me?" Prepare one student to perform a dramatic monologue. The character should explain feeling hand-cuffed by sin. In a conversation with God, the actor should wonder out loud whether Jesus could ever forgive his or her sins. Pass out copies of Repro Resource 5, but have students fill out the resource by writing about the sins that keep them "handcuffed" with God.

STEP 3

Hold a trial to determine if Jesus should forgive an average young teen for his or her sins. Have the students determine a "crime" common to junior highers: cheating, lying, etc. Then break the students into the "defense" team (which argues the defendant should be forgiven) and the "prosecution" team (which argues the defendant should not be forgiven). A student playing the part of defendant should admit to the crime and be repentant. When both sides have finished, you (playing the part of judge) should read 1 John 1:9 and declare the defendant "forgiven." Then use the optional activity in Step 3.

STEP 4

Give students an opportunity to confess their sins to God. Have students write their sins on slips of paper and pray silently, asking Jesus to forgive them. Have students place their folded papers in a metal container and have a leader ignite the paper and let it burn until it's gone (this is best done outside with proper safety precautions). Read Jeremiah 31:34b and Psalm 103:12. Lead into Step 5 by saying: **If Jesus forgives us, shouldn't we forgive others?**

STEP 1

If your group would rather start with discussion than a game, divide into "depth groups" (optimal size: four to six students each). Ask groups to come up with a list of qualities that make a great friendship and another list of things that can ruin a friendship. Then have group members discuss: **How have you felt when a friendship has ended? Was there anything you could have done to save the friendship? Was there anything the other person could have done?** This will transition to Step 2, where you will discuss that forgiveness can save friendships from the "graveyard."

STEP 4

After talking about the way Jesus forgives us, what better way to worship than to hold a student communion service? Talk to leaders in your church to 1) see if this is appropriate and 2) get instruction on how your church administers the Lord's Supper. Since forgiving others is an important part of preparing for the Lord's Supper, pass out copies of Repro Resource 6 and give students a few minutes to write a letter to anyone they need to forgive. This is a great chance for you to teach how God's forgiveness of our sins is intricately connected with our forgiveness of others (see Matthew 6:14 and 18:21-25). Then lead your students in communion.

STEP 5

Have students write forgiveness letters as directed in the main lesson. Then, turn the lights down. Ask students to look up Ephesians 4:32 in their Bibles and spend time meditating on and memorizing the verse. Encourage them to ask God to provide courage to forgive the friends who have hurt them.

STEP 3

Instead of using the Great Debate idea, read the Scripture listed in Step 3 and have girls record what Peter might have been thinking after each scene. You'll especially want to focus on how he might have felt after he denied Jesus three times and how he felt after Jesus forgave him. At the end of the Scripture reading, let a few volunteers share their journal entries.

STEP 4

The most effective way to teach girls about forgiveness is to show them real-life examples. Write the following situations each on their own index cards:

• You are a basketball player. Jill, the star of your team, needed to pass her history test so she could play in the game today. She got caught using a cheat sheet, failed the test, and was disqualified from the game. Your team lost the big game by four points. Does Jill deserve a second chance?

• You've been trying to be nice to the new girl, Kelly. In fact, you invited her to a sleepover. She was supposed to bring over two movies, but she forgot about the sleepover and didn't come at all. All your friends were mad at *you* because they couldn't watch the movies. Does Kelly deserve a second chance?

• Come up with additional situations as you like.

Pass out the cards. Whoever gets a card should read it. Then discuss: **Would it be hard or easy to forgive the person? How might you feel "handcuffed" if you didn't forgive? What are some of the consequences you would have to deal with if you didn't forgive?**

STEP 1

Have students compete in the "Handcuffed Challenges" in Step 1 while tied at the wrist to just one partner. Time the guys, award one point for the fastest duo in each challenge, and keep track of an overall winner. In addition to the challenges in Step 1, add these: tie/untie your shoes, do 10 sit-ups, write or draw something, make a pyramid of paper cups, hit a baseball off a tee, shoot a basketball into a hoop.

STEPS 4/5

While students do one of the "hands on" activities below, read Matthew 18:21-25 and discuss questions like: **Why is it hard to forgive someone if he or she wrongs you more than once? Why is it hard to forgive someone if it doesn't seem like he or she is sorry?**

• Serve Crosses: Have guys bring in pocket knives from home and "whittle" sticks while you discuss forgiveness. (Review safety rules—the most important are to always cut down and away, and to treat the knife with respect, not as a toy. Insist on strict compliance.) Carve or write the word "deserve" into the sticks, then discuss the fact that Jesus forgave us though we didn't deserve it. Crack or cut the sticks in half between the letters "e" and "s" so that the word "serve" is now on one section of the sticks. Tie the two sections of stick with twine to make a cross.

• Give each student a block of wood. Tell him to write on it the initials of people who are hard to forgive. Toward the end of the discussion, bring out some wood burners and have each guy burn a large "70 x 7" on the wood over the initials he wrote there, reminding him that Jesus said to forgive others not 7 times but 70 times 7.

STEP 1

Use the bubble gum and jumping jacks challenges to begin, then lead your teams to an obstacle course you've set up. (If you have a large group, you may want to divide into more teams.) Ideally, you'll want to set up your obstacle course outside. If you have a children's playground at your church or you can access one at a nearby park or school, it will make a great obstacle course. Otherwise, you could set up one in your meeting room using a creative arrangement of chairs and tables. Walk through the course yourself first, or have an untied student walk it as you direct. Make sure the obstacle course is difficult enough, but remember that the students will have limited use of their hands. "Spot" the teams as they move through the most precarious elements to ensure that no one gets hurt.

STEP 2

Take your group to a cemetery and have the students make tombstone rubbings to set up the "Friendship Graveyard" exercise described in the lesson. Give each student a few pieces of paper (larger paper works better) and a crayon. Have each student fold the paper on the front of a tombstone, then rub the side of the crayon across it. The raised or recessed writing on the tombstone will show up in color on the paper. After this exercise, take advantage of the setting and switch gears from Extra Fun to Extra Serious. Have students walk around the graveyard silently and think about friendships that have "died" because of a lack of forgiveness. Throw out questions for them to think about silently like: **What could you have done to save the friendship?**

STEP 2

After playing a lighthearted game like "Handcuffed Challenges," use one of these ideas to transition to the heart of the lesson:

- **Forgiveness Interviews:** Make a home video of teens talking about either a time they were forgiven or a time they forgave someone. If possible, edit the video so that the clips start with people talking about situations that are hard to forgive, then moves to people talking about how freeing it is or was for them to forgive a friend.
- **Contemporary Song:** Play a song that has a forgiveness theme, like "Will You Forgive?" by the Newsboys on the *Take Me to Your Leader* CD.
- **Movie clip:** Play a scene or two from a move popular with your students and appropriate for your meeting that shows either: 1) A dramatic portrayal of forgiveness, or 2) A scene in which two friends have a hard time forgiving one another.

Whichever option you choose, discuss questions like: **Is it easy or hard to forgive? Why? What happens when we don't forgive others?**

STEP 1

Instead of taking the time to tie students' hands together, begin by having students stand in a circle. Tell students to reach across the circle and grab the wrists of two other people. Then see how long it takes for students to get untangled—they cannot let go of the wrists they are holding; the goal is to end up back in a circle where each person stands next to the two people he or she is holding wrists with. Discuss: **What are some things that "tangle" our friendships? What can untangle our friendships?**

STEP 3

As a group, read Luke 23:32-42 aloud—instead of the story of Jesus and Peter, this is the story of how Jesus forgave a criminal hanging on a cross next to Him. Keep students together in one group. Ask your students to brainstorm a few reasons why Jesus should NOT forgive the criminal. Then ask them to brainstorm a few reasons why Jesus SHOULD forgive the criminal. Read Luke 23:43 and then discuss: **Why did Jesus forgive the criminal? Do you think He should have? Why or why not?** Stress the fact that Jesus forgave the criminal, even though the criminal didn't deserve it.

STEP 5

If you're out of time at the end of the session, send students home with Resource 6 and have them fill it out on their own.

STEP 2

Many urban teens have witnessed or know of someone who has been murdered or otherwise died tragically. In preparation for the "Friendship Graveyard" discussion, ask: **How many of you know of someone who has been killed or murdered, especially someone close to you?** Secondly, ask if anyone has lost a friend or loved one to disease or illness. Afterward, discuss the power friendships have on us and how we must value friends and family members while they are here with us. Finally, use Resource 5 and the concluding comments at the end of Step 2.

STEP 3

Forgiving Peter is one thing, but what about the Judas in your life? Many city teens are living with Post Traumatic Stress Syndrome (PTSS). That is, they've witnessed murder or have been the victims of sexual or drug violence, police brutality, neglect, and abuse to name a few atrocities. Many teens can forgive the Peters in their lives—i.e., friendships which tear because of cowardice in commitments. But, true freedom can't emerge until they can forgive the Judases who have betrayed them outright, such as a parent who walked out of their lives or the murderer who killed a family member. This level of forgiveness is needed because much of their present stress, anger, and trauma may be related to not forgiving those who have wounded them forever. Give a short Bible study comparing Judas' betrayal (Matthew 26—27; Mark 14; John 18); Jesus' statement of forgiveness on the cross (Luke 23:34); and His mandate to forgive enemies (Matthew 5:44, Luke 6:27).

STEP 1

As an alternative to the handcuffs theme, give each student two rocks. For best results, give out the rocks one week ahead of time, and require students to carry the rocks around with them no matter where they go on the day before your meeting. The more frustrated they are with the rocks by the time of the meeting, the better. Use the rocks as a symbol of the consequences of unforgiveness wherever the lesson talks about "handcuffs." Instead of playing "Handcuffed Challenges" in Step 1, try the same challenges while students hold the rocks. Later, talk about how Jesus took one of our rocks away—He forgave us of our sins. Now we need to get rid of our other rock by forgiving others.

STEP 2

Instead of filling out the "Friendship Tombstones," this idea will get students talking about their friendship conflicts: Simulate an argument with a student or adult. For example, you might argue with another adult leader about how the "Handcuffed Challenges" in Step 1 should have been done. In the mock argument that ensues, make reference to the fact that there's a larger issue under the surface—something for which the two of you haven't forgiven each other. Don't let anyone else know what's going on. Start to go on with the meeting as if nothing happened, then stop a few minutes later as if you're just too distraught about it to go on. Ask students for advice. See if anyone advises you to forgive the person. Then admit that it was all an act. This simulation should make students more ready to talk about their own experiences with hard-to-forgive situations.

STEP 1

Have a large number of plastic grocery bags and permanent markers available. Ask the students to write on the grocery bags some words or phrases of things that can damage friendships. Begin a chain by tying the ends of one bag together to make a loop. Then connect another bag by tying it through the loop of the first bag and continue this process to form a chain of words. Have the students tie all their chains together to form one long chain. Seat two volunteers on chairs back to back and carefully put the chain of words all the way around both of them and the chairs. Talk about the words that have been written on the bags. **What effect could any of these words have on a friendship? Do you think these words really hurt? Is this permanent or would you be able to get out the chain? How can you get out of words or actions that hurt a friendship?** (Forgiveness.)

STEP 5

Distribute paper and pencils, and instruct the students to write the letters to the words "I FORGIVE" down the left side of the paper. Explain that they are to write a word or phrase about forgiveness by using each letter in those words. For example, on the line with the letter F, write "God **F**orgives me." Ask for volunteers to read what they have written. Talk about how we learn about forgiveness from Jesus' example.

DATE USED:

Approx. Time

STEP 1: *Unhand Me!* _____
- ❏ Extra Action*
- ❏ Small Group*
- ❏ Large Group
- ❏ Heard It All Before
- ❏ Fellowship & Worship
- ❏ Mostly Guys
- ❏ Extra Fun
- ❏ Short Meeting Time
- ❏ Combined Junior High/High School
- ❏ Sixth Grade
Things needed:

STEP 2: *The Friendship Graveyard* _____
- ❏ Little Bible Background
- ❏ Extra Fun
- ❏ Media
- ❏ Urban
- ❏ Combined Junior High/High School
Things needed:

STEP 3: *The Great Debate* _____
- ❏ Small Group
- ❏ Heard It All Before
- ❏ Little Bible Background
- ❏ Mostly Girls
- ❏ Short Meeting Time
- ❏ Urban
Things needed:

STEP 4: *...Second-Chance Friend* _____
- ❏ Small Group
- ❏ Large Group
- ❏ Little Bible Background
- ❏ Fellowship & Worship
- ❏ Mostly Girls
- ❏ Mostly Guys*
Things needed:

STEP 5: *Putting Forgeness into...* _____
- ❏ Extra Action
- ❏ Fellowship & Worship
- ❏ Short Meeting Time
- ❏ Sixth Grade
Things needed:

* two combined steps

Fox-Hole Friends

YOUR GOALS FOR THIS SESSION:
Choose one or more

☐ To help students learn that Jesus held the disciples accountable during an intense time in the Garden of Gethsemane.

☐ To help students understand a mind-blowing idea about accountability: Jesus wanted the support of the friends who lived in the "fox hole" with Him.

☐ To help students become Fox-Hole Friends—friends that keep each other accountable to specific spiritual goals.

☐ Other:_____
_____

Your Bible Base:

Matthew 26:36-46

Up for Grabs

(Needed: two paper bags with approximately six identical food items in each bag. Suggested food items are a hard-boiled egg, a small jar of baby food, an onion, licorice, a warm can of cola, and a container of yogurt).

Begin the lesson by asking: **Is anyone hungry today?** Choose two hungry volunteers—for best results choose one guy and one girl. Give them each a bag of food and explain that the goal of the game is to see which student can eat all of the food in his or her bag first.

Encourage the audience to cheer for the contestants. After one of the students has finished his or her second food item, point to the student who is losing and explain: **I think [name of the student who is behind] needs some help.** Ask for two other volunteers in the audience who are the same gender as the student who is falling behind. They should help by grabbing and eating their own food items out of the losing student's bag. Inevitably, this team of three people will end up beating the one student who remains alone in the game. Let the student who was at first winning express his or her displeasure about how unfair the contest was. Tell him or her it was all for the sake of making a point and thank the contestant for being a good sport. Let the winning team express what it was like to get to work as a team.

It's easier to do most things when somebody helps us. So why don't we ask for help more often?

Do you think your friends think more of you or less of you when you ask for help?

What kind of friendships would you have if you never asked for help or never let your friends help you?

STEP 2

Stories from the Front Lines

(Needed: copies of Repro Resource 7)

Pass out copies of ""On the Front Lines" (Repro Resource 7). Ask for a few volunteers to take turns reading the story aloud.

Many veterans of foreign wars seem to have a strong bond with the people they fought with on the front lines. Why do you think that is?

When two friends have an important purpose for their friendship and they fight for that purpose side by side, it can create the kind of bond we call a Fox-Hole Friendship. Besides friendships between veterans who fought together, where else do you tend to see close, "fox-hole" kinds of friendships?

Do you ever see Fox-Hole Friendships between Christians? Do you know of any examples?

Are most Christian friendships more like couch potato friendships or Fox-Hole Friendships? Why? What are yours like?

OPTIONS

HEARD IT ALL BEFORE

LITTLE BIBLE BACKGROUND

FELLOWSHIP & WORSHIP

MOSTLY GIRLS

MEDIA

SHORT MEETING TIME

URBAN

SIXTH GRADE

STEP 3

Freeze Frame

(Needed: Bibles, posterboard, pens)

Introduce the Scripture reading by saying: **Many Christians suffer from "Do-It-Yourself Syndrome." This syndrome is often marked by thoughts like:** *I'm not doing well spiritually, but I can't tell anyone what I'm struggling with because then they'd know I'm not a perfect Christian.* **Or, on the flip-side:** *I know my friend is struggling spiritually but I can't say any— thing because I might make him upset.* **The Do-It-Yourself Syndrome is one of the biggest obstacles we face if we**

OPTIONS

SMALL GROUP

SHORT MEETING TIME

JR. HIGH HIGH SCHOOL COMBINED

SIXTH GRADE

want to build Fox-Hole Friendships. What would Jesus say about the Do-It-Yourself Syndrome? Let's find out.

Divide into four teams. Assign each group one of the Scripture passages below. Have each group create "Freeze Frame" pictures for its passage. To make "Freeze Frame" pictures, students become characters or inanimate objects in the story, frozen in a portrayal of what happened in their scene. One person in each group should be the narrator and explain the pictures.

Assign these passages:
Scene 1: Matthew 26:36-39
Scene 2: Matthew 26:40-41
Scene 3: Matthew 26:42-44
Scene 4: Matthew 26:45-46

Jesus was going through one of His toughest times while He was here on earth. He knew He was going to die. He knew very soon He would be hung from a cross. In that critical time for Him, why do you think He wanted His friends to join Him in prayer?

Explain that Jesus had an "inner circle" of disciples, people He taught and included in more ways than the others. It was these three "inner circle" disciples—Peter, James, and John—whom Jesus asked to pray with Him.

Part of being a Fox-Hole Friend is keeping others accountable, or on track spiritually. That's why, when Jesus found His disciples sleeping, He woke them and asked them to continue praying. But the disciples were already tired and were unable to stay awake.

Note what Jesus said to His disciples when He found them sleeping. He asked them tough questions like, "Can't you pray with me?" and "Are you still sleeping?"

These questions are called "accountability" questions. Jesus asked tough questions of His disciples because He wanted to keep them "on track" in their commitments.

Did anyone catch the mind-blowing idea about accountability in this passage? Jesus wanted to have His Fox-Hole Friends with Him during this tough time in the garden. He kept them accountable to what He asked them to do and asked for their support. During tough times, even Jesus didn't want to do it alone.

STEP 4

How to Be Fox-Hole Friends

Introduce the small group activity by saying: **Jesus is our model for friendship. He taught us that it's important to have Fox-Hole Friends. He also taught us what Fox-Hole Friends do. First, they make themselves accountable to one another. They have a commitment to listen to each other and to keep working together at growing closer to Jesus. Second, they keep each other accountable. That means they ask each other tough questions because they care and want their friends to do the right thing.**

Divide into small groups of six to eight students. Have each group come up with a skit that illustrates how one Fox-Hole Friend could keep another accountable. They should show a real-life situation that would cause one of the friends to struggle in his or her walk with Christ. Then have a friend or a group of friends do something to help that person stay on track.

If groups are stuck coming up with situations, here are two ideas to prime the pump: a friend is getting busy with school and sports and is deciding not to spend time with God; or, a friend made the cheerleading squad and now she's been attending many of the popular kids' parties where she's starting to drink and smoke.

You may want to circulate among the groups to make sure they understand the assignment and are making progress in it.

After 10 minutes, ask the groups to reassemble. One at a time, have each group act out its skit.

Accountability in Action

(Needed: copies of Repro Resource 8 and 9, pens)

Ahead of time, ask one of your adult volunteers, another adult from your church, or a Fox-Hole Friend of your own (see Teacher Tip below) to share what accountability looks like. If possible, invite both partners in the accountability friendship to come and share with your students. In advance, write out the following questions and distribute them to a few students so that they can ask questions of these Fox-Hole Friends: **How did your Fox-Hole Friendship start? What are the toughest parts of being a Fox-Hole Friend? Are you ever scared to ask your friend tough accountability questions? What is the best part of having a Fox-Hole Friend?**

After the interview, pass out copies of "Tough Questions" (Repro Resource 8). Tell students to circle one of the tough questions they want to be asked or write their own. Explain that if students are ready to hold each other accountable, they should find a partner this week. Both partners should sign and date the "Fox-Hole Friendship Certificate" (Repro Resource 9). Encourage them to post the Certificate on their bathroom mirror or closet as a daily reminder of their commitment to Fox-Hole Friendships. Remind students that they can be Fox-Hole Friends with more than just one person.

Close in prayer, thanking God for giving us friends who climb into the Fox-Holes of life with us.

Teacher Tip: It may seem scary at first to invite one of your own accountability friends to speak, but the risk you take in opening up part of your own life to the group will encourage your students to do the same in their own lives.

NOTES

On the Front Lines

I didn't know how to handle war.

Now my hands were shaking furiously. My stomach was pulling, twisting. I couldn't do anything to stop it. I panicked. I flat out panicked. I blew my cover and stood straight up. Like a man gone stark raving mad, I shot a few rounds straight into the sky. In a matter of seconds, bullets from the brush whizzed by my left and right. Another land mine exploded in the distance. I was a sitting duck.

Stuff happens in war. People flip out.

I think Mitch must have flipped out, too, to do what he did. I was a scared, out-of-place 19 year-old. I wasn't the kind of guy someone like Mitch would risk his life for. But he did. He jumped right up without thinking. He tackled me. I fought him like a cornered dog. I didn't know what I was doing. Mitch dragged me kicking and screaming back into the foxhole.

We didn't talk much in the fox hole. I was a wreck. I was cold, shaky, scared to death. We just sat there, silent. He gave me his coat. He fed me his rations.

It must have been hours—it felt like days—that we sat there in the fox-hole. A foxhole was a hole you dug out to hide in. Soldiers like us who fought on the front lines had to dig a lot of fox-holes. Sometimes you had just minutes to dig a hole because there was no place else to hide for cover. Mitch saved my life when he pulled me into the fox hole.

I'm grateful for that day, that moment, when Mitch saved my life. Most often it's when I look at my children. You see, I've got a wife and three kids. So I guess I'm pretty normal, huh? But I'll never forget my Fox-Hole Friend. Each day I try to live with a little more courage because of him.

NOTES

Tough Questions

Circle the question that you most need to be asked to be held accountable during the next month because of the struggles that you are having right now.

How are you treating your brother or sister?

Are you obeying and honoring your parents or step-parents?

Are you completing your homework on time and honestly?

Are you gossiping about other people?

How is your friendship with Jesus these days?

Are you reading your Bible as much as you'd like?

Are you remembering to pray for others?

Are you honoring God with what you watch on TV and at the movies?

Are you honoring God with the language you use? (Are you using swear words often?)

Are you taking advantage of opportunities to introduce others to Jesus?

Other: _____

_____

_____

_____

_____

_____

Fox-Hole Friendship Certificate

On this _____ day of _____, _____, _____ and _____ commit to a Fox-Hole Friendship. We will:

1 Ask each other tough questions.

2 Support each other in our walks with God.

3 Never, never, never give up on our friendship.

_____
Your Signature

_____
Your Fox-Hole Friend's Signature

_____
Parent/Guardian or Other Signature

_____
Youth Worker's Signature

STEP 1

Before students arrive, tape a large piece of crepe paper shoulder high across a doorway. Everyone must make it over the "electric fence" (represented by the crepe paper). They can not go under, around, or touch the crepe paper. Once a person is over the fence, he or she may not return to the original side until all students make it across safely. Students will have to work together and think strategically to be successful. Give as little direction as possible. Discuss questions like: **Did anyone try to make it over alone? What was that like? How did this task require everyone to work together? What are some things that make it hard to work together in life? Why do you think we don't work together more often?**

STEP 5

Since a Fox-Hole Friendship is based on trust, let students symbolize this by participating in a modified trust fall. Each partner needs a group of eight people to "spot" his or her jump—four on the left and four on the right. The spotters stand facing each other with their arms extended while holding the spotter's wrists across from them. Have partners stand side by side, facing the spotters. Spotters should bend at one knee slightly. Have an adult spot the faller's head. Stress safety. Go through a number of practice runs. Jump from a safe distance; for most groups, falling from a chair will be high enough. Fallers should cross their arms over their chest. Before falling, fallers should shout "Falling!" and wait to hear the spotters yell back, "Fall on!" Before they jump together, have partners explain to the group what they are trusting each other for as Fox-Hole Friends.

STEP 1

Try meeting at an indoor rock climbing gym or a ropes course for the day. Or, if you really feel adventurous, arrange to go rappelling outdoors with an organization that provides equipment and guides. These activities teach more about "accountability" and trust than you ever can in a classroom. After the activity, debrief students about any lessons they learned about trusting, depending on, and challenging each other. Finish the meeting at the off-site location, if possible.

STEP 3

You may not have enough students to make three different "Freeze Frames." Instead, assign each of your students to a specific role in the story—Jesus, Peter, James, John, and other disciples as needed. After reading each scene, pause and have students act out a more detailed conversation that might have taken place between the characters. Interview the characters about what they are thinking and feeling. Use the discussion questions at the end of Step 3.

STEP 5

If you want to take your small group to the next level, ask students to make "fox-hole" commitments to the entire group. Then spend some time practicing what that means—have each student share with the group what tough question from Repro Resource 8 he or she wants group members to ask him or her consistently. Have students sign the "Fox-Hole Friendship Certificate" (Repro Resource 9) of other group members.

STEP 1

Divide into two large teams with an equal number of students on each team. Have the two teams face each other while sitting down in long, single-file lines. Each team should hold hands all the way down the line and they must look straight across at the other team the entire time. (If they look any other direction, award the other team a point.) At one end of the two lines, place a chair with a set of keys on it. Stand at the front of the line and hold the hands of the first two people in line. Squeeze one of the leader's hands. That leader should then squeeze the hand of the person next to him or her. That hand squeeze should be passed all the way down the line to the person next to the keys, who should pick them up. No sounds are to to be made at all! This is a great teamwork test. You'll find that the signal will get dropped in some lines and get falsely started in lines where it doesn't really exist. Teams earn one point for correctly grabbing the keys, and lose one point for incorrectly grabbing the keys. Play several rounds.

STEP 2

If possible, don't just tell a story—interview actual veterans who fought together on the front lines. For best results, have the veterans come to your class or you could videotape the interviews ahead of time and play them back for your group. One other variation: If you can't find two veterans who fought together, interview one and have him or her tell stories of the people he or she fought with. Make sure your interviewee(s) cover such topics as: what a foxhole is, the depth of friendship that's built while fighting on the front lines together, and the best and worst parts of fighting together. If you use this option, for the sake of variety don't use friendship interviews again in Step 4.

STEP 4

A lot of church kids are tired of hearing adults talk about being real but not modeling it. Surprise them with your honesty. Open up about a real problem you have. Forget generalities here. You need to be specific! Set up an accountability agreement with your group. Be willing to let them ask you how you're doing with your problem (as they agree to let you ask them about theirs). One youth worker had his group help him lose weight. He started each Sunday morning with a step on the scale. Do not cross appropriate boundaries between adults and students, but be as honest as you can.

STEP 1

Use this activity to introduce not only Fox-Hole Friendship, but also to teach an important lesson about the body of Christ. Divide into groups of six to eight students each and challenge each group to create a "human machine"—a machine must have various parts that move and work together. Groups can become anything from pinball machines to car engines. Give a prize to the most creative machine. Point out the way that everyone on each machine must do his or her unique and important job for the machine to function. Explain that this is how the body of Christ works, too—we each have different and unique things to add to each other; we must work together.

STEP 2

Many teens, especially those who haven't grown up in the church, mistake confronting others as judging them. Write the situations below on newsprint or white board:
1. You're watching your Dad change the tire on his car and you notice he forgot to put on one of the bolts.
2. You're walking to school with your best friend and he starts to gossip about another student.
3. Your friend asks if she can copy your homework because she couldn't do hers since her little brother was sick and she had to help take care of him.
4. Your friend tells you he's going to a party tonight and he's planning on trying drugs. For each situation, discuss: **What would you say or do? Why? Would you be judging or confronting the person? What's the difference?**

STEP 2.

As youth leader, you probably know of at least one or two Fox-Hole Friendships that already exist among your students—where students are committed to keeping each other accountable and supporting each other on the front lines of following God. Celebrate these friendships. Tell stories you know that make good examples of Fox-Hole Friends. Let students talk about their friendships with one another. Let any student who wants to share statements like, "I am thankful for my friend _____, because he/she. . . ."

STEP 5

This option works best if students already have "Fox-Hole Friend" commitments to one another; or, allow time to choose Fox-Hole Friends during the lesson. Close your meeting by having your students sit on the floor with their partners. Take five minutes to sing some praise and worship songs, then have your students pray for one another in the areas they requested accountability.

STEP I

Use the "Up for Grabs" rules, but instead of an eating contest, have girls race to make friendship bracelets.

STEP 2

Some girls may not relate to the military-based "fox-hole" theme. Instead you may want to refer throughout to Accountability Partners instead of Fox-Hole Friends. Instead of reading the fox-hole story, pass out old magazines. Tell girls to clip out articles and pictures that remind them of something they know they're not supposed to do but might like to do. Discuss: **How would you feel if you had a friend who helped you avoid some of these tempting things? A friend who sticks by you and helps you avoid tempting situations is called an Accountability Partner. Do you have an Accountability Partner? Do you want one?**

STEP 4

Most teen girls are willing to share their struggles and fears openly with others. This activity will help them do that. Pass out paper and pens; ask students to pretend someone in the class is their Accountability Partner. Give girls four minutes to write an anonymous "Dear Accountability Partner" letter listing areas they're struggling with and asking for advice and accountability. Collect the letters, mix them up, and redistribute them to the class. Now give students four minutes to write advice, encouragement and/or Scriptural help on the letter they've received. Return letters to the original owners but be sensitive to the students who want to remain anonymous.

STEP I

This game will get your guys excited and ready to learn about Fox-Hole Friends. Set up a course that includes a starting line, a finish line, and a number of "fox-holes." In war, fox-holes are places soldiers hide for protection. So, in this situation a fox-hole could be an overturned table, a refrigerator box guys can crawl in, or anything else you can think of. Have two guys race through the course at a time. Arm all other guys with water balloons and set them up along the outside of the course. See which pair gets through the course fastest and "bombed" with water balloons the fewest times. If you're playing this game in a gym instead of outside, use tennis balls; if you're playing in a classroom, you can use paper wads. Use this game to introduce what "fox-holes" are.

STEP 5

Give each guy a rock and a marker. Have guys write their names on their rocks. Then pass the rocks around the circle and have each guy initial everyone else's rock. Then take the guys to a place where you can build your altar. This could be outside in some woods nearby or it could be in the building. Your location should be a place where the rocks won't be seen or disturbed. One at a time, have the guys place their rocks in a pile. As they do this, each guy needs to say one way that he needs the rest of the group to hold him accountable. When you are done, you will have a little "altar" to remember your commitments by.

STEP I

Try some of these teamwork games or make up your own:
• **Stand Up:** Groups of three sit on the ground with their backs together, and try to stand up without using their hands at all.
• **Handicapped Obstacle:** Assign various handicaps to group members (no sight, one leg, no arms, no speaking). Then have them complete a simple obstacle course together—no time limit, just teamwork.
• **Beam Pass:** Have students stand on a beam or log with both halves of the line facing the middle. Everyone must get to the opposite-side position without stepping off.
• **Few Feet:** Challenge your group to see how few feet they can have touching the ground (total of the group).

STEP 5

If your students are ready, help them get into Fox-Hole Groups—groups of friends who make accountability commitments to one another. Leave a few minutes for them to sign one another's Fox-Hole Friendship Certificates. Then give the new Fox-Hole Groups a chance to compete together. This will help close the meeting on an upbeat note. Review the rules for "Up for Grabs" in Step 1. Give each team a bag filled with the same 6-10 food and drink items. (It would be best if these are different items than the ones you used in Step 1!) See which team can eat all the items first. Give the team that wins a jar of baby food for a prize.

STEP 1

For a shorter opening try the following video opening. Take your video camera to a couple of local schools right before classes let out. After asking permission from the administration, shoot short clips of kids together: groups by the locker, walking through the halls, playing basketball, holding hands, talking to a teacher. Make sure each shot is less than five seconds, with the total footage less than three minutes. If you keep the shots short, you won't have to spend time editing the piece. When you play the video for the students, play the theme song from the movie *Toy Story* in the background ("You've Got a Friend in Me").

STEP 2

Look for ways to use additional media to introduce your discussion of "Fox-Hole Friendship." For example:
• Show clips from old war movies of soldiers fighting in fox-holes (screen them for appropriateness for your group).
• Show a clip from a documentary of "Desert Storm" (the war against Iraq) where military leaders discuss the strategic importance of fox-holes.
• Bring in a magazine like LIFE from the World War II era, or a book with pictures of soldiers fighting in fox-holes.

The goal for this activity is to get them thinking: **What would it be like in a fox-hole? Who would I want in *my* fox-hole?**

STEP 1

Instead of waiting for everyone to arrive, start playing "Up for Grabs" when the first guy and girl arrive. As others arrive, girls should jump in to help the girls team, and guys jump in to help the guys. Instead of a long discussion, have students discuss with one or two people next to them: **If we can get more done when we work together, why don't we ask for help more often?**

STEP 2

After reading Resource 7, tell a story about one of your own friendships. Use it as an example of what it means to have a Fox-Hole Friendship that involves keeping a friend accountable as you both live the "front lines" of following God.

STEP 3.

Instead of making "living collages," have your three small groups each write a short newspaper account of the scene you assign them. Use the questions at the end of Step 3.

STEP 4/5

You can accomplish the goals for both Steps 4 and 5 with one set of student or adult testimonies. Tell your speakers to get very specific about their friendship, including actual situations that involved asking each other tough, confronting questions. Also, allow your speakers an opportunity to encourage the rest of the group to be accountable. In closing, pass out copies of Resources 8 and 9 for students to complete at home. *(Needed: guest speakers.)*

STEP 2

Urban groups may not relate as well to the "fox-hole"/war imagery. Instead introduce the concept of being on the "front lines" in a way they can relate to with this simulation activity. Break into three teams and announce that teams are television reporters for the city's Christian TV station—WGOD. Each team was covering a routine story when a city-wide riot broke out. Each team must give two TV reports, one as if during the crisis and the other reporting how they got out safely by depending on God and working together as friends on the front lines.
• TEAM 1 was en route to the station when it got caught in gang cross-fire. It is now reporting from between two trucks. The gangs are closing in on the reporters' location.
• TEAM 2 has been kidnapped by four armed bank robbers. The thieves have allowed Team 2 to report their demands, but they have threatened to detonate a bomb and destroy millions of dollars in property if they do not get $1 million in one hour.
• TEAM 3 is doing a story from the city's highest security prison. There's been a prisoner uprising. The team and the guards are confined in cells. The team is reporting the demands from Cell Block 4. The prisoners are threatening to kill one cell block group per hour.

STEP 4

If groups get stuck coming up with ideas for the temptation situations in Step 4, here are two ideas with urban twists:
(1) Fyseen has sworn to wait for sex until marriage, but now he's telling you he's been getting hot and heavy with Rasheeda.
(2) Han-Min wants to get rid of her Christian CDs because she's into only Gangsta Rap now.

STEP 3

Find a quiet, relaxing place outside or a special place in your church or home where your group can "get away." Before moving to this "garden," discuss: **Have you ever faced a really tough morning when you knew your day would be difficult?** (First day at a new school, parents' divorce, funeral, etc.) Help students understand that Jesus was facing an excruciatingly tough day—He knew He was going to die. Move to the "garden" area. Read Matthew 26:36-46. In addition to the questions and comments in Step 3, discuss: **Did Jesus' friends do a good job supporting Him? When you've been through tough times, were your friends there for you? What did they do?** Finally, give students time to think about what they've read while you play a song in the background.

STEP 5

Logistically, this step will work better for future follow-up if the partners attend the same school and if the partners are similar in life stage and corresponding temptations. Make this clear in your instructions and encourage middle school students to choose middle school partners and senior highers to choose senior high partners. Before you copy Resource 8 and distribute it to your students, you may also want to add questions such as: **Are you driving in a responsible manner? Are you honoring the curfew your parents have established for you? Are you drinking or using drugs?**

STEP 1

Many sixth graders would rather be an active participant instead of an observer. "Touch Tag" will keep them active. Choose two volunteers to be IT and IT 2. Explain that each person tagged by IT becomes part of IT—they must hold IT's hand, then use his or her free hand to tag others. Explain that anyone tagged by IT 2 also becomes a part of IT 2, but should hold to some part of IT 2's clothing with both hands and *not* tag others. Play until everyone has been tagged, Discuss: **Which team had the biggest advantage? Why? Is it easier to do things with help or on your own? Why? What are some examples? Is following God easier to do on your own or with someone else's help?**

STEP 2

Sixth graders may need a special introduction to the big word "accountability." Divide into three teams. Give each team a pile of cut-out letters that spell accountability. See which team can unscramble the word first. **What is accountability?** Supplement answers with this info: **It means holding someone responsible for his or her actions. For example, if my friend and I want to keep each other accountable to stop swearing, we could charge one another a quarter every time we catch each other saying a swear word. How else can we keep each other accountable?**

STEP 3

Instead of making "living collages," pass out markers and paper and have students draw the Bible story in a series of comic book frames. Divide into four groups and assign each group to draw one scene. Use the discussion questions at the end of Step 3.

DATE USED:

Approx. Time

STEP 1: *Up for Grabs* _____
- ❏ Extra Action
- ❏ Small Group
- ❏ Large Group
- ❏ Little Bible Background
- ❏ Mostly Girls
- ❏ Mostly Guys
- ❏ Extra Fun
- ❏ Media
- ❏ Short Meeting Time
- ❏ Sixth Grade

Things needed:

STEP 2: *Stories from the Front Lines* _____
- ❏ Heard It All Before
- ❏ Little Bible Background
- ❏ Fellowship & Worship
- ❏ Mostly Girls
- ❏ Media
- ❏ Short Meeting Time
- ❏ Urban
- ❏ Sixth Grade

Things needed:

STEP 3: *Freeze Frame* _____
- ❏ Small Group
- ❏ Short Meeting Time
- ❏ Combined Junior High/High School
- ❏ Sixth Grade

Things needed:

STEP 4: *...Be Fox-Hole Friends* _____
- ❏ Heard It All Before
- ❏ Mostly Girls
- ❏ Urban

Things needed:

STEP 5: *Accountability in Action* _____
- ❏ Extra Action
- ❏ Small Group
- ❏ Fellowship & Worship
- ❏ Mostly Guys
- ❏ Extra Fun
- ❏ Combined Junior High/High School

Things needed:

Stretcher Friends

☐ To help students learn how four friends found a creative way to introduce their paralyzed friend to Jesus.

☐ To help students understand a mind-blowing idea about introducing Jesus: Jesus can meet your friends' needs.

☐ To help students become Stretcher Friends—friends that find creative ways to introduce the people in their lives to Jesus

☐ Other:_____

_____

Your Bible Base:

Mark 2:1-5-12

STEP 1

Human Stretcher

(Needed: colored candies)

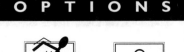

Instead of just saying "Get into groups of three!" use this creative way to break into small groups. Hand out one candy to each student. Explain that students should put the candy on their tongues but leave their mouths open and then find four other people who have the same color candy and sit down as a team. For best results, ahead of time organize your candies into multiples of five per color. NOTE: If your group won't divide equally into groups of five, you will have some students "left over" after this mixer. Allow them to join whatever team of five they want.

Introduce the game "Human Stretcher" by saying: **Has anyone ever been carried on a stretcher? When?** Pause for responses, then continue: **Has anyone ever actually been part of a stretcher? I didn't think so. Well, today you're going to have a chance to be part of a human stretcher.**

Designate the smallest member of each team the "stretcher." The other four or five students are the stretcher bearers. Two students should each grab one ankle and two students should each grab one arm. Let students practice carrying the "stretcher" around the room. Then, line the teams up and let them race from one side of your room to the other. Declare a winner.

Congratulate teams on their great job being human stretchers. Then say: **There's another way we can be "human stretchers" to our friends. Many of our friends don't know Jesus. When we bring our friends to Jesus we are like human stretchers.**

The Closet Jesus Fan

Ahead of time, prepare one student to roleplay the part of a Closet Jesus Fan in a mock interview you will conduct. A Closet Jesus Fan is someone who is afraid of telling others about Jesus. Instruct your actor to act according to certain guidelines during the interview. He or she should avoid mentioning anything about being a Christian, going to church, or knowing Jesus; act shy and nervous; speak only in vague terms about being a Christian; and keep trying to change the subject to something less challenging like lunch, a recent movie, or homework.

Tell students to find partners. Explain that they are going to practice introducing each other before you talk about introducing Jesus. Students have three minutes to learn as much about their partners as they can by asking questions such as: *Where were you born? What's your favorite restaurant? What do you like best about your brothers and sisters?* Explain that each student will use this information to make a brief introduction of his or her partner.

After three minutes, give each student a chance to introduce his or her partner by sharing three things he or she learned from the interview.

Say: **Sometimes it's hard to know how to introduce our friends. And it can be even harder to introduce our friends to Jesus. I've asked [name of the student actor you've prepared] to come and show us what it might be like to introduce Jesus.**

Interview your student actor with the questions like:

- **So, do you go to church?**
- **Have you ever invited any of your friends to go to church with you?**
- **What do you think of Jesus?**
- **Do you want to tell the group anything about Jesus?**
- **Is there anything you particularly like about Jesus?**
- **You don't seem to be too excited about your faith in Jesus. Isn't Jesus supposed to be your best friend?**

After the interview, discuss: **How would you summarize the introduction style of this student?**

Did this person give Jesus an effective introduction? Why or why not?

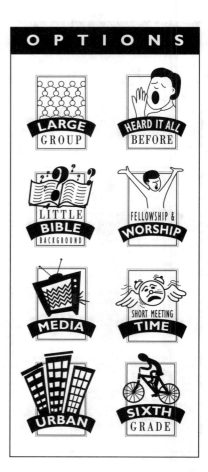

O P T I O N S

LARGE GROUP

HEARD IT ALL BEFORE

LITTLE BIBLE BACKGROUND

FELLOWSHIP & WORSHIP

MEDIA

SHORT MEETING TIME

URBAN

SIXTH GRADE

It's probably obvious to you that this person was what we'll call a "Closet Jesus Fan." He was terrified of telling others about Jesus. He probably keeps his faith hidden, as if in a closet. How many of you find it awkward or even scary to try to introduce Jesus?

What are some things someone might find scary about introducing Jesus?

Let's face it. None of us wants to introduce Jesus if it's going to make us look like a geek, right? The problem is our fear often keeps our faith locked up. Instead of being Stretcher Friends, we end up being Closet Jesus Fans. Today we're going to talk about how to introduce Jesus without looking like a geek.

STEP
3

Stretcher Friends Melodrama

(Needed: Repro Resource 10, one candy bar or piece of candy per student)

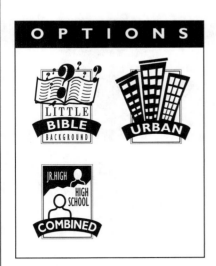

Ahead of time, prepare a student to wait outside your room at a place where he or she can hear you without being seen. In the lesson below, you will say at one point, "You may not know it, but Jesus died for you because of how much He loves you." That will be your actor's cue. He or she should burst into the room and say, "They're giving away free candy bars outside. Come on! Hurry outside!" This simulation will help start a discussion about why we should introduce others to Jesus.

Before we study about how to introduce Jesus, let's talk a little about friendship. I'm wondering something. What do you think is the most extreme act of friendship someone could ever do? Take a few responses, then ask: **What about dying for a friend? Don't you think dying for someone is the greatest act of friendship? Has anyone ever died for you? You may not know it, but Jesus died for you because of how much He loves you.** *Student enters.*

At this point, your lesson may get a little chaotic. The student that you prepared ahead of time should burst in the room and yell, "They're giving away free candy outside. Come on! Hurry outside!" Some of your students may immediately get up and head outside. Others may stay, watching you for a cue. Go ahead and excuse your students to go outside and each get the candy. You may want to recruit an adult ahead of time to stand outside and distribute the candy.

Call your students back to the room. Explain: **Wasn't that great of (the student's name) to run in here and tell us about the free candy bars?**

Get back to the lesson by saying: **Dying for someone is the ultimate act of friendship. When Jesus died for us on the cross it was the greatest act of love, sacrifice, and friendship ever. But the second most extreme act of friendship is to introduce someone to Jesus. So many times we keep the good news of our friendship with Jesus to ourselves. Instead, we should be just like the student who burst into our class-room to tell us about the candy. Our news about Jesus is so much better than a candy bar, and yet we hesitate to introduce others to Him.**

In a melodrama, volunteers act out the story as you read it. Give these directions: **We're about to read a melodrama. And while I want you to have fun with this, see if you can find a mind-blowing idea about friendship in this melodrama.** Assign nine of your most vocal, outgoing students to the roles listed on "Stretcher Friends Melodrama" (Repro Resource 10). Other students who want to participate can be "People." Read the script and have your actors and audience act out the scene as you read.

How were the four friends in this story different from the Closet Jesus fan?

What would have happened to the paralyzed guy if the friends had done nothing?

Why do you think the four friends were so motivated to bring their friend to Jesus?

What can this story teach us about introducing Jesus to our friends?

Did anyone catch the mind-blowing idea about introduc-ing Jesus? Like you and me, these four friends just might have been terrified about introducing Jesus. After all, their paralyzed friend could have rejected Jesus and refused His help, and the four guys could have looked like geeks. But get this: Those four friends understood that Jesus can meet your friends' needs. Jesus can heal your friends wherever they hurt. That's a mind-blowing idea about introducing Jesus, isn't it?

How to Be Stretcher Friends

(Needed: copies of Repro Resource 11 and 12)

Ahead of time, assign three volunteers the three monologues on "A Friend in Need" (Repro Resource 11). Prepare them with a copy of Repro Resource 11 and encourage them to practice so that they can read their lines as convincingly as possible on the day of your meeting. If you used Repro Resource 2 in Step 4 of Session 2, these three characters will be familiar. For best results, choose the same actors from Session 2 to read their characters' lines again here. This resource is a follow-up to Repro Resource 2.

Introduce the monologue reading by saying: **It's one thing to admire what these four friends did and another thing to be Stretcher Friends in our own world. Sit back and listen now to the stories of three teens who have needs only Jesus can meet. Pay close attention because in a few minutes we'll discuss what it would mean to be a Stretcher Friend to these people.**

Have your actors perform their monologues.

Ask students to go and stand by one of the three characters that they would like to help introduce to Jesus. Groups don't have to be equal in size. If any group is larger than 4-5 students, break it into smaller groups as necessary. Pass out pens and copies of "I Will Introduce You to Jesus" (Repro Resource 12). Each small group should brainstorm answers to the questions on the resource sheet as they relate to the character they've chosen. Give groups about 10 minutes to brainstorm answers. Then have one spokesperson per group present his or her small group's answers.

STEP 5

Stretcher Friends in Action

(Needed: a wooden cross, or large branches and nails, or two pieces of wood and nails; tape, index cards, pens)

OPTIONS

EXTRA ACTION

HEARD IT ALL BEFORE

FELLOWSHIP & WORSHIP

MOSTLY GUYS

EXTRA FUN

URBAN

Bring in a large wooden cross and put it on one side of your room. You can make a wooden cross by nailing two large branches or pieces of wood together in the shape of a cross.

Your friends who don't know Jesus have needs that only Jesus can meet. Their lives could change if only someone would step up and introduce them to Jesus. We've spent some time today starting to answer the question "HOW do we introduce our friends to Jesus?" Now we need to decide WHO we can introduce to Jesus.

Give pens and an index card to each student. Ask students to indicate the person that they will try to introduce to Jesus on the card by writing his or her name, drawing a picture, or writing something that reminds them of him or her. On the back side of the card, ask them to write two specific actions that they will take to introduce their friend to Jesus. Encourage them to use some of the ideas that they shared when they discussed their "I Will Introduce You to Jesus" handouts. Or they can come up with their own ideas to be Stretcher Friends in action.

After three or four minutes, point to the cross at the side of your room. Ask students to come forward and tape their index cards to the cross. **Every time we look at this cross it will be a reminder of our commitments to introduce one friend to Jesus.** If possible, leave the cross where it is for the next few weeks as a reminder. Make sure you set an example by putting an index card on the cross with one of your own friend's names on it.

Finally, close in prayer. Ask God to provide your group with opportunities to be Stretcher Friends and introduce others to Jesus.

Stretcher Friends Melodrama

Characters:

Jesus	Frank (Friend #1)
The People	Fran (Friend #2)
The Stretcher	Fred (Friend #3)
Pete, the paralytic	Frieda (Friend #4)
Two roof shingles	

One day Jesus was walking along. He decided to enter a house. A bunch of people heard that Jesus was in the house, so they crowded in. In fact, it was so crowded that some of the people were sitting on top of one another. The people were on the edge of their seats. They "shushed" anyone who made any noise that kept them from hearing Jesus' preaching.

The four friends, Frank, Fran, Fred, and Freida, tiptoed up to the house so that they wouldn't disrupt Jesus' teaching. Peering inside, they saw how crowded it was. Well, all except Freida, who was so short that she had to climb on top of Fred's back to see inside. Frank, Fran, Fred, and Freida were very sad because they had really hoped that their friend Pete, who was paralyzed, could see Jesus so Jesus could heal Pete. But there were too many people. They were so sad that they couldn't even walk; they could only crawl away from the house.

Suddenly Fran jumped to her feet and yelled, "Wait. I have an idea."

"What?" yelled Frank.

However, Fran was partly deaf so she screamed louder, "What?" to Frank.

Frank returned the favor by yelling at the top of his lungs, "What?"

This time Fran heard him. She yelled, "We could go through the roof."

All four friends leaped for joy. They were still leaping for joy when Fred yelled, "Hey, we can bring Pete, our paralyzed friend with us." Still leaping for joy, all four friends yelled together, "What a great idea!"

They found a stretcher lying on the side of the road and picked it up. Then they found Pete, picked him up, and put him on the stretcher. They got lost on the way back to the house so they had to walk a little extra.

Finally they found the house. They pried up two of the roof shingles. Being very careful, they lowered the stretcher and Pete in front of Jesus. All four friends were smiling at Jesus. Jesus smiled big back at them. Jesus said to Pete, "Your sins are forgiven."

At that point, Pete got up off the stretcher and walked out of the house. He was so excited that he could walk, he hopped around a little. Then he jumped. Then he skipped around Jesus. Everyone in the house was shocked and gasped in unison. Together they said, "Praise God!" The four friends began leaping for joy again and giving each other high fives.

The end.

A Friend in Need...

Try to put yourself into the shoes of these students as you read their thoughts and feelings aloud.

Student #1: Clothes Carol

I feel like everyone is judging me every time I walk onto our school campus. If I could read their thoughts, they'd probably be thinking stuff like, "She's so out of style," or "Her clothes are so lame." Why do they judge me so much? And why do I even care that they judge me in the first place? Why is it so important to me that other people approve of how I look? I wish I didn't care so much, but I can't help it. I guess that I'll never have the clothes it takes to be accepted.

Student #2: New Girl Nancy

It's been a whole month at this school and I still feel like a loner. There was that other new girl who started having lunch with me, but pretty soon she joined the basketball team and made some new friends and ditched me. Now it's just me eating lunch alone again. I just hate sitting at that lunch table alone. I try to pretend as if I'm reading my English homework so that nobody will guess how alone I feel. I may be able to hide my loneliness from other people, but not myself.

Student #3: Failing Frank

I'm still not cutting it. I try in math, but the numbers just don't make sense. My other classes are OK, but not math. Even my older brother tried to help me, and he did help a bit, but not enough. I just wish I didn't have to take math. My parents are really getting mad at me. They say that I'm messing up my chances of going to a good college. But that feels so far away. All I care about is finishing this school year and passing my last math test.

I Will Introduce You to Jesus

I will **pray** for ...

What kind of **needs** could Jesus meet in your friend's life?

What are some **creative ways** you could introduce your friend to Jesus?

 **I could ...**

 **I could ...**

 **I could ...**

 **I could ...**

5 I could ...

NOTES

STEP 1

Instruct the group to stand in a circle. Choose one person to be the starter and lay one hula hoop on the starter's right shoulder and the other on his or her left shoulder. Next, have students grab hands. On your signal, the group must race to get the hula hoops around the circle in opposite directions and back to the starter. They do this by stepping through the hoop, then darting their head through. They must keep their hands clasped together at all times. At some point the hoops will intersect, which will make things more interesting. Discuss: **Have you ever heard the saying "I had to jump through hoops for him"? What does it mean? Some of your friends may think they have to "jump through hoops" to know Jesus. But all they have to do is come to Jesus as they are. We're going to talk today about how to help our friends do just that!**

STEP 5

Junior high students are not always comfortable sharing important information. But if you get them involved in an active game, they just might start sharing before they even know it. Choose one person to be "It." Play like "Freeze Tag" (whenever It tags someone, he or she must stand "frozen") with this variation: to get "unfrozen" students must shout out their answers to this question: **What's the name of one unchurched friend you will pray for?** Each round, switch "Its" and questions. Other questions include: **What are you most afraid of about sharing your faith?** and **What's one lesson you learned today about sharing your faith?**

STEP 1

Here are two suggestions for getting more personal with your small group:
• School Trip: Take a field trip to one of the schools your students attend. Take a walk around the school and tell students to picture in their minds some of their friends who don't know Jesus.
• Yearbook Discussions: Gather recent yearbooks from your students' schools. As students enter, encourage them to thumb through the books. This is sure to stimulate plenty of "Look, there's so and so" kinds of comments. Ask as many questions as you can about who your students' friends are, what the various people are like, etc. This will get students thinking about specific people. After either of the activities, discuss: **Do you believe every person needs Jesus? Why or why not? Do the people at your schools need Jesus? Who might God want you to introduce to Jesus?**

STEP 4

One of the best ways to practically prepare students to share their faith is to help them write "testimonies." These are 1-2 minute personal stories about 1) What the subject's life was like before he or she knew Jesus; 2) How he or she became a Christian; and 3) What it means to "walk with God" and have a "relationship with God" in the subject's own words. Tell students to write out their testimonies in two or three paragraphs. Then ask for volunteers to give their testimonies to the class. Discuss the best ways they can share their testimonies with their friends.

STEP 1.

Capitalize on the energy of a large group. Divide into two or more affinity groups (guys vs. girls, 7th vs. 8th grade, etc.) Have each group send up five team representatives and have them race as instructed in Step 1. Encourage the audience to cheer loudly.

STEP 2

Sometimes the standard of expectations for drama performances is higher among teens in a large group. Instead of the "Closet Jesus Fan" skit, ask your drama team or two or three actors ahead of time to write and perform their own "life without Jesus" monologues. These should be stories that detail how life would be different if the actors didn't know Jesus. They should be written, however, in the present tense; for example: "My life looks good on the outside, but I'm missing something. I don't feel satisfied." At the end of the monologues, have the students write down three things that would be different in their own lives if they didn't know Jesus or three things that might change if they committed their lives to Christ for the first time.

STEP 4

Break down into small groups of six to eight students each. Pass out one copy of Resource 11 to each group. Tell the groups to choose three people to read the parts of the three characters to the rest of the group. Then ask the group to choose one of the three characters to whom they'd like to be a Stretcher Friend. Ask one person in each group to be the "scribe" and record any ideas the group comes up with on Resource 12. Afterward, have the scribes share their answers with the rest of the class.

STEP 2

Call the local fire department and see if you can get an Emergency Medical Technician (EMT) to come visit for a short introduction about emergency response. Have the guest talk about what it's like to be on the scene of a life and death situation. Prepare students to ask questions like: **How does it feel to deal with people in crisis? What's the toughest accident you've ever dealt with? What's the most extravagant length you've ever gone to for somebody else? Did you put yourself at risk to help someone else?** After the guest leaves, discuss: **How can we be like "EMTs" to our friends? What kinds of crises are your friends facing? Have you ever seen yourself as an EMT for Christ?**

STEP 5.

If your students have "heard it all before," this is another opportunity to challenge them to start living it out. Use the time you have for Step 5 to introduce a special "Introduction Night"—an event to which your students can bring the unchurched friends for whom they have committed to pray. Ask students to help you brainstorm an event that would help them effectively introduce Jesus to their friends. Possibilities:

• A dinner at your house or the church.

• A fun activity—anything from a lock-in or "road rally" to a night at the movies.

• A special Sunday school or mid-week service with a special format that will help introduce unchurched students to Jesus.

You might prepare a few students to give their testimonies. Or you might give a short talk to help introduce Jesus.

STEP 2

Some students in your group may not yet be spiritually mature enough to relate to the "Closet Jesus Fan" illustration. Instead, start by discussing: **What's the greatest act of love anyone's ever made for you?** Then, when you discuss the following questions, have students move to the left if they agree with the first choice, and to the right if they agree with the second choice. **Which do you think is a greater act of love: Someone climbing the highest mountain to be with the one he or she loves, or someone leaving, even though he or she doesn't want to, because it's the best thing to do for the one he or she loves? A son dying for his father, or a father dying to save his son?** Add as many other questions as you can. Then detail as best you can the ultimate act of love God made on our behalf—He sent His Son, Jesus, to die for our sins.

STEP 3

Another Bible story for a group with little Bible background might be Jesus' encounter with the woman at the well. Read John 4:4-26. Use the "melodrama" idea in Step 3. You'll have to write a simple script yourself. Here are a few lines to get you started: **Most Jewish men hated Samaritan women. They held their noses up in the air when they saw one. They made disgusting, snobbish sounds. But when Jesus met a Samaritan woman, He went out of His way to serve her.** You can tie in the "Stretcher Friends" terminology in two ways: 1) Some students might need to get on the "stretcher" like the woman at the well did and come to God through Jesus for the first time. 2) Discuss how the Samaritan woman, once she experienced a relationship with God through Jesus, went on to be a Stretcher Friend to many other Samaritans by introducing them to Jesus.

STEP 2

Before getting too far in the lesson, take some time to review what students have been learning in the series. Ask students to walk around outside your meeting room (or provide a number of various, random objects if going outside is not possible). Tell students to find one object that summarizes a lesson they have learned about Jesus' friendship during this series. Have each student share and explain the object he or she found. Encourage students to share with an attitude of worship, thanking Him for serving us, valuing us, forgiving us, and modeling accountability for us. Lead your students through the following discussion: **Don't all these things make you glad that you know such a great God? Don't you wish everyone could experience God's forgiveness, friendship, and other great qualities? How can we share what we're learning with our friends?**

STEP 5

Make Step 5 more worshipful and reflective with these variations. First, while students are filling out their cards, play a recording of a challenging song like Al Denson's, "Be The One." (This song talks about accepting the call to share our faith with the world.) Second, as students tape the names of their friends on the cross as a commitment to share their faith, have a basketful of nails available at the foot of the cross. Encourage students to take a nail and keep it with them as a physical reminder to share their faith. Finally, have students pair up with a close friend and spend a few minutes praying for their friends who need to be introduced to Jesus.

MOSTLY GIRLS

STEP 1

Sometimes girls are more willing to start off with discussion instead of an activity. This step will help them build relationships by sharing some of their fears. Ahead of time, make multiple sets of index cards that include questions about fear like: *What's the scariest amusement park ride you've ever been on? What's the scariest movie you've ever seen? What are you most afraid of?* Add more question cards as needed. Divide students into groups of three or four and give each group one of the cards. Each student should answer the question. Rotate the cards around the groups. Before moving on, ask for volunteers to answer this question: **What scares you about sharing Jesus with your friends?**

STEP 4

Teen girls love solving problems. With that in mind, help students get even more in depth with the Step 4 activity. You may want to have a few concordances handy. Make sure students know how to use them. After students listen to the three monologues (as directed in Step 4), have them look up Scripture that would encourage and support one or more of the three characters. Pass out three bandage strips to each girl. Have them write the Scripture references they've found on the bandages and give them to the appropriate character. Point out that what most unbelieving people need to know most is that Jesus can help them heal where they hurt—somewhat like bandages.

MOSTLY GUYS

STEP 1

Guys and roleplays are not always a great mix. Instead, give your guys a physical challenge. Divide into groups of five and in each group, designate one guy to be the "paralytic" and the other four to be his "Stretcher Friends." The friends must carry the paralytic through a course that you lay out ahead of time. Make sure the course is difficult enough to be challenging. Discuss: **How did you like that activity? Was it difficult? Did you get tired? Did you ever resent your friend or the fact that you had to carry him? How can we "carry" our friends who don't know Jesus? How might they feel similar to how the "paralytic" felt in this exercise? What feelings do you have about sharing your faith with your friends that compare to what you felt during this exercise?**

STEP 4

Have students make videotapes of their testimonies—one or two minute personal stories about what Christ has done in their lives.

STEP 5

Follow the directions for Step 5 up to the point where students write their friends' names on index cards. Instead, bring in blank business cards (or paper cut to that size). Have students write the names down on these cards to keep in their wallets. This might be a less intimidating idea for guys than taping cards to a cross.

EXTRA FUN

STEP 1

Have teams race around a course carrying one team member on a hospital gurney. These are a little hard to come by. But if you ask a local hospital community relations department, you might be able to borrow two gurneys. Make a course in a gym or outside using cones or chairs as turn-around points. Have teams race head-to-head, or have them go one at a time. (This latter option makes the fun possible even if you can only get one gurney). If you are unable to get a gurney from a hospital, consider renting one for a day from a hospital equipment rental store.

STEP 5

After you finish the cross exercise in Step 5, have your kids plan a party. The party's goal might be: 1) To review the things learned during this friendship series, or 2) To invite the visitors your students wrote down in Step 5. If your group is small, involve everyone in the planning of every aspect. If your group is more than a dozen kids, divide them into smaller groups to plan different aspects of the party: games, decorations, food, entertainment.

STEP 1

Record on your VCR clips from movies or TV shows that feature emergency room scenes of doctors saving lives. Show the video, then discuss: **Why do you think the characters were motivated to save lives? Do you think they cared about the people they were saving?** Help students see that people who don't know Jesus are in an "emergency" situation—their eternities hang in the balance. Discuss how students can be used by God to help "save" their friends who don't know Jesus.

STEP 2

Gather up recent yearbooks from the schools your students attend. Film 2-5 second clips of a number of faces. If possible, intersperse these clips with one or two teens stating common objections to sharing their faith: *I don't want to judge them; they have their own beliefs; who am I to tell them what to do?* When you show the clips, play a song in the background that motivates students to introduce others to Jesus. Discuss: **Do you really think *everyone* needs Jesus? Do you think Jesus could make your friends' lives better? Why or why not? Why is sharing our faith so hard?**

STEP 1

Step 3 in the main lesson calls for one student to interrupt the class by shouting, "There's free candy!" If you do this to start your lesson, you'll not only have a succinct introduction to today's theme, you'll also shave some time off of Step 3. Discuss: **Do you appreciate the fact that (name of person who announced the free candy) decided to share with others instead of keeping it all to herself? We have Great News about Jesus. Are you going to keep that to yourself or share it with others?**

STEP 2

Ahead of time, ask two students to share about how they came to know Jesus and about the stretcher friends who were involved. Try to find two students who have different stories about how they were introduced to Jesus. When they finish, ask if anyone else would like to share how they were introduced to Jesus. Discuss: **What's the best way to introduce someone to Jesus? What ways are effective? What ways aren't? Why?**

STEP 4/5

Instead of choosing volunteers to read the monologues off Resource 11, make up your own story simulations to read. Find out ahead of time what the names and needs are of some of the unchurched peers in your students' circle of influence. Write and then read hypothetical stories about how they came to know Christ and the difference it made to them. Follow the directions for Step 5 here as written in the lesson.

STEP 2

Sometimes the pressure involved in taking a stand for Jesus can be more intense in urban areas. Peers may call your students "God Nerd" or "Whacked Hallelujah Freak." Discuss: **Are you willing to look like a geek in the eyes of some in order to serve Jesus? What will the consequences be of sharing your faith?** Be aware that in some cases it may be physically dangerous to share one's faith. Help students work through this critical issue, then use Step 2 as written in the lesson.

STEP 3

If you are working with a super-low budget try using a bag of marshmallows, candy corn, or Hershey's Kisses in Step 3.

STEP 5

Have teens bring in their favorite Christian hip-hop, rap, and gospel music (like Kirk Franklin, Out of Eden, Hezekiah Walker, etc.) Celebrate all five of the friendship lessons they've learned in this series. Make a party of it—don't forget refreshments and decorations. Have a "rap off" and see which teen can put together the best lyrics on the five types of friendship. Give a prize to the winner. Further, give a prize to those who can "break off somethin' proper" [translation: put the best music together] using the following styles for the following types of friendship:
- Extreme Friend Rap
- Bleacher Friend Rasta
- Second-Chance Friend Hip-Hop
- Fox-Hole Friend Blues
- Stretcher Friend Gospel Music

STEP 3.

Instead of offering free candy bars, have a student interrupt your meeting and yell, "I'll give $10 to the first person who shakes my hand!" The $10 prize is certain to get the interest of your older students.

STEP 4.

Here's a practical way to get both middle school and high school students to practice sharing their faith: Read the following quotes then have volunteers suggest ways to follow-up with a comment that would bring up Jesus. Statements:
• "I don't know what to do! My mom's having surgery tomorrow. I'm really scared." (Possible response: "Can I pray for you?")
• "Allison's so mean. I think I hate her. How can you still be polite to her after all she's said about you?" (Possible response: "I've said things that are stupid, too. But God keeps loving me and wants me to keep loving others.")

STEP 2

The learning ability of most sixth graders is enhanced when they use a variety of senses in the learning process. Plan ahead of time for the students to create and film a TV commercial no longer than 2-3 minutes. The commercial should explain why Jesus is the best friend for anyone who doesn't know Him. Have the students first prepare a script that includes information, such as: **What is it like to be Jesus' friend? What are the benefits of having Jesus for a friend? What are the disadvantages when you don't know Jesus?** Show the commercial to the entire class.

STEP 4

Instead of writing responses to Repro Resource 12, have students roleplay possible conversations with the characters on that sheet. How might they start a conversation? How could they find a way to introduce what Jesus had to offer? Let as many volunteers roleplay these situations as you have time for. You may want to play the part of the characters from Repro Resource 11 during the roleplays. Give students feedback.

DATE USED:

Approx. Time

STEP 1: *Human Stretcher* _____
❑ Extra Action
❑ Small Group
❑ Large Group
❑ Mostly Girls
❑ Mostly Guys
❑ Extra Fun
❑ Media
❑ Short Meeting Time
Things needed:

STEP 2: *The Closet Jesus Fan* _____
❑ Large Group
❑ Heard It All Before
❑ Little Bible Background
❑ Fellowship & Worship
❑ Media
❑ Short Meeting Time
❑ Urban
❑ Sixth Grade
Things needed:

STEP 3: *Stretcher Friends...* _____
❑ Little Bible Background
❑ Urban
❑ Combined Junior High/High School
Things needed:

STEP 4: *How to Be Stretcher...* _____
❑ Small Group
❑ Large Group
❑ Mostly Girls
❑ Mostly Guys
❑ Combined Junior High/High School
❑ Sixth Grade
Things needed:

STEP 5: *Stretcher Friends in Action* _____
❑ Extra Action
❑ Heard It All Before
❑ Fellowship & Worship
❑ Mostly Guys
❑ Extra Fun
❑ Urban
Things needed:

NOTES

Unit Three: Which Way to God?

Talking to Junior Highers about Other Religions

by Darrell Pearson

It's one of the most frustrating things about the Christian faith, for group members and leaders alike. But Jesus did say it—He claimed to be the only way to God. And junior highers *really* don't like it.

That leaves the leader with a real dilemma: How do you present to your group members the Way, the Truth, and the Life, without it seeming so unfair that group members will never buy it?

The word *unfair* is the key here. Junior high and middle school students are into this word. Just try to change the rules of an intense game right in the middle of a competition and you'll know what taking a risk with your life is all about. These kids want something *fair*, and that includes their God. They have a very tough time accepting a God who seems to think so narrowly.

In our seventh grade membership class, we used to have a true-false question that stated, "Jesus is the only way to God." I was always amazed at how many students answered "false," until I realized that they did it only because it seemed unfair not to.

Unfortunately (or so they might think), God is not fair. He's way beyond that. And that *is* fortunate for all of us. But getting kids to understand it can be a very tough problem. Here are a few ideas to help kids see God in the right perspective as we talk about other religions.

Sincerity Does Not Equal Truth

I'll never forget several eighth-grade girls who came up to me after our Wednesday night program with serious expressions on their faces. Their dilemma had to do with a friend at school who practiced a different religion. After their initial rejection of their friend's belief system, they found that their friend was far more serious about *her* faith than they were about *theirs*. That made them question their own beliefs and wonder if their friend really had it all figured out. It was difficult for their junior high minds to consider whether anything was true or false in this matter, because they were focused on their friend's sincerity. "It's not fair that she and her family practice their faith so hard, and yet they might go to hell!" was the essence of their concern.

I tried not to downplay their friend's faith, but instead tried to help them see that if they were concerned about the issue, they should think about taking their own faith more seriously.

It might take some creative teaching to bring the point home, but I think it would be worthwhile to pursue the concept that sincerity does not equal truth. You want to help group members see that just because someone is "into" a belief system, doesn't mean he or she necessarily holds the key to life. The key is to discover what is real and true.

What Do Other Religions Say?

Very few junior highers have any kind of developed concept of what other religions believe. In fact, very few youth *leaders* have such a developed concept. We tend to assume that all religions have at their core the same purposes and quests. Not so! You could do a great Sunday morning series focusing on different religions (maybe visits from people of other religions or dramatizations by adults who could handle this sensitively) to help kids see what the purposes of other faiths really are. Through a series like this, kids could develop an appreciation for the contributions other religions have made to the world, while still seeing those religions accurately for what they are.

We had an exchange student from Japan in our group last year who caused some other group members discomfort as he struggled with our Christian beliefs. Many kids expected him to be a Buddhist, but in fact, he was an agnostic. To him, Buddhism was an interesting historical/cultural religion from his homeland, but not something to follow. Many kids also assumed that the purpose of Buddhism was to find God—which, in fact, is *not* the goal of Buddhism. Without knowing the religion or the person, group members had a difficult time communicating with him. He was eventually very open to studying the message of the Bible, once he decided that the other people in the group accepted him (one of the *real* issues of religions and junior highers).

Keep Pointing Back to Christ

Group members always want to put the focus on outside issues, rather than deal with the simple concept of examining what Jesus said and responding to that. There is nothing as impactive about the Christian faith as studying the person of Christ. As you get to know Him by reading about Him and His teachings, you can't help but be struck by the person Himself.

Group members can discover this too, but they need to be challenged to do it. Junior highers who have questions about the Christian faith and other religions have the possibility of finding answers when they study Jesus, as He is revealed in Scripture. This is not a cop-out for answering questions about other religions; it is a prime ingredient for getting at the truth. After all, doesn't it seem fair to study Christ more completely too?

Know Your Subject Matter

It's easy to dismiss junior highers' questions about faith issues as being the result of ignorance or lack of concern, but I would encourage you to take them seriously. I read an interview with singer/composer John Denver in which he was asked about his religious beliefs. A major spokesperson for the New Age movement, Denver said he started developing his New Age thinking at age 12, when his Sunday school teacher ignored his questions about the validity of Christianity. "There had to be something better," he stated. Never ignore a student's questions on faith issues.

Becoming familiar with the issues is actually a fun and rewarding endeavor in itself. There are a lot of good resources out there to help you become better acquainted with some great answers. Along with C. S. Lewis's classic work, *Mere Christianity*, I would encourage you to read Hans Kung's two volumes, *On Being a Christian* and *Does God Exist?* These books are well written and fascinating, and will equip you with more ideas than you can probably ever use. Lewis's book is not as complete, but his comments on other religions are very helpful. It would also be worth the time to check out a book from the library on the great religions of the world to enhance your own appreciation of what they stand for. It might seem like an enormous investment of time, but the well-prepared youth leader is ready to confront questions on Christianity as well as questions on other religions.

God Isn't Fair!

No, He's not—and that's fortunate for us. If God were completely fair, we'd all be in trouble. God is not concerned about fairness, but about people. A youth leader would be wise to explain to group members that fairness is not as important as God's concern for them individually. This includes concern for people of all religions.

I've always been fascinated with the parable of the laborers in the vineyard, in which the men working just one hour got paid as much as the ones who worked twelve hours. Unfair! Every one of us would be equally frustrated that the boss paid someone the same amount of money for far less work. We're just like junior highers! But help your group members imagine that, instead of being the first person hired, they're the last. There they are, seventh graders with no money, no one interested in hiring them, needing $30 for the school sports participation fee. They've got no hope. And then some guy hires them to do one hour of lawn mowing and pays them for a whole day. How would they feel? Filled with incredible gratitude and wonder, I'd guess.

That's the God of Christianity, the God you need to help your group members see. He's not fair, even when junior highers demand fairness, because He's way beyond it. He actually loves people so much that He'll do whatever it takes to care for them. When group members have questions about other religions, take them seriously, appreciate the contributions other religions have made to the world, but point kids to the God who loves so "unfairly." Bringing them continually back to the person of Christ will ultimately make the difference with their questions.

Darrell Pearson is co-founder of 10 to 20, an organization dedicated to presenting high-involvement events for teenagers.

The images on these two pages are designed to help you promote this course within your church and community. Feel free to photocopy anything here and adapt it to fit your publicity needs. The stuff on this page could be used as a flier that you send or hand out to kids—or as a bulletin insert. The stuff on the next page could be used to add visual interest to newsletters, calendars, bulletin boards, or other promotions. Be creative and have fun!

Is Christianity the Only Way?

If Christianity is right, does that mean other religions are wrong?
What do other religions believe, anyway?
Does it really matter what religion you are—as long as you're sincere?
You'll find answers to these and other questions when we start
a new unit called *Which Way to God?*

Who:

When:

Where:

Questions? Call:

Unit Three: Which Way to God?

Special delivery.

(Write your own message on the bundle.)

What's so funny?

(Write your own message on the book.)

What do you think?

Where Did Religions Come From?

Choose one or more

☐ To help kids recognize that God has made His presence known to people throughout the ages.

☐ To help kids understand that even though people hunger after God, many have ignored the truth about Him.

☐ To help kids pray for people of other faiths.

☐ Other:_____
_____

Your Bible Base:

Psalm 19:1-4
Romans 1:18-25

Do-It-Yourself Religion

(Needed: Copies of Repro Resource 1, pencils, prizes)

Have group members form pairs. Distribute copies of "Prehistoric Worship" (Repro Resource 1) and pencils to each pair. Read aloud the first two paragraphs on the sheet while your group members follow along.

Then have the members of each pair work together in answering the questions on the sheet. Encourage the pairs to put thought, creativity, and detail into their answers. Announce that you will be awarding prizes to the pair that gives the most complete answers.

Give the pairs a few minutes to work. When everyone is finished, go through the questions one at a time and have each pair share its responses. Afterward, award prizes to the pair that gave the most complete answers.

Use the following ideas to supplement the pairs' responses.

How would you feel about the boulder? Would you be happy to have it in your village? Would you be afraid to go near it? Explain. (Some may be happy, because they believe that no harm or trouble could come to the village as long as the boulder is there. Others may be afraid of doing something wrong around the boulder and being punished for it.)

What kinds of rules and rituals would you come up with concerning the boulder? How would you show your respect and worship for this higher power? (Some may suggest marking off the area around the boulder and not allowing anyone to go near it. Others may suggest bowing your head and showing reverence every time you pass near the boulder. Still others may suggest that once a year, in a ritual to commemorate the boulder's arrival, someone in the village climbs to the top of the mountain and hurls himself off to the village below.)

What would be the benefits of obeying these rules and following these rituals? (Some may suggest that obeying and following protects a person from being struck by other falling boulders.)

What would be the penalty for disobeying these rules and not following these rituals? (Some may suggest that disobeying and not following is punishable by death—from a falling boulder.)

How would you explain to others what the boulder means to you? (Some may suggest drawing the events surrounding the boulder's arrival on cave walls. Others may suggest bringing people of other villages to see the boulder.)

Afterward, point out to your group members that they actually "created" a religion ("boulderism") in this exercise.

Then ask: **How many people do you think you could get to follow your religion today—if you really tried?** Get a few responses.

Where Did They Come From?

(Needed: Chalkboard and chalk or newsprint and marker, copies of Repro Resource 2)

Not counting boulderism, how many different religions would you say there are in the world today? Encourage several group members to offer their opinions.

Then have a brief contest to see which group member can name the most religions. When you say, "Go," the first person to jump to his or her feet gets to name a religion. If the person is correct, he or she gets a point. Then you will say, "Go" again, and the first person to stand will name another religion. Continue until your group members are out of answers. Then declare the person with the most points the winner.

The list of religions might include Christianity, Judaism, Hinduism, Buddhism, Islam, satanism, etc. (You may need to point out that different Christian denominations like Baptist, Methodist, and Lutheran are not separate religions.)

Ask: **Do all these religions believe basically the same things?** (No. Their beliefs are very, very different from each other.)

Then how did they all get started? Who created them? Who came up with all their different rules and rituals? You're not necessarily looking for answers here. You just want group members to begin thinking about how different religions got started.

What might cause someone to want to create a religion? If no one mentions it, suggest "a hunger for God"—the desire to know whatever is beyond ourselves. Some people go so far as to say that religion is an *instinct* in humans, that we have an empty space inside us that only God can fill.

Point out that different religions have been around since the beginning of history. Distribute copies of "Religion Through the Ages" (Repro Resource 2).

O P T I O N S

HEARD IT ALL BEFORE

MOSTLY GIRLS

MOSTLY GUYS

SHORT MEETING TIME

URBAN

SIXTH GRADE

Give group members a few minutes to look over the sheet. Then say: **Compared to some of the other religions on this time line, Christianity is just a youngster. Religions like Egyptian mythology and Babylonian astrology were around centuries before Christianity.**

If Christianity wasn't the first religion, how can it be the best one? Why is it better than any of the other religions that sprung up over the centuries? In other words, how do we know we're right? Encourage several group members to offer their opinions.

STEP 3

Futile Thinking and Foolish Hearts

(Needed: Chalkboard and chalk or newsprint and marker, Bibles)

Explain: **Before we start comparing Christianity with other religions, we need to talk about *why* there are so many different religions.**

Have group members turn in their Bibles to Romans 1:18-25. Explain: **As I read each of these verses, hold your arms up in the air. If a verse is talking about what human beings are like, point to yourself—we're assuming that everyone here today is a human being. If a verse is talking about God, point upward. If a verse is talking about both human beings and God, point in both directions.**

Read aloud verse 18 and then wait for group members' responses. Ask a couple kids to explain why they responded as they did. Continue the same process with verses 19-25.

Use the following suggestions to supplement group members' responses.

Verse 18—This verse talks about both God and human beings. It describes the wrath of God from heaven. It also describes the godlessness and wickedness of people who suppress the truth.

Verse 19—This verse talks about God. It tells us that God has made Himself plain to us.

Verse 20—This verse talks about both God and human beings. It describes God's invisible qualities (His eternal power and divine nature).

OPTIONS

EXTRA ACTION

LARGE GROUP

HEARD IT ALL BEFORE

URBAN

SIXTH GRADE

It also tells us that we are capable of recognizing and understanding God's invisible qualities, so we are without excuse if we don't believe in Him.

Verse 21—This verse talks about human beings. It describes people who "knew" God, but didn't glorify or thank Him. The thinking of these people became futile and their hearts were darkened.

Verse 22—This verse talks about human beings. It describes people who claimed to be wise, but who became fools.

Verse 23—This verse talks about human beings. It describes people who worship images of men, birds, animals, and reptiles rather than the immortal God.

Verse 24—This verse talks about both God and human beings. It describes how God gave some people over to their sinful desires. It also describes how some people gave in to sexual impurity and degraded their bodies.

Verse 25—This verse talks about human beings. It describes how some people exchanged the truth of God for a lie, and worshiped created things rather than the Creator.

Have someone read aloud verse 21 again. Then ask: **What is "futile thinking"?** (Useless thinking, not sticking with what you know is right.)

How could futile thinking and foolish hearts lead to the creation of religions that don't glorify God? (It's a matter of refusing to recognize God and what He's done.) If no one mentions it, point out that the Israelites built and worshiped a golden calf—instead of God—just after they'd seen the miracles God performed during the ten plagues. They quickly forgot what God had done.

Why does it seem to be so easy for us human beings to forget about God and all the things He's done for us? Get a few responses.

STEP 4

God Made Plain

(Needed: Bibles)

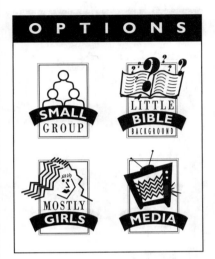

OPTIONS

SMALL GROUP

LITTLE BIBLE BACKGROUND

MOSTLY GIRLS

MEDIA

Have someone read aloud Romans 1:19 again. Then ask: **How has God made Himself plain to us? Other than the Bible, what evidence is there in the world that God exists?** (Creation itself points to the existence of a Creator. Something as complex as the universe must have been created by an intelligent being.)

Have someone read aloud Psalm 19:1-4.

Then ask: **How has God made Himself plain in people's lives?** (Some group members may mention God's personal appearances to people like Adam and Eve and Moses. Others may mention the fact that He makes Himself known through our consciences—He's given us an inbred sense of right and wrong. Others may mention the fact that He makes Himself known through answered prayers.)

If no one mentions it, suggest that the most obvious way God made Himself plain to us was through Jesus. Jesus was God in human flesh. We have actual historical accounts of God's words and actions on earth.

Christianity is based on the fact that God has made Himself known to us through Jesus. It is supported by the historical record in the Bible of Jesus' words and deeds. Jesus Himself said that He is the *only* way to God. That's why we believe Christianity is the "right" religion.

Ask: **If God has made Himself plain to us, why are there so many different religions?** (Some people refuse to see the evidence for what it is, and prefer to follow their own ideas. Others realize that following Christianity would mean a change in their lives, and they're not willing to change. Still others look for religions that "make them feel good" rather than ones based on truth.)

STEP 5

Religious Who's Who

Explain: **In the next few weeks, we're going to look at how the world religions of Judaism—the religion of Jewish people, Islam—the religion of Muslims, Hinduism, and Buddhism compare with Christianity.**

Do you know anyone who follows one of these religions? Explain that you're not looking for specific names of people. You're just trying to find out how much exposure your group members have to people of other religions.

You may want to point out that Judaism is widely practiced in the United States, as well as Israel; Islam is practiced in many Middle Eastern and Asian countries; Hinduism is practiced primarily among Asian Indians; and Buddhism is practiced among Chinese, Japanese, and southeast Asian people.

Say: **If you don't know someone who is Jewish, Muslim, Hindu, or Buddhist, chances are good that you will soon. For example, in the United States, the number of people who practice Islam has doubled within the last ten years.**

Because so many world religions are becoming popular in the West, we as Christians have to decide how we're going to respond to people with these beliefs.

One thing we can do is pray for these people to believe in God and His Son, Jesus Christ. But we need some kind of a reminder to help us remember to pray for these people.

Have each group member think of a sound he or she hears regularly—the sound of a telephone ringing, the sound of the zipper on a school backpack, the sound of a siren, etc. For the next week, whenever he or she hears that sound, he or she should say a sentence prayer for people of other religions.

Close the session in prayer, thanking God for creating us with a hunger for Him. Ask Him to help your group members be concerned for, yet respectful of, people of other religions.

PREHISTORIC WORSHIP

Imagine that you're a member of a primitive tribe of cave dwellers in prehistoric times. You've been taught that some kind of "higher power" lives in the sky. However, the only thing you know about this higher power is that it often gets angry and sends water from above. This water is often accompanied by terrifying flashes of light and loud, crashing noises.

One day while your tribe is gathered together, you hear a loud rumbling sound from above. But this time, instead of water falling from the sky, a huge boulder comes crashing down into the middle of your village. *At last,* you think, *the higher power has come down to make itself known to us!*

How would you feel about the boulder? Would you be happy to have it in your village? Would you be afraid to go near it? Explain.

What kinds of rules and rituals would you come up with concerning the boulder? How would you show your respect and worship for this higher power?

What would be the benefits of obeying these rules and following these rituals?

What would be the penalty for disobeying these rules and not following these rituals?

How would you explain to others what the boulder means to you?

NOTES

Religion Through the Ages

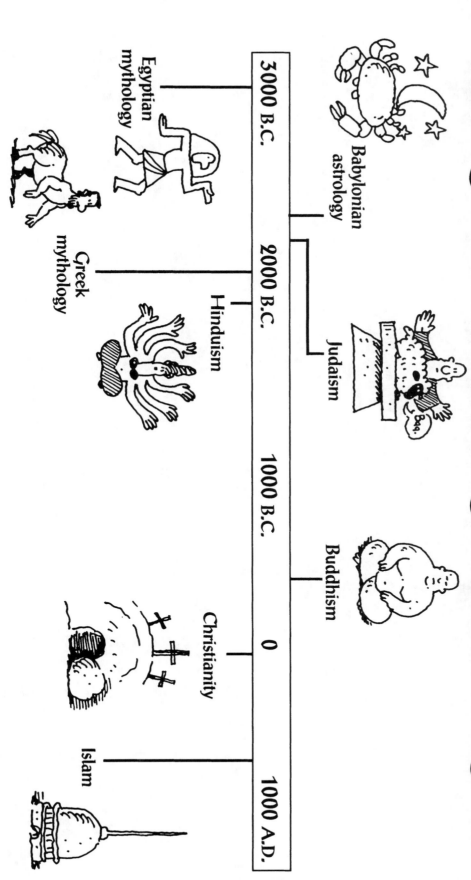

Babylonian astrology

3000 B.C.

Egyptian mythology

2000 B.C.

Greek mythology

Hinduism

Judaism

1000 B.C.

Buddhism

0

Christianity

1000 A.D.

Islam

NOTES

STEP 1

Instead of having group members simply fill out and discuss Repro Resource 1, have them form teams of four or five for a brief competition. The teams will compete in an "Invent-a-Religion" contest. Give the teams five minutes to read through Repro Resource 1 and come up with the following:

- Name of the religion
- Secret ritual handshake
- Tribal dance
- Anything else that would add to this new religion.

After the teams present the rituals they came up with, you will choose the one that most creatively expresses the team's religion. This activity could be an effective lead-in to Step 2.

STEP 3

Have your group members participate in a brief demonstration of something futile and something foolish. First, have them stand up, hold their noses, and hum a simple song (perhaps "Row, Row, Row Your Boat") together. It's impossible (futile)! Then have group members try singing the song backward, adding whatever actions they wish.

"Dream a but is life

Merrily, merrily, merrily, merrily

Stream the down gently

Boat your row, row, row"

You might want to have group members try to sing the backward song as a round. After sharing a few laughs, point out how foolish the activity was. It made no sense! Tie this into the futile thinking and foolish hearts mentioned in Romans 1.

STEP 1

Use the same idea as Repro Resource 1, but instead of using "boulderism," allow group members to make up their own religions. Provide individuals or pairs with paper and pencils and instruct them to think up a religion. Encourage them to consider the following: who or what they will worship, how they will feel about this being or thing, how they will worship it, how they will please it, and what their rewards or punishments might be. After a few minutes of brainstorming, have them write a paragraph describing their religion. (They could illustrate it if they wanted.) After a few more minutes, have group members read their descriptions. Discuss as a group what the descriptions have in common. Then have group members discuss how many followers they think they could get for their religion and why.

STEP 4

Before examining what the Bible teaches, get the kids to share their own reasons for knowing God exists. Encourage them to be personal. (You might start them off with an example from your own life in which you saw evidence of God's hand at work.) To make things more interesting, you may want to stipulate that they share their reasons without speaking. They could do this through pantomime, drawing, sculpting, etc. (You would need to make materials available.) After group members have shared their reasons, discuss the biblical teaching: the witness of creation, the Bible, and Jesus Christ. You may find that kids have already raised these points. You may also find that they gave examples of answered prayer.

STEP 1

Rather than pairs, have group members work in teams of three or four. As an alternative to filling out Repro Resource 1, have group members use the questions as a guide in making up skits to demonstrate "boulderism." They might act out a worship service or punishment ritual, or they might develop the "Ten Commandments of Boulderism." Encourage creativity and zaniness in the skits, but get kids thinking about the components of religion.

STEP 3

Have group members form eight teams. Assign one of the verses in Romans 1:18-25 to each team. After providing paper and markers, have each team draw a cartoon depicting what its verse teaches about God and/or human beings. The cartoons may be single- or multiple-framed (like a comic strip). For example, for verse 18, team members might draw some symbol for God—looking angry, sending bolts of lightning at people on earth. These people may be shown practicing various forms of godlessness: stealing, worshiping idols, saying God doesn't exist, and so on. After a few minutes, have the teams display their pictures and explain their verse. Then discuss why people reject God's truth.

STEP 2

Get your group members' interest by having them play devil's advocate against Christianity. Have them pick one of the religions mentioned on Repro Resource 2 and come up with several arguments for believing it instead of Christianity. (Emphasize that they don't have to believe the arguments they come up with.) Make a list on the board of these arguments; then discuss which seem strongest and why. Discuss arguments for as many of the religions as you have time for. As you look at biblical truths in the next step, draw attention to the way those truths counteract the arguments for other religions.

STEP 3

Before examining the Bible, challenge your group members' thinking with a debate that raises some difficult questions. Write each of the following statements on index cards, making two cards for each statement. (1) Some of the smartest people in the world, including physicist Stephen Hawking and the philosopher Plato, haven't been Christians. Therefore, Christianity can't be true. (2) You're only a Christian because your parents are Christians. If you had been born in a Saudi Arabia, you'd be a Muslim like your parents. (If you like, make up different or additional statements to use.) Have group members form two teams. Give each team a copy of both statements. Explain that one team will argue that the statement is true; the other will argue that it is false. Give the teams a few minutes to prepare some arguments; then let them debate. After they've argued for a while, stop the action and read aloud Romans 1:18-25. Emphasize that God says all people everywhere have knowledge of Him. (It's not just a cultural issue.) Emphasize also that even smart people have given themselves to futile thinking, ignoring God's truth for their own "wisdom."

STEP 4

The meaning of these passages may not be readily apparent to kids with little Bible background, so help your group members understand these passages by examining them in more depth. As a group, discuss what phrases like "heavens declare," "skies proclaim," "pour forth speech," and "display knowledge" mean. Point out that the psalmist is using metaphoric language to show that the natural world, by its existence, gives evidence of God's existence.

Kids may also have difficulty thinking of other examples of how God reveals Himself. If so, have them look up some of the following passages (or similar ones of your own choosing): Genesis 3:8-20; 18:1-3; Exodus 3:1-6; John 1:1-18. In each of these passages, God reveals Himself to someone in the Bible, culminating in the incarnation—God with us in the flesh.

STEP 5

Use the following activity to help group members prepare for the upcoming sessions. For each major religion (Judaism, Islam, Buddhism, and Hinduism), have your group members answer these questions: **What do we know? What do we want to know?** List the answers on the board as they are given. (Some of your group members' "knowledge" may be inaccurate. As they study the religions, encourage them to evaluate the accuracy of what they "know.") After group members have answered the questions, divide into four teams. Give each team a poster board and markers, and assign it one of the religions. Instruct each team to make a poster that has three columns or sections: "What We Know," "What We Want to Know," and "What We've Learned." Team members should fill in the first two columns, using the answers on the board. Collect the posters and save them for use in upcoming sessions. You can use the posters as guides in preparing for future sessions.

STEP 1

Play a variation of "spin the bottle" to get kids thinking about religions and revealing themselves. Have group members stand in a circle. Place a soda bottle on the floor in the center of the circle. Have someone spin the bottle. Whoever the bottle ends up pointing to has to complete this statement: "If I wasn't a Christian, I would be a (name a religion) because . . ." Keep playing until everyone has had a chance to respond. If someone gets pointed at twice, he or she should re-state his or her religion choice and give a second reason. If some of your kids aren't Christians, modify the statement to say, "Besides Christianity, I am interested in (name a religion) because . . ."

STEP 5

Wrap up the session with an expanded prayer time, focusing on our longing and need for God. To prepare, have a volunteer read aloud Psalm 42, which describes longing for God as a deer pants for water. Point out that this passage expresses the hunger that people have for God. Have your group members make up their own similes for God-hunger, using contemporary language and settings. (Examples might include "I long for God as a marathon runner longs for Gatorade" or "I long for God as a dieter longs for chocolate.") Encourage them to incorporate these into the prayer time. Begin the prayer by praying, "Dear God, we hunger for You . . ." Then have volunteers complete the statement with their similes. Then have volunteers pray for Muslims, Jews, Buddhists, and Hindus. (You will want to arrange this with the volunteers beforehand.) Close the prayer by asking God to help group members be faithful in praying for people of other religions.

STEP 2

Before distributing "Religion Through the Ages" (Repro Resource 2), ask your group members to define the term "a hunger for God." Ask: **What are some ways people know they have this "hunger"? What do people do about this? When have you experienced it? Since some churches have more women than men, do you think girls have more "hunger for God" than guys do? Why or why not?**

STEP 4

Explain to your group members your experience of learning the truth about Christ and how He made Himself plain to you. Then ask them to think back over their own experiences. Ask: **When did you first consider the evidence for yourself? What helped you to understand who God—the God of the Bible—is?**

STEP 1

Instead of using "boulderism," have your group members make up a religion involving baseball (or some other sport). Ask: **What would you worship? How would you show respect? What would you be required to do? What would you be required to avoid? What would be the purpose or benefit of this religion?** For example, the religion of "baseballism" might require weekly attendance at ballpark services called "games." A person might study the rules of baseball to find out how to live properly, since baseball would be a model of the way the world should be. "Communion" might involve hot dogs and sodas. (If your group is fairly large, divide into teams and assign a different sport to each team.) Instruct group members to create a list of the "ten commandments" for this new religion.

STEP 2

Liven up this step with a team competition. Have group members form teams of three or four. Instruct each team to brainstorm a list of as many religions as it can think of. (Make sure the teams don't allow other teams to overhear their ideas.) Give the teams two minutes to make their lists. Afterward, have the teams read and compare their lists. If more than one team listed a religion, they should cross it off their lists. Teams get a point for each religion they list that no one else does. Of course, the teams will all guess the more common religions, but you may find some obscure ones listed too. From this, you may get a sense of how familiar your group members are with other religions. Here are some religions the teams may list: Confucianism, Shintoism, Taoism, atheism, agnosticism, and ancestor worship. Some teams may also list cults like Jehovah's Witnesses, Christian Science, Mormonism, New Age, Scientology, the occult, etc.

STEP 1

Before the session, make up sets of cards (enough sets so that there will be one card per group member). On one card, write the name of a religion (e.g., Islam); on another card, write a statement about that religion (e.g., "Mecca is the holy place"). As group members arrive, tape a card to each one's back. Have them mill around asking questions to determine what their card says. After they find out, they should try to find their partner. When they think they've found their partner, they should come to you for verification. Depending on the size of your group, you may need to make several sets of cards about the same religion. Here are some sample ideas: Judaism—studies the Torah; Buddhism—seeks nirvana; Hinduism—believes cows are sacred; and Christianity—believes Jesus is the Savior. You can look to information in Sessions 2-5 for further ideas.

STEP 5

End the session with a costume party. Have group members form four teams. Assign one of the four major religions addressed in this book (Judaism, Islam, Hinduism, and Buddhism) to each team. You will need to supply encyclopedias with information about religions as well as art supplies, such as scissors, tape, construction paper, and perhaps even old clothes. Have the teams skim the encyclopedias to learn about the dress and customs of their assigned religion (or at least some of its practitioners). Have them choose a couple of elements and make something to wear that reflects those elements. (For example, the Judaism team might make skullcaps from construction paper.) When the teams are finished, serve refreshments. Group members can explain their costume items to each other while they eat.

STEP 4

Help your group members strengthen their sense of God's reality and recognize ways that He has shown Himself by having them make videos. Have group members form teams. Give each team a camcorder and a time limit. Team members might record things like nature scenes while a narrator explains their significance or reads appropriate verses. They might get people to read and explain what the Bible says about God. They might give personal testimonies about ways God's existence has been evident to them. If you have time and if other groups are meeting in the building, ask permission for kids to interview some adults on this question. Afterward, have each team present and explain its video.

STEP 5

Bring in a supply of local newspapers, particularly sections that have information on religion (usually found in the Saturday paper). Instruct your group members to find information on different churches, mosques, synagogues, and temples in your area. Have group members cut out and save the information they find. (They can use the clippings as prayer reminders.) You might also have volunteers read some of the articles on religion they find in the newspapers. These resources could help inform your kids about religious issues, preparing them for prayer.

STEP 1

Skip this step or condense it by going through Repro Resource 1 as a group. Read the introductory paragraph and discuss the questions as a group. Another alternative would be to open the session with this question: **What does every religion need?** Have group members list the components on the board. Some of the things they may mention are something or someone (a power) to worship, rules of conduct, ways of showing reverence, and rewards and punishments.

STEP 2

In order to save time for studying the Bible in later steps, condense this step in the following ways. (1) Don't play the game involving naming religions. Instead, just list the major religions. (You may also ask group members for a few more suggestions.) (2) Distribute Repro Resource 2 for the sake of your group members' information, but don't discuss it. Instead, after discussing the reasons for religions, move right into the Bible study in Step 3.

STEP 2

Have group members form two or three teams. Announce: **It has just been made public that since some religions are more popular than others, as of tomorrow, all religious faiths will no longer be valid. Starting tomorrow, all religions will have the opportunity to "start from scratch." Therefore, any group of at least three people has the opportunity to create a new world religion.** Give the teams the following questions to answer in creating their new religions (1) **What are the main beliefs of your new religion? (2) Does God exist in this new religion? If so, what is He like? (3) Who will lead this new religion? What responsibilities will the leaders have? (4) If people of another religion were to get violent with you, how would the people of your religion respond? (5) What is the utmost goal of your religion? (6) According to your religion, is there life after death? If so, what is it like? (7) How would someone be able to tell that you're a member of this religion? (8) How will you make sure the next generation won't change this religion?** Give the teams several minutes to develop and present their religions. Wrap up the activity by discussing what makes Christianity more than just "another religion." Focus on the fact that God loved us enough to die for us and that Jesus rose from the dead.

STEP 3

To add a little variety to the study of Romans 1:18-25, have group members form teams to paraphrase the passage in some new way. Choose one or more of the following challenges and see what kinds of translations group members come up with.
• Using one-syllable words only
• Using street slang
• Using flowery language (big words)
• Using rap

STEP 1

Have group members form teams. If possible, put junior highers and high schoolers on different teams. Instruct the members of each team to create a religion that is geared especially toward kids their age. In particular, have them think about what the religion would need to be like to attract as many followers as possible. They should consider things like the following: who or what to worship; what rules, if any, to follow; what the rewards or benefits would be; what worship would be like. They should also explain why they think their religion would attract kids. They may describe the religion in a paragraph or just make a list of the religion's qualities. After a few minutes, have each team describe its religion. Discuss what the different religions have in common; then compare them to religions that actually exist.

STEP 5

Make a list of all the schools represented by your group members. Under each school, list the various religions that are represented by individuals (teachers and students) at those schools. Try to rank the religions in order of most common to least. Use the following questions to generate some discussion about the lists.

• What percent of the kids at your school who would be identified as Christians would you say have a strong commitment to Jesus Christ as Lord of their lives?

• If you lived in a country in which only one percent of the population was Christian, how would life be different for you? How would you feel? What laws concerning religious freedom would be important to you? How would you feel if you had to go to school on Christmas and other "sacred" days? How would you feel if other kids tried to get you to adopt their religion? Would it be easier or harder to share your faith in Jesus? Why?

STEP 2

As you begin Step 2, ask your sixth graders to define the word "religion." (One definition of the word is "a system of faith and worship of something or someone perceived as supernatural, having more than natural powers."). Then ask: **Does everyone have a religion? Why or why not?**

STEP 3

Help your sixth graders focus on the basic truths expressed in the verses discussed in this step. Go through the activity of having kids respond to each verse; but before returning to verse 21 and discussing the word "futile," have group members form four teams. Ask the members of each team to paraphrase (express in their own words) one of these passages from Romans 1: verses 18 and 19, verse 20, verse 21, verse 25. After the team members have had time to talk together and write a paraphrase, ask each team to choose someone to read its verse to the rest of the group.

DATE USED:

Approx. Time

STEP 1: *Do-It-Yourself Religion* _____
- ❏ Extra Action
- ❏ Small Group
- ❏ Large Group
- ❏ Fellowship & Worship
- ❏ Mostly Guys
- ❏ Extra Fun
- ❏ Short Meeting Time
- ❏ Combined Junior High/High School

Things needed:

STEP 2: *Where Did They Come From?* _____
- ❏ Heard It All Before
- ❏ Mostly Girls
- ❏ Mostly Guys
- ❏ Short Meeting Time
- ❏ Urban
- ❏ Sixth Grade

Things needed:

STEP 3: *Futile Thinking and Foolish Hearts* _____
- ❏ Extra Action
- ❏ Large Group
- ❏ Heard It All Before
- ❏ Urban
- ❏ Sixth Grade

Things needed:

STEP 4: *God Made Plain* _____
- ❏ Small Group
- ❏ Little Bible Background
- ❏ Mostly Girls
- ❏ Media

Things needed:

STEP 5: *Religious Who's Who* _____
- ❏ Little Bible Background
- ❏ Fellowship & Worship
- ❏ Extra Fun
- ❏ Media
- ❏ Combined Junior High/High School

Things needed:

Judaism and Christianity

YOUR GOALS FOR THIS SESSION:

Choose one or more

☐ To help kids discover the principal beliefs of Judaism and how those beliefs differ from Christian beliefs.

☐ To help kids understand that Jesus' resurrection is the central proof that He is the Son of God.

☐ To help kids choose not to discriminate against people of the Jewish faith.

☐ Other:_____
_____

Your Bible Base:

Matthew 22:37-39;
27:26—28:15
John 14:6
1 Corinthians 15:3-8

STEP 1

Hate Crimes

(Needed: Copies of Repro Resource 3, chalkboard and chalk or newsprint and marker)

Have group members form teams of three or four. Distribute copies of "Signs of the Times" (Repro Resource 3) to each team.

Explain: **As you read the first two articles on this handout, think about how you might use one of them as an opening scene in an action-adventure movie. The movie is about a superhero who especially hates hate crimes. For example, you could have your superhero appear in the nick of time to stop the hate crime from being committed or you could have the superhero avenge the crime in some way.**

Encourage group members to put as much detail as possible into their stories. For instance, what's the name of this superhero? What dark secret from his or her past causes him or her to hate hate crimes so much? What powers does he or she have to battle hate crimes?

Give the teams a few minutes to work. When they're finished, have each team share its ideas.

Then give group members a minute to read the third article on Repro Resource 3.

Ask: **What does this article tell us about hate crime?** (That it's widespread—it doesn't just occur in big cities. Many of the people involved in hate crimes are teenagers.)

Do you know someone who's been the victim of a hate crime? Do you know someone who's guilty of a hate crime? Explain that you're not looking for specific names here. You just want general details about the events that occurred and how people felt about them.

On the board, draw a picture of a cross with a circle around it and a slash through it.

How would you feel if someone painted this symbol on your house or on your backpack or on your bike? (Fearful, embarrassed, angry, frustrated, numb.)

How would you answer Mrs. Lesser's question from the first article: "Why would they do this?" (Kids who are angry at their parents or at their schools sometimes focus their anger on a group that their society has persecuted—usually a minority group. Other kids pick up the prejudices of their parents or neighborhood. Gang members, for example, pick up gang prejudices so that others will accept them. Hate for a certain group binds the gang together.)

Explain: **Many minorities are victims of hate crimes. But today we're going to look at one group in particular— Jewish people.**

A Brief History of Judaism

(Needed: Copies of Repro Resource 4, pencils)

Distribute copies of "Tangled Web of Words" (Repro Resource 4) and pencils. Explain that each of the scrambled words on the sheet relates to Jewish people and their history. Instruct group members to unscramble the words on the left and then match them with their correct definitions on the right.

Give group members a few minutes to work. When everyone is finished, go through the words one at a time and have group members call out their responses.

The correct answers are as follows:

(1) Abraham—(d) the "father of Judaism."

(2) Jacob—(h) the Old Testament man who had twelve sons who became the tribes of Israel.

(3) Passover—(a) the ceremony still celebrated today that commemorates the miraculous escape from Egypt of the Jewish people.

(4) Torah—(c) the Hebrew name for the first five books of what we call the Old Testament, which Jewish people consider very important.

(5) Nazis—(b) the political party in Germany that slaughtered six million Jewish people.

(6) Zionism—(g) the movement to reestablish a Jewish homeland in the land of Palestine.

(7) Israel—(f) the name of the Jewish homeland which is now an established nation.

(8) Sabbath—(e) the day that Jewish people consider sacred—it begins at sundown on Friday and ends at sundown on Saturday.

As you go over the answers, ask your group members to call out what they know about each topic. Use the following information to supplement your discussion.

God made a promise to Abraham that He would make a great nation of Abraham's descendants. This nation, Israel, would be God's chosen people. Abraham's grandson, Jacob, had twelve sons. These sons later became the twelve tribes of Israel. One of the sons, Joseph, was sold into captivity in Egypt by his brothers. While Joseph was captive in Egypt, God looked out for him and caused him to prosper. Eventually Joseph became second-in-command of Egypt. His responsibility was to prepare the country for a coming famine.

To protect his family during the famine, Joseph provided for them in Egypt. Over the years, the descendants of Joseph and his brothers remained in Egypt. But the attitude of the Egyptians began to change toward the Israelites. In time, the Egyptians made slaves of God's chosen people.

God called Moses to lead the Israelites out of slavery in Egypt. When Pharaoh, the leader of Egypt, refused to let the Israelites go, God sent ten plagues on the Egyptian people. The tenth plague—the one that finally convinced Pharaoh to let the Israelites go—was the death of the firstborn son of every family in Egypt. The only people who escaped this plague were the Israelites who painted their doorposts with lamb's blood. Their houses were "passed over" by this plague of death. Jewish people today still celebrate the Passover, commemorating this event.

From Egypt, God led the Israelites through the wilderness to the "promised land," or Israel. There is a continuing movement, known as Zionism, to establish in Israel a homeland for all Jewish people.

The Old Testament of the Christian Bible is the primary book of the Jewish faith. Jewish people would not call it an "Old Testament," for the Hebrew Scriptures are their total Bible. Jewish people consider the first five books of their Scriptures—the Torah—to be especially important. These are the books that contain God's laws, including the Ten Commandments. God's laws concerning the sabbath provide guidelines for Jewish worship today.

Throughout history, Jewish people have been mistreated and discriminated against. The most horrible example of this was the massacre of millions of Jewish people at the hands of the Nazis during World War II.

STEP 3

Reopening the Investigation

(Needed: Copies of Repro Resource 5, pencils, chalkboard and chalk or newsprint and marker [optional])

OPTIONS

LARGE GROUP

LITTLE BIBLE BACKGROUND

MOSTLY GIRLS

SIXTH GRADE

Ask: **Since Jewish people appear so often in the Bible and since they're God's chosen people, does that mean they're Christians?** (No.)

Jewish people believe in God. They use our Old Testament as Scripture. They acknowledge that Jesus died on the cross. So what's the difference between Jewish beliefs and Christian beliefs? (The major difference is that Christians believe Jesus ["Yeshua" to Jewish people] is the Messiah, the Son of God, and that His sacrifice on the cross pays for our sins. Most Jewish people do not believe Jesus is the Messiah; in fact, many believe the Messiah hasn't come yet.)

What proof do we have that Jesus is who He says He is— the Messiah, Savior, and Son of God? There are plenty of answers group members could give. For instance, the Bible supports Jesus' claims. Also, Jesus fulfilled hundreds of Old Testament prophecies concerning the Messiah.

If no one mentions it, suggest that Jesus' resurrection is the *ultimate* proof of His claims. If Jesus had the power to conquer death, then we can certainly believe that He is who He says He is.

Explain: **Most Jewish people do not believe that Jesus rose from the dead after He was crucified. Therefore, they do not accept Him as the Messiah. Over the years, several theories have been used to explain away the idea of Jesus' resurrection. Let's take a look at a few of them.**

Distribute copies of "Conspiracy Theories" (Repro Resource 5) and pencils. Have group members form three teams. Assign each team one of the theories on the sheet. Instruct the teams to read Matthew 27:26–28:15 and I Corinthians 15:3-8. (You may want to write these passages on the board.) Then, based on the information in these passages, each team should draw a conclusion about its theory and offer evidence to back up its conclusion.

Give the teams a few minutes to work. When they're finished, have each one share its conclusions.

Use the following information to supplement the teams' responses.

Theory #1: Jesus Didn't Really Die.
- After having been flogged (beaten with a whip), beaten by the soldiers, and nailed to the cross, Jesus was in no condition to move the large stone that blocked His tomb.
- Besides having to move the stone, Jesus also would have had to remove His tightly wrapped grave clothes. In His condition after the crucifixion, He couldn't have done it. He also would have had to either overpower or sneak past the Roman guards posted at His tomb. Neither scenario is very likely.
- There were over 500 witnesses who saw the resurrected Jesus.

Theory #2: The Disciples Stole Jesus' Body from the Tomb.
- The disciples are mentioned very little in the events surrounding Jesus' trial and crucifixion. Peter was so scared that he denied knowing Jesus. The rest of the disciples probably had scattered and were hiding. So it's unlikely that they had the courage to band together to steal Jesus' body.
- The disciples would have had to either overpower or sneak past the Roman guards posted at the tomb. Because the Roman guards were well-trained, the disciples probably couldn't have overpowered them. And because they would have had to move the large stone in front of the tomb, it's unlikely that the disciples could have sneaked past the guards.
- There were over 500 witnesses who saw the resurrected Jesus.

[NOTE: You might want to point out that most of the disciples later were put to death because they preached that Jesus was the Messiah who had risen from the dead. It doesn't make sense that the disciples would have died for something they knew was a lie.]

Theory #3: The Jewish Officials Secretly Removed Jesus' Body from the Tomb.
- When the guards reported Jesus' body missing, the Jewish officials paid them a large sum of money to say that the disciples had stolen the body. If the Jewish officials had taken the body, they could have simply produced the body to squelch the rumors of Jesus' resurrection.
- There were over 500 witnesses who saw the resurrected Jesus.

Have someone read aloud John 14:6. Summarize: **Jesus Himself claimed to be the Messiah, the *only* way to God. We have the choice whether to believe Him or not. Many Jewish people choose not to believe Him.**

STEP 4

A Conspiracy of Prayer

(Needed: Bibles)

Ask: **Why do you think Jewish people have been so perse-cuted throughout history—even by people who claimed to be Christians?** (Some people have said that it's the fault of the Jewish people that Jesus was crucified. Others stereotype Jewish people as ruthless business people who take advantage of others.)

Ask group members if they agree with these ideas. Then explain that Jewish people were not the only ones responsible for Jesus' crucifixion. Anyhow, Jesus forgave those who crucified Him, so we have no right to hold a grudge against any Jewish people. Also point out that all stereo-types are dangerous and misleading.

Have someone read aloud Matthew 22:37, 38. Then say: **Some people say that loving God with all your heart means hating those who don't recognize the truth about Him. Do you agree? Why or why not?** Get a few responses.

Then have someone read aloud Matthew 22:39. Point out that loving God (the first commandment) includes loving other people (the second commandment)—whether or not those people are Christians. So our reaction to Jewish people should be one of love.

Can you think of any "mild" forms of prejudice toward Jewish people that you've seen at your school or in your community? (Responses might include the following: excluding Jewish people from cliques or activities; telling jokes that put down Judaism or Jewish people; listening to or making negative comments about someone's Jewish background; generalizing or stereotyping Jewish people; etc.)

How could you show your love for Jewish people when you see or hear these "mild" forms of prejudice being practiced? (Some group members might suggest making a bold stand and publicly defending Jewish people. Others may suggest more subtle methods like not laughing at jokes about Jewish people.)

Close the session by praying for Jewish kids in your local schools and for Jewish families in your community. Ask God to keep them safe from hate crimes and to help them find "completion" in Christ—perhaps using your group members as instruments.

OPTIONS

EXTRA ACTION

HEARD IT ALL BEFORE

FELLOWSHIP & WORSHIP

MOSTLY GIRLS

MOSTLY GUYS

EXTRA FUN

SHORT MEETING TIME

JR.HIGH HIGH SCHOOL COMBINED

Signs of the Times

COUPLE'S HOME, CAR SCARRED BY ANTI-SEMITIC GRAFFITI

Sheri and Lawrence Lesser were startled by a loud banging noise outside their house about 12:15 A.M. Then someone shouted, "Die Jew." The Lessers are Jewish.

The couple found numerous swastikas painted on their house, driveway, front gate, and car. The words "Die Jew" were painted on a wall. The vandalized car was parked across the street from the Lessers' house, in front of a neighbor's home.

"It had to have been someone who knew the car was ours," said Sheri Lesser. "It had to be someone who has seen us in the car or who knows us. Why would they do this? There is no reason for it."

—Los Angeles Times, July 25, 1992

VOLUNTEERS BRUSH AWAY SYMBOLS OF HATE AT VANDALIZED SCHOOL

After church services ended Sunday morning, about fifty people from various churches traded their Sunday finery for T-shirts and jeans to clean up a Jewish high school hit by anti-Semitic graffiti. A few days before, Valley Torah High School had been spray-painted with more than three dozen swastikas. The vandals had done thousands of dollars of damage and stolen some equipment.

—Los Angeles Times, March 16, 1992

REPORTS OF RACIAL VIOLENCE GROW AS HATE CRIMES INCREASE

• Hate crimes in Idaho and its surrounding four states jumped from 60 to 263.
• In Boston, hate crimes are creeping back up after years of decline.
• In New York City last year, crimes involving bias more than doubled the previous year's crimes of that kind.
• Seventy percent of those arrested in New York City for bias crimes are younger than 19 and 40 percent are under 16.

—Christian Science Monitor, October 5, 1990

NOTES

Tangled Web of Words

_____ 1. RHAAAMB

a. the ceremony still celebrated today that commemorates the miraculous escape from Egypt of the Jewish people

_____ 2. CABOJ

b. the political party in Germany that slaughtered six million Jewish people

_____ 3. SRPOSVEA

c. the Jewish name for the first five books of the Old Testament, which Jewish people consider very important

_____ 4. HOTAR

d. the "father of Judaism"

_____ 5. ZASNI

e. the day that Jewish people consider sacred—it begins at sundown on Friday and ends at sundown on Saturday

_____ 6. ZOSINMI

f. the name of the Jewish homeland which is now an established nation

_____ 7. RESILA

g. the movement to re-establish a Jewish homeland in the land of Palestine

_____ 8. BHABAST

h. the Old Testament man who had twelve sons who became the tribes of Israel

CONSPIRACY THEORIES

THEORY #1: JESUS DIDN'T REALLY DIE.

On the cross, Jesus fainted from exhaustion and pain, but didn't die. In the coolness of the tomb, He regained consciousness and made His escape.
Important Issues to Investigate:
- What kind of physical condition was Jesus in after the crucifixion?
- What obstacles would He have had to overcome in escaping from the tomb?

THEORY #2: THE DISCIPLES STOLE JESUS' BODY FROM THE TOMB.

Jesus' disciples somehow overpowered the Roman guards posted by Jesus' tomb. They then rolled away the stone from in front of the tomb, removed Jesus' dead body, and hid it. Afterward, none of them ever told anyone what they'd done.
Important Issues to Investigate:
- What kind of attitude did the disciples have during Jesus' crucifixion? Did any of them run away? Did any of them stick around?
- What obstacles would they have had to overcome to steal Jesus' body?

THEORY #3: THE JEWISH OFFICIALS SECRETLY REMOVED JESUS' BODY FROM THE TOMB.

To prevent the disciples from stealing Jesus' body and claiming that He'd risen from the dead, the Jewish officials (with the help of the Roman guards) secretly removed Jesus' body and hid it.
Important Issue to Investigate:
- When rumors of Jesus' resurrection started circulating, what could the Jewish officials have done to disprove them?

STEP 2

Have group members form teams. Use the words on Repro Resource 4 to play a guessing game. Have each team send a pair of players to the front of the room. One person in each pair will give clues, the other will guess. Whisper the first word to the clue givers. To begin the game, Team A's clue giver will give a one-word clue; Team A's guesser will then have 15 seconds to guess the word. If his or her guess is wrong, Team B's clue giver will give a one-word clue to his or her partner, and so on. Keep alternating until one pair guesses the word. Award a point for each correct guess. When you're finished with the game, continue discussing Judaism, using the information in the session.

STEP 4

Before discussing prejudice toward Jewish people, allow your group members to experience discrimination firsthand. Select an arbitrary characteristic (perhaps people with tie shoes vs. those with slip-ons, people wearing rings vs. those who aren't, people whose first names begin with A-L vs. those whose names begin with M-Z, etc.). Divide your kids into one of two groups based on this arbitrary characteristic. Don't explain what the characteristic is. Penalize those in one group (by having them do a certain number of knee bends, push-ups, etc.) and reward those in the other group (by giving them small candies, letting them play a special game, etc.). See if your group members can determine what your basis for discrimination was. Try another round, if you have time, using a different criterion. Then move into the questions listed in Step 4.

STEP 1

Get your group members thinking about Judaism by having them free associate the word "Jewish." Encourage them to be honest about what comes to their minds (including stereotypes). They can say things even if they disagree or think they're wrong. You can do the free association one of two ways. (1) Go around the room and have each group member say something as quickly as possible. List the responses on the board as they are named. Continue around the room until each person has given two or three responses. (2) Distribute paper and pencils. Give group members two minutes to list as many things as they can think of. Then have them read their lists. Afterward, discuss which of the associations are factual and which have to do with stereotypes. You may want to point out that stereotypes contribute to hate crimes.

STEP 2

Before the session, cut up a copy of Repro Resource 4. Write each of the words on an index card and tape the appropriate definition to the card. Give at least one card to each group member. On the board, have each group member draw a picture of his or her word (as in the game *Pictionary*) while the rest of the group tries to guess what it is. Allow 30 seconds per drawing. When everyone has had a turn, use the words as a basis for discussing Judaism and its history.

STEP 2

Invite a Jewish Christian, a "complete" Jew, to speak to your group. If you don't know any, try contacting *Jews for Jesus* or a similar organization. Have this person describe and explain Jewish beliefs and practices, including the Jewish view of Jesus. Then have the guest explain how he or she became a Christian, especially what changed his or her mind about Jesus. Finally, have your guest explain how his or her family and Jewish friends have reacted. If you have time, let the kids ask additional questions.

STEP 3

Set up a courtroom scene in which to hold trials to determine if any of the "conspiracy theories" are plausible. You will need six teams. Teams A and B will take Theory #1, with Team A arguing that it's true and Team B arguing that it's false. Teams C and D will take Theory #2; and Teams E and F will take Theory #3. Give the teams time to study Matthew 27:26–28:15 and I Corinthians 15:3-8. While Teams A and B argue their case, have the other teams serve as judge, jury, and audience. Give the teams about five minutes to present their arguments and counter-arguments. If you like, encourage them to make the trials elaborate. For example, they could bring in "eyewitnesses" and "experts." After the teams present their cases, have the jury decide whether or not the theory is plausible. When all the verdicts are in, have the entire group discuss the arguments and verdicts.

STEP 1

Instead of opening with the activity on hate crimes and anti-Semitism, challenge your group members to think about their faith. Perhaps the challenge will shake some of them out of their apathy. Ask: **Why aren't you Jewish?** Give group members a few minutes to think about their answers. Then list their responses on the board. If you think it would work with your kids, take a slightly adversarial tone in commenting on group members' answers and test the validity of their responses. For example, if someone says he isn't Jewish because his parents aren't Jewish, point out that while his point is true, it's not a good reason for not being a Jew—especially if the Jews are right. This activity is designed to get your kids ready to discuss the truth of Christianity.

STEP 4

As your group members think about anti-Semitism, have them take a private "prejudice test." Ask: **Have you ever painted a swastika on someone's house? Have you ever called a Jewish person a slang name? Have you ever told a joke about Jewish people? Have you ever said something stereotypical about Jews? Have you ever laughed when someone else did one of these things?** If your group members answered yes to any of the questions, encourage them to think of a way to change this behavior in the future. Give them time to pray silently for God's help. Close by discussing ways kids could show their love for Jewish people.

STEP 2

If in the last session your group members made posters (with the categories "What We Know," "What We Want to Know," and "What We've Learned"), bring out the Judaism poster. Review what your group members know about Judaism and what they want to know. Then fill in what your group members have learned already in this session about Judaism. Use Repro Resource 4 as a guide. Check to see if what they already "knew" was accurate. What new questions does the new information raise? You may want to bring an encyclopedia or book on world religions to help kids find answers to the questions they still have.

STEP 3

Before your group members can understand that many Jews rejected Jesus as the Messiah, they need to know what the Messiah is as well as some of the prophecies about Him. Explain that the Messiah is the ruler the Jewish people looked for to free them from their oppressors and rule over them. There are many prophecies about the Messiah in the Hebrew Scriptures (Old Testament); although many Jews didn't (and don't) believe Jesus was the Messiah, He fulfilled those prophecies. Have your group members compare the following pairs of verses, which show Old Testament prophecies and Christ's fulfillment of them in the New Testament: Micah 5:2 and Luke 2:4, 5, 7 (born in Bethlehem); Zechariah 9:9 and Mark 11:7, 9, 11 (triumphal entry); Psalm 16:10 and Acts 2:25-32 (resurrection). Have group members also look at John 1:41, in which Andrew tells Peter he has found the Messiah.

STEP 1

As group members arrive, secretly assign several of them to be Jews. Announce to the group that there are ____ (the number you assigned) Jews in the group. The object of the activity is for the rest of the group members to figure which people are Jews. In doing so, they should ask yes or no questions. (However, no one may ask, "Are you one of the Jews?") When someone thinks he or she has identified all of the Jews, he or she should tell the leader. If the person is right, the game's over. If not, he or she has to sit out. After someone identifies all of the Jews, have your group members discuss the kinds of questions they asked people. Discuss what the questions show about what the group knows about Jews—and about the stereotypes of Jews.

STEP 4

Wrap up the session with a prayer service that includes praise, confession, thanksgiving, and supplication. Before the prayer time, discuss each part to encourage kids to think about what they want to pray. You will need to lead off each part of the prayer or assign a volunteer to do so. Begin with praise: **Dear God, You are . . .** Have group members complete the thought with their own phrases or sentences that acknowledge God's attributes, character, and deeds. Then pray: **We confess that our sins include prejudices.** Have a time of silent prayer in which kids can confess their prejudices. Then pray: **We thank You for Jesus, for His resurrection, and for the gift of faith.** Give group members time to add their own words of thanksgiving. Then pray: **We ask that You would help us love our Jewish neighbors.** Here group members could think of Jewish friends or a local synagogue. **And bring them to know Jesus. Amen.**

MOSTLY **GIRLS**

MOSTLY **GUYS**

EXTRA FUN

STEP 3

Make the events of Christ's trial, crucifixion, death, and resurrection more visual by having your group members read and pantomime these events before discussing "Conspiracy Theories" (Repro Resource 5). Have group members form teams. Assign each team one or more of the sections in Matthew 27:26–28:15, as divided in the New International Version. Ask each team to choose a narrator who will read the section while the other team members pantomime the events described in the verses. After all of the teams have presented their readings and pantomimes, ask someone to read aloud I Corinthians 15:3-8.

STEP 4

As you begin Step 4, divide your group members into two teams. Instruct one team to represent the point of view of Jewish people throughout the discussion. Ask: **How would you feel if you heard negative comments about you? What would you do in response?**

STEP 1

As you're discussing hate crimes, ask your group members some of the following questions.

• **Why do you think guys are often more involved in hate crimes than girls are?**

• **What satisfaction do you think people get from participating in hate crimes?**

• **Which of the following activities that you could engage in would you say might be potentially damaging to someone from another race or religion?**

(a) Overhearing someone tell a racially or ethnically insensitive joke

(b) Laughing at such a joke

(c) Telling such a joke

(d) Making a generalization about people of another race or religion like "That's just the way they are"

(e) Not wanting to associate with someone who's "different" from you

STEP 4

As you discuss prejudice, get your group members to discuss typical (or specifically) male ways of exhibiting prejudice. Also talk about male attitudes toward prejudice. Discuss whether guys show prejudice differently than girls do and, if so, why. Then discuss whether your group members have ever felt pressured to laugh at bigoted remarks. If so, how did they respond? How *should* they have responded?

STEP 1

Open the session with this story:

One day, a Jewish woman named Rachel saw her neighbor Miriam and cried, "You won't believe what's happened. My son has become a Christian." Miriam replied, "Have I got news for you—my son has also become a Christian!" Together they went to the deli owner. "Herschel," they said, "you won't believe what's happened. Both of our sons have become Christians!" Herschel replied, "Have I got news for you—my son has also become a Christian!" The three of them consoled each other, and decided to seek out a rabbi. "Rabbi," they cried, "you won't believe what's happened. All three of our sons have become Christians." The rabbi replied, "Have I got news for you—my son has also become a Christian!" Rachel then asked, "What should we do?" The rabbi suggested they talk to God. "Lord," the rabbi prayed, "You won't believe what's happened—all of our sons have become Christians," Then God said, "Have I got news for you!"

Ask: **Do you think this joke is insensitive to Jewish people? Why or why not? What does it suggest is the main difference between Judaism and Christianity? How much do you know about Judaism?**

STEP 4

Explain to your kids that Jews still celebrate Passover as a commemoration of the time the angel of death passed over the houses of the Israelites who sprinkled their doors with blood. Have your kids try some matzo bread (unleavened bread) or other food of the Passover feast. Make it clear to the kids that you're not celebrating Passover. Explain that, as Christians, we don't celebrate it since what happened in Egypt only served to point the way to God's method for saving us—Christ's blood.

MEDIA

STEP 1

Begin the session by explaining that hate crimes are crimes motivated by people's dislike for someone who differs from them in terms of race, ethnic origin, religion, or gender. You might use the articles on Repro Resource 3 as examples. Distribute several newspapers and magazines and have group members look through them for other examples. Discuss the parallels between the various examples they find. Also discuss why people commit hate crimes and the extent to which the perpetrator's age is a factor.

STEP 2

Find a Jewish person who is willing to talk about his or her faith. Tape or film this person answering a few questions. (The tape probably should not be more than fifteen minutes long.) Here are some questions you might ask. **Why are you Jewish? What do you believe about God? Who is the Messiah? What do you think about Jesus? On what points do you disagree with Christianity?**

SHORT MEETING TIME

STEP 1

Condense this step by skipping the part in which kids make up movie scenes. Instead, read and discuss the articles on Repro Resource 3 as a way of focusing on hate crimes. You could also begin the session by asking group members to define *hate crime* and discuss why it happens. Then you could look at the examples on the sheet to further the discussion and introduce the topic of anti-Semitism.

STEP 4

Condense this step by eliminating the discussion of the sources of anti-Semitism. Have group members concentrate on situations in which anti-Semitism is demonstrated in their schools. Then have them come up with one way to show love to Jewish kids in one of these situations.

URBAN

STEP 1

Rather than going through Repro Resource 3, ask your group members to talk about hate crimes they've witnessed or heard of (or perhaps even been victims of).

STEP 2

Most city teens come in contact with Jewish people every day, but probably know very little about Jewish people. Use the following information to supplement a discussion of Judaism.
A Brief History of Anti-Semitism
• In biblical days—Jews were slaves in Egypt (Exodus 1-11)
• In Roman days—Jews were hated for not accepting Roman gods or food
• In medieval days—People thought Jews were condemned by God for Jesus' death
• In romanticism days—Jews were scapegoats for German economic wrongs
• In the early twentieth century—Millions of Jews were killed in Hitler's holocaust
Jewish Holidays
• Sabbath (Shabbat)—Day of rest for godly reflection
• Passover (Pesach)—Commemorates Israel's release from Egypt
• Feast of Weeks (Shavuot)—Commemorates receiving the Ten Commandments
• New Year (Rosh Hashanah)—First days of creation celebration
• Day of Atonement (Yom Kippur)—Day for reconciliation with God
• Feast of Dedication (Chanukah)—Commemorates retaking of the temple
Types of Jewish People
• Orthodox Jews—Traditionalists who believe in the literal Torah
• Reformed Jews—Liberals striving for modern religious relevance
• Conservative Jews—Traditionalists who reinterpret Jewish law for modern conditions
• Reconstruction Jews—Those who see the evolution of Jewish religion as a product of social needs
• Messianic Jews—Those who recognize Jesus as the Messiah

STEP 2

Have a contest between junior highers and high schoolers to see which group has the greatest multicultural awareness. Get a player from each team to stand in front of you. Read one of the definitions on Repro Resource 4. The first player to signal a response gets a chance to answer the question. (The signal could be raising a hand, banging on a table, or shouting "buzz.") Award a point for each correct answer; deduct a point for each wrong answer. If you want extra questions, you could have group members make them up based on what they know about Judaism. (You would need to verify the accuracy.) Or you could get a dictionary of religions and come up with more yourself.

STEP 4

Divide group members into teams according to the schools they attend. Have the teams rate the level of anti-Semitism at their school on a scale of one to ten (with ten being highest). Also have the teams discuss the forms that anti-Semitism takes at their school. Then, based on this assessment, have the teams create public service messages for their school, discouraging anti-Semitism and encouraging acceptance. Provide the teams with paper and markers so they can make posters or bumper stickers, or do T-shirt designs. Encourage them to come up with catchy slogans.

STEP 2

Instead of having your sixth graders work alone on unscrambling the words on "Tangled Web of Words" (Repro Resource 4), have them work in teams of three or four. Assign different words to the teams so that each team is working on only two or three words. When the teams have figured out their assigned words, have them share their answers with the rest of the group so that everyone can complete Repro Resource 4. Then ask all of the teams to work on matching the words and definitions.

STEP 3

Help your sixth graders visualize the events in Christ's trial, crucifixion, death, and resurrection. Before distributing "Conspiracy Theories" (Repro Resource 5), have group members form teams. Assign each team one or more of the sections in Matthew 27:26–28:15, as divided in the New International Version. Ask each team to choose a narrator who will read its section(s) while the other team members pantomime the events described in the verses. After each team has made its presentation, ask someone to read aloud I Corinthians 15:3-8.

DATE USED:

Approx. Time

STEP 1: *Hate Crimes* _____
- ❏ Small Group
- ❏ Heard It All Before
- ❏ Fellowship & Worship
- ❏ Mostly Guys
- ❏ Extra Fun
- ❏ Media
- ❏ Short Meeting Time
- ❏ Urban

Things needed:

STEP 2: *A Brief History of Judaism* _____
- ❏ Extra Action
- ❏ Small Group
- ❏ Large Group
- ❏ Little Bible Background
- ❏ Media
- ❏ Urban
- ❏ Combined Junior High/High School
- ❏ Sixth Grade

Things needed:

STEP 3: *Reopening the Investigation* _____
- ❏ Large Group
- ❏ Little Bible Background
- ❏ Mostly Girls
- ❏ Sixth Grade

Things needed:

STEP 4: *A Conspiracy of Prayer* _____
- ❏ Extra Action
- ❏ Heard It All Before
- ❏ Fellowship & Worship
- ❏ Mostly Girls
- ❏ Mostly Guys
- ❏ Extra Fun
- ❏ Short Meeting Time
- ❏ Combined Junior High/High School

Things needed:

Islam and Christianity

YOUR GOALS FOR THIS SESSION:

Choose one or more

☐ To help kids discover the principal beliefs of Islam and how those beliefs differ from Christian beliefs.

☐ To help kids understand why people can't earn God's favor.

☐ To help kids avoid unfair statements about Muslims.

☐ Other:_____
_____

Your Bible Base:

Romans 5:8
Ephesians 2:1-10

Paper-Wad Shoot

(Needed: Paper, masking tape, trash can, prize, obstacles [optional])

OPTIONS

FELLOWSHIP & WORSHIP

MOSTLY GUYS

EXTRA FUN

SHORT MEETING TIME

Before the session, you'll need to make three ball-shaped paper wads. You'll also need to mark (using a strip of masking tape) a "free-throw line" somewhere in your meeting area. Place a trash can (which will serve as a basketball hoop) several feet away from the free-throw line. If possible, set the trash can in a place where it will be difficult to see from the free-throw line. You could use obstacles to block the view.

To begin the session, choose three or four group members to participate in a free-throw shooting contest. Explain that the first person to hit three shots in a row will win a prize.

You'll need to offer something pretty desirable as a prize—perhaps a jumbo-size candy bar—so that group members will be competing hard to win it.

Hold up the three paper wads. Explain: **You will only have three shots at the basket, so if you miss once, you're out.**

Ask one of the remaining group members to move his or her chair next to the basket to retrieve the paper wads. It might be a good idea to recruit this person before the session, and explain to him or her what you're going to do.

Hand the paper wads to the first contestant, and have him or her shoot. When he or she misses, give the paper wads to the next person in line, and have him or her shoot. Continue this process until you get to the final person in line.

[NOTE: It's important that you set up the trash can in such a way that it will be practically impossible for anyone to hit three shots in a row.]

Before the last person shoots, say to him or her: **Wait a minute. At this rate, no one's going to win the prize. If you want to, you can have** (the person sitting next to the trash can) **shoot your shots for you. If he** (or she) **makes all three shots from where he** (or she) **is sitting, you get the prize.**

When the person sitting next to the trash can makes all three shots, award the prize to the contestant.

Explain: **Having a substitute can make a big difference sometimes, can't it? In today's session, we're going to be talking about just *how much* of a difference a substitute can make.**

STEP 2

What Do Muslims Believe?

(Needed: Copies of Repro Resource 6, colored markers)

Ask: **How many of you have heard of the Islamic religion?**
If some of your group members haven't heard of it, ask: **How many of you have heard of Muslims?** Probably most of your group members have heard of Muslims. Point out that Muslims are people who follow the religion of Islam.

When you think of Muslims, what images come to mind?
(Some of your group members may have images of terrorists or religious fanatics. Others may know some Muslims and may have a more tempered view of them.) Try not be judgmental as group members share their opinions. Encourage them to be open and honest. You'll address the issue of stereotypes later in the session.

What do you know about the religion of Islam? What do Muslims believe? Get answers from as many group members as possible.

Have group members form pairs. Distribute copies of "A Very Brief History of Islam" (Repro Resource 6) to each pair. Also set out several colored markers for the pairs to use.

Explain: **This sheet gives us some information about how Islam got started. As you read it over, you'll probably find some similarities between Islam and Christianity. You'll also find several differences between the two religions. Choose two different colored markers. With one color, highlight all the statements about Islam that could also apply to Christianity. With the other color, highlight all the statements that disagree with Christian beliefs.**

Give the pairs a few minutes to work. When they're finished, have them share the statements they highlighted.

Use the following information to supplement the pairs' responses.
Statements That Could Apply to Christianity
- "Muhammad had an intense hunger for God"
- Muhammad was "upset [because] the Arab people around him worshiped many gods."
- Muhammad preached that there "is only one God."
- Muhammad "said that all people should submit to [God] and follow Him."

OPTIONS

EXTRA ACTION

SMALL GROUP

HEARD IT ALL BEFORE

URBAN

SIXTH GRADE

Statements That Disagree with Christianity
- Muhammad's revelations stand behind "the Koran, which became the holy book of Muslims."
- Muhammad preached that "God . . . is called Allah."
- "Muhammad taught that Jesus was a prophet of Allah, not the Son of God."
- "Muhammad could not accept the idea of the Trinity."
- "Muhammad also taught that Jesus did not die on the cross. (In fact, he taught that *Judas* died on the cross!) Therefore, Jesus has nothing to do with our salvation."

Ask: **Based on this sheet, what would you say is the biggest difference between Islam and Christianity?** (Islam teaches that people must earn their salvation through good works. Christianity teaches that salvation is a gift from God—all we have to do is accept it.)

STEP 3

The Five Pillars

(Needed: Copies of Repro Resource 7, pencils)

Have group members remain in the pairs they formed in Step 2. Distribute copies of "The Five Pillars of Islam" (Repro Resource 7) and pencils to each pair.

Say: **Muslims believe they can earn salvation by performing various tasks. These tasks are summarized in the "five pillars of Islam." Unscramble the words on the sheet to discover what these tasks are.**

Give the pairs a few minutes to work. The first pair to correctly unscramble all the words on the sheet wins. If none of the pairs is finished after about five minutes, the pair with the most words unscrambled at that time wins.

The correct answers are as follows:
- Pillar #1—*Reciting* the creed
  Muslims must recite the *following words* at least *once a day*: *"There* is no *God* but *Allah* and *Muhammad* is his *prophet."*
- Pillar #2—*Praying*
  Five times a *day*, Muslims must *bow toward* Mecca—their *holy city*, located in Saudi Arabia—and *pray*.
- Pillar #3—*Giving* alms to the *poor*
  One-*fortieth* of a Muslim's *income* must be *given* to charity.

- Pillar #4—*Fasting*
  The *month* of Ramadan is *holy* to Muslims. In that *month*, they must fast during the *daytime*.
- Pillar #5—*Making* a pilgrimage
  All Muslims must *travel* to Mecca at least *once* in their *lives* (or send *someone* in their *place*) to *worship* at the *holy* shrines there.

That's Impossible!

(Needed: Bibles, chalkboard and chalk or newsprint and markers)

Ask: **How would you feel if you had to earn your salvation by doing certain tasks?** (Some of your group members may say they'd be uncomfortable relying on their own actions for salvation. Others may say that earning your own salvation seems fair—in other words, you get what you deserve.)

Ask for a volunteer to come to the front of the room and try the paper-wad activity (from Step 1) again.

Explain: **Some people might say that salvation is like this paper-wad activity. Earlier, several people tried to hit three shots in a row, but couldn't do it. But then when we had a substitute shoot the shots, hitting the trash can three times in a row was easy. In the same way, earning our own salvation is difficult. But when we have a substitute—Jesus—earn our salvation for us, it's a lot easier.**

How many of you would agree with this comparison? Encourage several group members to offer their opinions. Then hand the paper wads to the volunteer and have him or her prepare to shoot.

Just before he or she throws the first paper wad, say: **No, that comparison's not quite right. Let me make a quick adjustment.** Walk over and turn the trash can upside down. **Now the comparison's accurate.**

Ask your volunteer: **Do you think you could hit these shots now?** (No. It's impossible.)

Explain: **When the trash can was turned right side up, it would have been pretty hard to make three shots in a row, right? But it still would have been possible—perhaps for someone who practiced a lot or someone who got lucky.**

OPTIONS

LARGE GROUP

LITTLE BIBLE BACKGROUND

MOSTLY GUYS

SHORT MEETING TIME

In our comparison, that would have meant that earning our own salvation may be hard, but that it is possible. And that's not true. Earning our own salvation is impossible— just like throwing paper wads into an upside-down trash can is impossible.

Have group members turn in their Bibles to Ephesians 2:1-10. Ask volunteers to take turns reading the passages aloud.

Afterward, ask: **How does verse 1 describe human beings?** (As being "dead in [our] transgressions and sins.")

Point out that if we're considered "dead," there's not much hope for us saving ourselves.

What do you think verse 3 means when it says, "we were by nature objects of wrath"? (Because God is holy, He can have nothing to do with sin. He demands that sin be punished—by death [Romans 6:23]. Because we've all sinned, we are deserving of God's wrath and punishment.)

If we deserve death for our sins, why did God send Jesus to take our punishment for us? (Verse 4 says it's because of His "great love for us.")

Have someone read aloud Romans 5:8. Then ask: **What can we do to get God to love us?** (Absolutely nothing. God loves us no matter what. It has nothing to do with our actions. He sent His Son to die for us "while we were still sinners.")

Look at Ephesians 2:8, 9 again. Why is it important for us to know that salvation is a gift, and not the result of our works? (So that we can't boast about how we saved ourselves.)

How is the description of good works in verse 10 different from Islamic beliefs about good works? (Verse 10 says that God created us to do good works. Doing what we were created to do brings us fulfillment—but it has nothing to do with how we are saved. In Islam, salvation is based on good works.)

Trouble with Stereotypes

(Needed: Chalkboard and chalk or newsprint and markers)

Ask: **Why do many people in the western world have negative attitudes toward Muslim people?** (Many people associate Muslims with terrorist activities such as taking hostages and hijacking planes. Others may associate Muslims with the actions of Iraq during the Gulf War.) You might want to remind group members of some of the things they mentioned concerning Muslims in Step 2.

Ask: **Do you think these negative attitudes are justified?** (No. Most Muslims have nothing to do with terrorist activities or violence. This is an unfortunate stereotype.)

What are some stereotypes people have of Christians? (That Christians are a bunch of "goody two-shoes" who never do anything wrong; that Christians are hypocrites who say one thing, but do another; that Christians never have any fun; that all Christian preachers wear polyester suits, con little old ladies out of their money, and commit adultery with women in their congregation; etc.)

Are these stereotypes fair? (No. Although some Christians may fit some of these descriptions, most Christians don't.)

How can we avoid stereotyping other people—particularly Muslims? (By focusing on their positive points.)

What is there to respect in the Muslim faith? (Their dedication to do good works means that faithful Muslims are usually hard working, devout people who pray and fast more than most Christians!)

How would you talk to a Muslim about your faith, what you believe? Get responses from as many group members as possible.

If no one mentions it, point out that the Islam religion lacks grace—loving people no matter what they do. Perhaps the best way for Christians to witness to Muslims is to show them what grace really is by respecting them and refusing to stereotype them. Then, once trust has been established, we might earn the privilege of being able to share Bible passages such as Ephesians 2:1-10 with them.

Close the session in prayer, asking God to help your group members respect Muslims and be open to following His leading in bringing the love of Jesus Christ to Muslim people.

A Very Brief History of Islam

around 600 years after Christ, there lived a man named Muhammad. Muhammad had an intense hunger for God. It upset him that the Arab people around him worshiped many gods. (Worshiping many gods is called polytheism, in case you want to impress someone with a five-syllable word).

Muhammad claimed to have revelations from God. These revelations were written down in the Koran (or Qur'an), which became the holy book of the Muslims. He began to preach that there was only one God, who is called Allah. He said that all people should submit to Allah and follow Him.

Muhammad taught that Jesus was a prophet of Allah, not the Son of God. If God is God and Jesus is God, Muhammad reasoned, that would mean there is more than one God. (As we mentioned earlier, the fact that there is only *one* God is one of the key beliefs of Islam.) Muhammad could not accept the idea of the Trinity—that God is one being in three Persons: the Father, the Son, and the Holy Spirit.

Muhammad also taught that Jesus did not die on the cross. (In fact, he taught that *Judas* died on the cross!) Therefore, Jesus has nothing to do with our salvation. According to Muhammad, Muslims "earn" their salvation through the five "pillars" of the Islam faith.

THE
FIVE PILLARS OF ISLAM

Unscramble the following words to discover how Muslims believe they can "earn" their salvation.

PILLAR #1 **eitricgn** the creed

Muslims must recite the **ginlowlof sodrw** at least **ceon** a **yad:** "**erthe** is no **odg** but **lahal** and **madumham** is his **rophept.**"

PILLAR #2 **yingrap**

vefi esmit a ady, Muslims must **obw wartod** Mecca—their **loyh ticy,** located in Saudi Arabia—and **ryap.**

PILLAR #3 **viggin** alms to the **opor**

One-**frietthor** of a Muslim's **comein** must be **vigen** to charity.

PILLAR #4 **fantsig**

The **thomn** of Ramadan is **oylh** to Muslims. In that **tomnh,** they must fast during the **datimey.**

PILLAR #5 **kingma** a pilgrimage

All Muslims must **velart** to Mecca at least **ceno** in their **elvis** (or send **soonmee** in their **eclap**) to **shiprow** at the **yolh** shrines there.

STEP 2

Distribute copies of Repro Resource 6. Have group members mark up the sheet as indicated in the session. Then, instead of simply having kids share the statements they highlighted, try another method. Read the information on the sheet slowly; instruct group members to stand up when you read statements that could apply to Christianity and bow down (facing east) when you read statements that disagree with Christianity. (Kids should remain seated during the other parts.) You might want to pause at various points during the reading to ask kids why they are standing or bowing down.

STEP 3

Instead of using the unscrambling activity on Repro Resource 7, try a more active alternative. Write down the five pillars of Islam on five different slips of paper. Put these slips of paper inside (or tape them to the outside) of some type of "pillar" that can be knocked over with a ball. (You could use empty two-liter bottles, paper towel tubes, or plastic bowling pins.) Label the pillars one through five. Set the pillars at the opposite end of the room, far enough apart that only one could be knocked down at a time. Have kids line up at the other end of the room. One a time, give them an opportunity to toss or roll a ball at the pillars. When a pillar is knocked over, the person who hit it should read the slip of paper. Briefly discuss that pillar of Islam. Continue play until all five pillars have been knocked over. If you have time, play a second round. This time, have kids try to recite each pillar from memory after it's knocked over.

STEP 2

Before having kids read Repro Resource 4, distribute paper and markers. Instruct group members to draw a Muslim. They should draw what they think most people see in their minds when they think of Muslims. They should include as many details and images as possible. Some pictures may verge on caricature. For example, if some group members think other people view Muslims as terrorists, they might draw their figure holding a machine gun or bomb. When group members are finished, have them share their pictures. Discuss to what extent their own images of Muslims are similar to those in the pictures.

STEP 5

Have kids pair off and discuss with their partners a time that they have been discriminated against for any reason. If they have trouble thinking of such times, use the following suggestions to help them. Perhaps they've been in a store in which the employees followed them around, convinced that all kids are shoplifters. Or maybe if they're female and blonde, people assume they are stupid. Or perhaps they've been made fun of for being "goody-two-shoes" since they're Christians. Afterward, have the partners roleplay one or both of the experiences. Get the kids to talk about how they felt, especially how unfair it was to be the subject of generalization. Help them see that stereotypes about Muslims are just as unfair and hurtful. Then discuss ways to show God's grace to Muslims we meet.

STEP 4

After discussing the impossibility of being righteous or perfect, have group members form teams of four. Distribute paper and pencils to each team. Instruct the teams to read Ephesians 2:1-10 and Romans 5:8. Based on these passages (and team members' knowledge), have each team make a flow chart of salvation, illustrating how a person gets into heaven. The charts should show, for example, what happens to the "perfect," to the sinners who believe in Jesus, and to the sinners who don't believe in Jesus. Encourage group members to show as many of the steps, options, and moments of decision in the process as possible. When they are finished, have the teams explain and compare their charts. Emphasize that no one is perfect and that it is only through Christ that we can get to heaven.

STEP 5

Invite a guest speaker to address your group. Consider one of the following options in inviting your speaker. (1) Focus on prejudice by inviting a Muslim to discuss the prejudices and negative attitudes he or she has experienced. (2) Focus on the differences between Islam and Christianity by having a converted Muslim explain his or her conversion. (3) Focus on evangelization by having a missionary to Muslims discuss his or her ministry and experiences.

STEP 2

Before going through Repro Resource 6, give a short quiz to your group members to see how much they really know about Islam.

(1) Who is the founder of Islam? (Muhammad.)

(2) What does the term *Islam* mean? (Submission to the will of God.)

(3) In what century did the founder of Islam die? (632 a.d.)

(4) What are the two major sects of Muslims? (Sunnis and Shi'ites [Shiahs].)

(5) True or false: There are more Muslims than Christians in the world. (False. Of the world's population, 29.9% claim to be Christian; 19.2% claim to be Muslim.)

(6) What percent of Muslims have never heard the Gospel? (Over 80%.)

(7) What do Muslim people call God? (Allah.)

STEP 3

After group members have unscrambled the five pillars of Islam, get them thinking about Muslims' devotion and sincerity. Ask them how sincere they think someone who follows these pillars must be. Ask if they think such Muslims are more devoted than Christians. Finally, discuss whether or not Muslims are more deserving of heaven than most Christians. This discussion should prepare you for Step 4, in which you discuss the fact that salvation can't be earned.

STEP 3

If in Session 1 your group members made posters (with the categories "What We Know," "What We Want to Know," and "What We've Learned"), bring out the Islam poster. Review what your group members know about Islam and what they want to know. Then fill in what your group members have learned already in this session about Islam. Use Repro Resource 7 as a guide. Check to see if what they already "knew" was accurate. What new questions does the new information raise? You may want to bring an encyclopedia or book on world religions to help kids find answers to the questions they still have.

STEP 4

Your group members may not understand the fact that Christ is a substitute. Help them see that Christ substituted for us in two ways. You will need to explain briefly the plan of salvation, emphasizing our need for perfect righteousness to go to heaven and our death sentence for sinning. Emphasize that having failed to live absolutely perfect lives, we deserve to die. Jesus was perfect and didn't deserve to die, but He let God kill Him instead of us. In that way, He paid for our sins. He also, in a sense, "loaned" us His own righteousness. You might have group members look up these passages: I Peter 2:24, Philippians 3:9; Romans 3:21-26. You might also want to read aloud the section in C. S. Lewis' *The Lion, the Witch, and the Wardrobe* in which Aslan willingly dies as a sacrifice for Edmund's treason.

STEP 1

Allow group members to become better acquainted by having them share honestly about who they would like to be besides themselves. Ask: **If you could be someone else, who would you be and why?** Give each person an opportunity to answer this question. (If your group is large, break into teams of four and let kids answer to their teammates.) After everyone has shared, discuss some of the reasons group members wanted to be someone else. Point out that the things we would want to change reveal our sense of our own imperfections. We know that we aren't perfect. Remind kids of this fact later in the session as you discuss the Muslim belief in salvation by works and God's demand for absolute perfection.

STEP 5

End the session with a time of praise and thanks to God that Christ is our substitute. Divide into three teams. Have one team choose several songs that are appropriate to this theme, such as "I've Been Redeemed," "Not What My Hands Have Done," or "Wonderful Grace of Jesus." Have the second team choose Scripture passages that discuss Christ as substitute, such as I Peter 2:4. (You will probably need to make a concordance available.) Have the third team be responsible for the prayer time. The members of this team could write a group prayer, several shorter prayers, or enlist volunteers to write personal statements of thanks.

STEP 3

Have group members form five teams. Distribute copies of "The Five Pillars of Islam" (Repro Resource 7) to each team. Ask each team to unscramble the words of one of the pillars. Then have each team come up with one reason why the task described in its pillar could be *good* for people to do, and one reason why that task might be *inappropriate* for people to do. After the teams are finished, have them share their information with the entire group.

STEP 5

As you begin Step 5, ask your group members to define the word *stereotype* (a fixed concept of a person, group, or idea held by a number of people, which represents an oversimplified opinion and allows for no individuality or critical judgment). Ask: **What is God's attitude toward people as separate individuals? Can we have Christ's love for others and keep our stereotypes? Why or why not?**

STEP 1

Rather than having only a few volunteers try the paper-wad shoot, divide group members into two teams. Let the players on one team use the "substitute" to make their shots; but don't allow the players on the other team to use the substitute. Afterward, talk about the advantage of having a substitute in this situation.

STEP 4

After discussing the paper-wad-shoot analogy, have group members form two teams. Instruct the teams to read Ephesians 2:1-10 and Romans 5:8, and come up with a set of questions based on the passages. Have the teams write each question (and answer) on a slip of paper. Ask one player from a team one of the questions written by the opponents. If he or she answers the question correctly, he or she gets to take a shot. (Remove the obstacles so that the shot is difficult, but not so difficult that no one will make it.) When you have asked all the questions, the team with the most points wins. (As an alternative, you could have teams study the passages and then answer questions which you make up.) When you are finished with the game, emphasize that salvation is a gift received by faith; it is not something we can earn through our works, which is what Islam wrongly teaches.

STEP 1

To introduce the topic of religions based on good works, have group members compete in a relay race called "Pilgrimage." Divide the group into teams of four. Clear out a large area in your meeting room. Explain that the teams are going on a "pilgrimage" to a holy place and that they must cross some difficult terrain to reach it. Each team member will be responsible for crossing a different part of the terrain. The first person has to "cross the desert" by crawling across the room and back; the second must "ride a camel" by getting a teammate to carry him or her across the room and back; the third must "cross the ocean" by crabwalking; and the fourth must "carry supplies" by balancing a book on his or her head. The first team finished wins. Afterward, discuss whether group members would like to have to go on a real pilgrimage to earn their way to heaven.

STEP 5

Wrap up the session with a "desert party." Decorate the room like a desert. You could serve refreshments at an "oasis." Consider serving *sand*wiches and water out of canteens. Play one or more of the following games:

• Camel races—Have group members form pairs. The pairs will compete in a contest in which one partner rides piggyback (or camelback) on the other.

• Flying carpet relay—Have group members form teams. Give each team two carpet squares. The object is to get the whole team to the other side of the room, stepping only on the carpet squares.

• Sand castles—Go to a place that has a lot of sand. Have group members form teams. See which team can build the most elaborate sand castle.

• Urban turbans—Have group members form teams. The teams will compete to see which one can balance the most paper cups and paper plates (alternating cup, plate, cup, plate) on one team member's head.

STEP 3

Before the session, tape-record or video-tape an interview with a Muslim in which he or she talks about his or her faith. Ask this person to explain what he or she believes about God, Jesus, the Bible, the Koran, and eternal life. Have the person describe his or her daily religious practice, particularly focusing on the five pillars. After playing the interview, supplement it with information from Repro Resource 7 ("The Five Pillars of Islam"). Have the kids discuss how good, sincere, or devout the interviewee seems. Ask them to compare this person to the majority of Christians they know. Kids may find the Muslim to be more sincere and devoted. If so, explain that sincerity and devotion do not earn a person's way to heaven. We can only get there through Christ's perfection.

STEP 5

As a lead-in to a discussion about stereotypes people have concerning Muslims, play (or simply discuss) selected scenes from various movies that feature Arabic people or Muslims. Some possibilities might include *Raiders of the Lost Ark*, *Lawrence of Arabia*, *Malcolm X*, or *Aladdin*. Discuss how recent events have fueled certain stereotypes people in the Western world have about Muslims. Point out that Islam is still one of the fastest-growing religions in the world.

STEP 1

Eliminate this step, beginning the session instead with Step 2, which focuses on what group members know about Islam. Because you are skipping the paper-wad shoot, you will need to adjust the beginning of Step 4, since you won't be able to refer to that activity as an object lesson. Instead, emphasize the impossibility of keeping God's law perfectly.

STEP 4

This activity will work especially well if you followed the "Short Meeting Time" option for Step 1. Explain that we must be absolutely perfect to go to heaven—without even one little mistake. Have group members stand up and take a quiz to determine how perfect they are. Read the following questions. Explain to the kids that if they answer yes to one of the questions, then they should sit down. **Have you ever killed anyone? Have you ever stolen something big, like a car, or robbed a bank? Have you ever stolen something small, like a candy bar or money from your mother's purse? Have you ever called someone a name?** (Probably everyone will be sitting by now.) **Have you ever felt like calling someone a name?** (This should get any possible holdouts.) Point out that none of your group members is good enough to go to heaven. Then follow the session in reading and discussing Ephesians 2:1-10. Emphasize how wonderful it is to have Christ substitute His perfection for our imperfection.

STEP 2

In most urban communities, there are two types of Muslims: orthodox (which this session focuses on) and the Nation of Islam (Black Muslims). Use the following information to supplement a discussion of Black Muslims.

A Brief History of Black Muslims
Rooted in black oppression, Wallace Fard preached that he was Allah (God) and of a "Caucasian devil." When Fard vanished, his spokesman, Elijah Muhammad, taught that the white race was created evil and that the Nation of Islam is the real religion for black people. Malcolm X, who was recruited in jail, became the Black Muslims' greatest evangelist until he broke from the group and started emphasizing the dignity of human rights rather than racial separation. Today the Nation of Islam is headed by Louis Farrakhan.

General Beliefs
• Islam is black man's religion.
• Europeans used Christianity to pollute and exclude blacks.
• Blacks need as many connections to Africa as possible.
• The black community must be improved by blacks working together economically and socially for empowerment.
• Whites cannot be trusted.

Evangelizing Nation of Islam Teens
(1) Don't downplay the cultural beauty teens find in the religion.
(2) Don't bash their Qur'an and dietary rules.
(3) Initially speak of Jesus as the *Word* of God, as in the Qur'an, and later as *Son*.
(4) Be genuine.
(5) Tell them you're a "Muslim" for Jesus. *Muslim* means one who submits to God.
(6) Present Malcolm X as a man who changed anger into faith.
(7) Dedicate yourself to praying for them.

STEP 5

Also discuss stereotypes people have of Black Muslims. Ask: **What would you say to a Black Muslim about Jesus?**

STEP 3

Since some high schoolers may not enjoy unscrambling the sentences on Repro Resource 7, try one of the following alternatives in covering the material. (1) Ask if anyone can name the five pillars of Islam. List the answers on the board, filling in what group members don't know. (2) Use the information on the sheet in a quiz. For example, for Pillar #1, you could have group members complete this statement: **There is no God but Allah . . .** For Pillar #2, you could ask things like **How many times a day must Muslims pray?** or **When praying, Muslims must bow toward what city?** You could do the quiz together as a group or have kids take it individually. Afterward, point out that Muslims believe they must keep these pillars in order to earn eternal life.

STEP 5

Before discussing stereotypes people have concerning Muslims, instruct your junior highers to make a list of stereotypes people have of high schoolers. At the same time, have your high schoolers make a list of the stereotypes people have of junior highers. After a few minutes, have group members share their lists. Discuss how these stereotypes might have originated and whether there is any validity to them. Ask: **How does it feel to be lumped together with all other people your age, especially when the association is negative? Why do people tend to stereotype others?**

STEP 2

Instead of having your sixth graders work in pairs on "A Very Brief History of Islam" (Repro Resource 6), have them form teams of three or four. Give each team a highlighter. Instruct half of the teams to look for statements about Islam that could also apply to Christianity. Instruct the other teams to look for statements that disagree with Christian beliefs. Afterward, ask the teams to share the statements they highlighted.

STEP 3

Simplify the unscrambling process on "The Five Pillars of Islam" (Repro Resource 7). Instead of using pairs of sixth graders to work on the resource, have group members form teams. Give each team one or more of the pillars to unscramble; then ask the team to share its information with the entire group.

DATE USED:

Approx. Time

STEP 1: *Paper-Wad Shoot* _____
- ❏ Fellowship & Worship
- ❏ Mostly Guys
- ❏ Extra Fun
- ❏ Short Meeting Time
Things needed:

STEP 2: *What Do Muslims Believe?* _____
- ❏ Extra Action
- ❏ Small Group
- ❏ Heard It All Before
- ❏ Urban
- ❏ Sixth Grade
Things needed:

STEP 3: *The Five Pillars* _____
- ❏ Extra Action
- ❏ Heard It All Before
- ❏ Little Bible Background
- ❏ Mostly Girls
- ❏ Media
- ❏ Combined Junior High/High School
- ❏ Sixth Grade
Things needed:

STEP 4: *That's Impossible!* _____
- ❏ Large Group
- ❏ Little Bible Background
- ❏ Mostly Guys
- ❏ Short Meeting Time
Things needed:

STEP 5: *Trouble with Stereotypes* _____
- ❏ Small Group
- ❏ Large Group
- ❏ Fellowship & Worship
- ❏ Mostly Girls
- ❏ Extra Fun
- ❏ Media
- ❏ Urban
- ❏ Combined Junior High/High School
Things needed:

Eastern Religions and Christianity

YOUR GOALS FOR THIS SESSION:
C h o o s e   o n e   o r   m o r e

☐ To help kids discover the basic beliefs of eastern religions such as Hinduism and Buddhism.

☐ To help kids understand how those beliefs differ from the beliefs of Christianity.

☐ To help kids choose to respect people who follow eastern religions, but reject their beliefs..

☐ Other:_____
_____

Your Bible Base:

Genesis 1:1
John 14:6
Romans 3:10-12
Hebrews 9:27-28

STEP 1

Give and Take

OPTIONS

(Needed: Copies of Repro Resource 8, pencils, a large bowl filled with jelly beans)

Before the session, set out a large bowl filled with jelly beans. You'll need to have at least 20 jelly beans for each group member.

As group members arrive, distribute copies of "What Do You Know about Eastern Religions?" (Repro Resource 8) and pencils. Instruct group members to fill in their answers for each question and then take (or give back) the specified number of jelly beans.

Give group members a few minutes to work. When everyone is finished, go through the questions one at a time and have volunteers share their responses.

Those who answered every question correctly should have one jelly bean left. As a reward, you may want to allow those who answered every question correctly to take a handful of jelly beans from the bowl.

Use the following information to supplement your discussion of Repro Resource 8.

(1) In the world today, how many followers are there of Hinduism and Buddhism? (d—Approximately 1 billion.) There are approximately 650 million Hindus and 310 million Buddhists in the world today.

(2) Who founded Buddhism? (b—Siddhartha Gautama.) Siddhartha Gautama was born about 550 years before Christ. He was known as a brilliant and holy man. His teachings developed as an offshoot of Brahmanism, the ancient Indian religion which later became Hinduism. He was later given the title of Buddha, which means "Enlightened One."

(3) Who founded Hinduism? (a—No one knows.) The religion of Hinduism evolved over several thousands of years. No one is specifically credited with founding it. Both Buddhism and Hinduism are offshoots of Brahmanism.

(4) Which of the following is not *a holy book of Hinduism?* (a—The Darths.) The Vedas contain the earliest hymns, prayers, and other sacred writings of Hinduism. The Upanishads deal with Hindu philosophy. The Bhagavad Gita is a sacred Hindu poem, used for devotion and philosophy.

(5) Which of the following is not *one of the major gods of Hinduism?* (a—Shaka.) According to Hindu teachings, Brahma is the creator; Vishnu is the preserver; and Shiva is the destroyer.

(6) Which of the following terms is not associated with Hinduism or Buddhism? (a—rasha-vidi.) The major form of Hinduism says that God is within us. To be one with God, we must break through our ordinary awareness of life. Yoga is a series of physical and mental exercises some Hindus use to unite with God. Achieving Nirvana is the ultimate goal of Buddhists.

(7) Which of the following is not a truth preached by Buddha? (c—Desire is the result of neuromuscular impulses.) The Buddha taught that life is full of suffering, that desires cause suffering, and that eliminating desires frees us from suffering.

STEP 2

Ultimate Goals

Ask: **Aside from the information on this quiz, what do you know about Hinduism? What do you know about Buddhism?** Get responses from as many group members as possible. You're not necessarily looking for "expert" answers here. You're looking for group members' ideas about what Hinduism and Buddhism are like.

Then ask: **What would you say is the ultimate goal for people who follow the Christian faith?** (Some group members may say heaven is the ultimate goal. Others may say it's living according to God's will or knowing God and worshiping Him.)

Explain that the ultimate goal for many people who follow the classical (or major) form of Hinduism is to become one with God in the same way a raindrop becomes one with the ocean. To do this, a person must break through his or her ordinary awareness of life. This can be accomplished in several ways, including yoga and meditation.

The ultimate goal for people who follow Buddhism is to achieve Nirvana—a state in which their personal identity no longer exists. The Buddha taught that suffering is the result of desire; so the goal is to free one's self of desire.

Say: **These are just some of the differences between Christianity and Eastern religions like Buddhism and Hinduism. There are many others. But there are also some similarities.**

Comparison Shopping

(Needed: Cut-apart copies of Repro Resource 9, envelopes, pencils, Bibles)

Have group members form three or four teams. Distribute to each team a cut-apart copy of "Similar Yet Very Different" (Repro Resource 9)—with the cards set face-down so group members can't see what's on them, two envelopes, and a pencil. Instruct someone from each team to label each envelope with one of the following headings: "Similar to Christianity" and "Different from Christianity."

Explain: **Each of these cards contains a belief of Hinduism or Buddhism. Your job is to read each card and determine whether that belief is similar to or different from Christian beliefs. Once you've reached a conclusion, put the card in the appropriate envelope.**

Give the teams a few minutes to work. When everyone is finished, have each team share and explain its responses. If two teams differ on a certain response, encourage them to briefly debate their positions.

Use the following information to supplement your discussion of the material.

Similar to Christianity
- *Hinduism and Buddhism both emphasize that there is more to life than the physical things people experience on earth; that is, there is a spiritual dimension to life that is even more important.* This probably could go in either category. John 15:35 tells us that, as Christians, we do not belong to the world. Matthew 6:19-21 tells us to "store up [our] treasures in heaven," not on earth. However, our actions on earth *are* important. Everything we do should be done for God's glory (I Cor. 10:31).
- *Hinduism and Buddhism emphasize the importance of devotion, good works, and self-control.* Ephesians 2:10 tells us that God created us to good works. Devotion and self-control are two important results of Christianity (see I Cor. 7:35 and Galatians 5:22-23).
- *Hinduism and Buddhism both involve a desire to be free from human weakness.* Paul details his struggle with human weakness in Romans 7:15-20.

Different from Christianity

- *According to classical Hinduism, a person seeks God within himself or herself.* When a person becomes a Christian, the Holy Spirit dwells in his or her body (John 14:15-17). However, this is not the same as the Hindu belief that people are already a part of God. Our goal is not to "be absorbed" into the Holy Spirit; our goal is to allow the Holy Spirit to guide our lives.
- *According to the Buddha, the study of or pursuit after God interferes with one's quest for ultimate truth.*

Explain: **One of the main differences between Christianity and Eastern religions like Buddhism and Hinduism is their beliefs about God. The Buddha taught that the study of or pursuit after God interferes with one's quest for ultimate truth. But as Christians, we are encouraged to study about God and strive to know Him personally. Many Hindus believe that God is within them, and that they must strive to the perfect understanding that they are one with God. Christians believe that God stands over and above His creation.**

Have someone read aloud Genesis 1:1. Then ask: **How does this verse compare with Buddhism's beliefs about God?** (According to the Bible, not only does God exist, He's the creator of everything.) Note that the Bible never makes any attempt to explain God's existence. The first five words of Scripture are "In the beginning God created."

Have someone read aloud Romans 3:10-12. Then ask: **How does this verse compare with Hinduism's beliefs about God?** (According to this passage, our sin has separated us from God. It prevents us from understanding and seeking Him.)

- *Hindu leaders throughout history have been honored in the same way gods are revered.* Point out that Paul and Barnabas rebuked the people of Lystra for referring to them as gods (Acts 14:11-15).
- *Both Hindus and Buddhists consider Jesus a great teacher, but not the Son of God.*

Have someone read aloud John 14:6. Then ask: **How does this verse compare with the teachings of Hinduism and Buddhism?** (According to this verse, Jesus is not just a great teacher, He is the *only* way to God. We cannot "become one" with God; we need Jesus as a go-between.)

- *Both Hindus and Buddhists believe in reincarnation.* Hindus believe that after a person dies, his or her soul returns in another living being. This process continues until a person achieves true oneness with God (or Brahma). Buddhists believe that different aspects of a person's identity separate at death and rearrange into another living form. This process continues until a person reaches Nirvana (or the cessation of life).

Have someone read aloud Hebrews 9:27-28. Then ask: **How many times does a person die?** (Once.)

What happens after that? (He or she faces judgment.)

How does this passage compare with the teachings of Hinduism and Buddhism? (It contradicts the belief of reincarnation—that people get several chances to die and come back.)

  • *Devotion, good works, meditation, and self-control are paths to the ultimate goal of Hinduism and Buddhism.* Ephesians 2:8-9 tells us that only by faith can God save us. We are incapable of doing anything to save ourselves.

From what we've studied, it's easy to see that Christianity and eastern religions are different. As we've said in other sessions, we can respond to these differences by loving people of these religions. We can pray for them, send missionaries to these countries and even witness to people in our country.

STEP
4

OPTIONS

Accept, Respect, and Reject

(Needed: Chalkboard and chalk or newsprint and markers)

Ask: **How should we respond to people who follow Hinduism or Buddhism?** Get responses from as many group members as possible.

While group members are responding, write the following on the board:

Accept   people of other religions
Reject   their culture
Respect   their beliefs

Ask volunteers to come to the board and draw lines to indicate what we should respect, accept, and reject concerning other religions.

The answers are as follows:
  • Respect people of other religions.
  • Accept their culture.
  • Reject their beliefs.

Ask: **How can we show respect for people of other religions and acceptance of their culture?** (Listen to them. Ask them practical questions about how they feel about their religion. Don't treat them like they're weird because they have a different philosophy of life. Pray for them and for opportunities to share your faith with them. Avoid stereotyping people based on their religious beliefs.)

Why is it important to reject their beliefs? (As Christians, we believe that God's truth is found in the Bible. We must not be afraid to disagree in a loving manner with beliefs that contradict the Bible. We must let others know what we believe concerning God, Jesus, the Holy Spirit, etc., and not be swayed by false beliefs.)

Close the session in prayer, asking God to help you and your group members respect people of other religions and accept their culture—while at the same time rejecting their beliefs.

WHAT DO YOU KNOW ABOUT
EASTERN RELIGIONS?

_____ **1. In the world today, how many followers are there of Hinduism and Buddhism?**
   a. Less than 500,000 (*If you chose this answer, don't take any jelly beans.*)
   b. Approximately 2 million (*If you chose this answer, take one jelly bean.*)
   c. Approximately 100 million (*If you chose this answer, take two jelly beans.*)
   d. Approximately 1 billion (*If you chose this answer, take three jelly beans.*)

_____ **2. Who founded Buddhism?**
   a. No one knows (*If you chose this answer, don't take any jelly beans.*)
   b. Siddhartha Gautama (*If you chose this answer, take one jelly bean.*)
   c. William "Bud" Hissom (*If you chose this answer, take two jelly beans.*)
   d. Kantiasi Sa-Rong (*If you chose this answer, take three jelly beans.*)

_____ **3. Who founded Hinduism?**
   a. No one knows (*If you chose this answer, give back one jelly bean.*)
   b. Siddhartha Gautama (*If you chose this answer, don't take any jelly beans.*)
   c. Mohatma Ghandi (*If you chose this answer, take one jelly bean.*)
   d. Lawrence Hindulman (*If you chose this answer, take two jelly beans.*)

_____ **4. Which of the following is *not* a holy book of Hinduism?**
   a. The Darths (*If you chose this answer, give back one jelly bean.*)
   b. The Vedas (*If you chose this answer, don't take any jelly beans.*)
   c. The Upanishads (*If you chose this answer, take one jelly bean.*)
   d. The Bhagavad Gita (*If you chose this answer, take two jelly beans.*)

_____ **5. Which of the following is *not* one of the major gods of Hinduism?**
   a. Shaka (*If you chose this answer, give back one jelly bean.*)
   b. Shiva (*If you chose this answer, don't take any jelly beans.*)
   c. Vishnu (*If you chose this answer, take one jelly bean.*)
   d. Brahma (*If you chose this answer, take two jelly beans.*)

_____ **6. Which of the following terms is *not* associated with Hinduism or Buddhism?**
   a. rasha-vidi (*If you chose this answer, give back one jelly bean.*)
   b. God (*If you chose this answer, don't take any jelly beans.*)
   c. yoga (*If you chose this answer, take one jelly bean.*)
   d. Nirvana (*If you chose this answer, take two jelly beans.*)

_____ **7. Which of the following is *not* a truth preached by Buddha?**
   a. Life is full of suffering. (*If you chose this answer, give back one jelly bean.*)
   b. The cause of suffering is desire. (*If you chose this answer, don't take any jelly beans.*)
   c. Desire is the result of neuro-muscular impulses. (*If you chose this answer, take one jelly bean.*)
   d. If we could be free of desire, we'd be free of suffering. (*If you chose this answer, take two jelly beans.*)

HOW MANY JELLY BEANS DID YOU END UP WITH? _____

NOTES

SIMILAR YET VERY DiFFeRent

Hinduism and Buddhism both emphasize that there is more to life than the physical things people experience on earth; that is, there is a spiritual dimension to life that is even more important.	According to classical Hinduism, a person seeks God within himself or herself.	According to the Buddha, the study of or pursuit after God interferes with one's quest for ultimate truth.
Hindu leaders throughout history have been honored in the same way gods are revered.	Both Hindus and Buddhists consider Jesus a great teacher, but not the Son of God.	Both Hindus and Buddhists believe in reincarnation.
Hinduism and Buddhism emphasize the importance of devotion, good works, and self-control.	Devotion, good works, meditation, and self-control are paths to the ultimate goal of Hinduism and Buddhism.	Hinduism and Buddhism both involve a desire to be free from human weakness.

NOTES

STEP 3

Designate one side of the room "Similar to Christianity" and the other side "Different from Christianity." Read one of the items on Repro Resource 9. Give kids a minute to think about which category the statement belongs in; then have them move to the appropriate side of the room. (Encourage group members to be honest and not to follow the crowd.) If responses are divided, have kids on each side explain their reasons. You may want to have volunteers read passages that are relevant to the statements. (See the session for appropriate passages.) Continue through all of the statements on Repro Resource 9.

STEP 4

After discussing what to accept, respect, and reject, have group members roleplay conversations in the following situations:

- **One day during history class, your teacher, who is a Buddhist, says that Christianity has done more harm in the world than good. He asks you what you think. You say . . .**

- **A friend from India invites you over for dinner. When you're there, nothing looks or smells edible to you. You suddenly have a craving for a Big Mac. Your friend's mom asks, "Aren't you hungry?" You say . . .**

- **A friend who used to come to your youth group tells you that she now believes in reincarnation. She asks you your view on the subject. You say . . .**

- **You invite the new kid at school to youth group. He seems interested, but it turns out that his parents are Hindu and are very offended that you were trying to convert their son. They complain to school officials. The assistant principal calls you in to ask if that's true. You say . . .**

STEP 1

After completing Repro Resource 8, gather your group members around a world map or globe. Instruct them to locate the top five Buddhist and Hindu nations (in terms of percent of the population that adheres to that religion). This will give kids a general idea of where these major groups of people are located. Finding some of the countries may be a real challenge!

Hindu

(1) Nepal (89.0%)

(2) India (82.0%)

(3) Mauritius (49.6%)

(4) Guyana (35.6%)

(5) Suriname (27.4%)

Buddhist

(1) Thailand (93.6%)

(2) Burma (87.0%)

(3) Kampuchea (85.0%)

(4) Sri Lanka (69.3%)

(5) Taiwan (65.0%)

STEP 3

Tape signs with the following words on them in different places around the room: "Strongly Agree," "Mildly Agree," "Mildly Disagree," and "Strongly Disagree." Reword each item on Repro Resource 9 to form a statement. For example, the top left item might read, *Life on earth isn't important. What is important is . . .* The top middle item might read, *A person should seek God within himself or herself.* As you read each of these statements, have group members stand by the sign that expresses their belief regarding the statement. Ask those who disagree to explain their views. Also, have group members read and discuss Scripture passages appropriate to each view (as outlined in the session).

STEP 2

To make it easier for group members to discuss their views, divide them into teams of four or five. Distribute poster board and markers to each team. Assign Hinduism to half of the teams and Buddhism to the others. Then have team members share everything they know about their assigned religion. Based on this knowledge (regardless of how accurate it is), each team should draw a picture of a Buddhist or Hindu that depicts the information. For example, a team might draw a Hindu leading a sacred cow or a Buddhist monk wearing an orange robe. At the bottom of the sheet, have team members write what they think is the goal of their assigned religion and what they think is the goal of Christianity. Have each team explain its poster. Point out any inaccurate information. Then discuss the purpose of religions, being sure to show how Christianity is different from other religions.

STEP 4

Invite a guest speaker to address your group. If possible, try to find either a Hindu or Buddhist convert to Christianity or a missionary to people of those religions. You might want to have group members develop a set of questions to ask the person. If the person is a convert, he or she could share about his or her conversion, who witnessed to him or her, what helped change his or her mind, and why he or she now believes in Christianity. You could also have this person suggest ways of sharing the Gospel with people of his or her former religion. A missionary could explain the challenges of witnessing to a person of these religions, share frustrations and blessings in his or her own ministry, point out what approaches tend to alienate unbelievers, and suggest how kids might witness to people of these religions.

STEP 2

At this point in the session, kids might think, *Here comes another "Christianity-is-right-and-everyone-else-is-wrong" lesson,* and tune you out. Many people are bothered by the exclusivity of Christianity. Some of your kids may be influenced by that thinking and be turned off to the Bible because of it. Try to keep their interest by getting them to acknowledge this objection to Christianity and then facing it head on. Begin by having kids brainstorm a list of related objections to Christianity. You might get them started with some of these: Christians are wrong to think their beliefs are the only way to God; being a Christian isn't as important as being spiritual; it's not fair to say that people of other religions go to hell. After you've developed a list, point out that one problem with these views is that they assume that all religions have similar views and goals. Explain that a close look reveals that this is not the case; consequently, we must choose among religions. Look first at the different goals of Christianity, Buddhism, and Hinduism.

STEP 4

Briefly discuss what Christians can accept, respect, and reject. Point out that doing these things isn't always easy. Divide into teams of three. Have each team think up a situation in which it would be difficult to apply these principles. You might give one or more of these examples: (1) A person says to you, "If you liked me as a person, you wouldn't criticize my beliefs." (2) You want to invite a Hindu friend over for dinner. You don't want to offend the friend by serving beef (which is forbidden for some Hindus because cows are sacred), but you don't want to support the false belief in sacred cows. Each team should choose one situation and write a "Dear Counselor" letter describing the problem. Have the teams switch letters; then have each team write a letter of advice in response to the other team's letter. Afterward, have the teams read the letters and explain their advice.

STEP 2

If in Session 1 your group members made posters (with the categories "What We Know," "What We Want to Know," and "What We've Learned"), bring out the Hinduism and Buddhism posters. Review what your group members know about Hinduism and Buddhism and what they want to know. Then fill in what your group members have learned already in this session about Islam. Use Repro Resource 8 as a guide. Check to see if what they already "knew" was accurate. What new questions does the new information raise? You may want to bring an encyclopedia or book on world religions to help kids find answers to the questions they still have.

STEP 3

Before kids can decide whether or not Buddhist and Hindu beliefs are similar to or different from Christianity, they need to improve their knowledge of the Bible. List the following passages on the board: John 15:35; Matthew 6:19-21; Ephesians 2:10; John 14:15-17; Genesis 1:1; Romans 3:10-12; John 14:6; Hebrews 9:27-28; Ephesians 2: 8-9. Depending on the size of your group, assign the passages to individuals or small groups. Have them read their assigned passages and then write statements that summarize what the passages say about God, human beings, or the relationship between the two. Have them read their statements to the rest of the group. Afterward, move into the Repro Resource 9 activity.

STEP 1

Have group members form teams of four. Give each team a piece of paper and pencils. Have the teams fold their paper (accordion-style) into eight sections. Assign Hinduism to half of the teams and Buddhism to the others. Explain that each team should write a poem about its assigned religion based on what the team members know and feel about the religion. The first person will write a line; then the next person's line must rhyme with the first person's, and so on. Make sure that each writer sees only the line written above his or her line. After all four team members have written a line, they should start a second stanza with a new rhyme. When the poems are complete, have the teams read and discuss them. You may want to supplement (and correct) their information with the material in the session.

STEP 4

Have group members answer the following questions to show their level of acceptance of other cultures and respect for people of other religions.

• **My favorite foreign food is . . .**
(Do not accept pizza, tacos, french fries, or chop suey!)

• **The foreign country I most want to visit is . . .**

• **The place in the world where it would be hardest for me to live is . . .**

• **If a Buddhist or Hindu asked me how our religions differ, I'd say . . .**

STEP 3

Before doing the activity with "Similar Yet Very Different" (Repro Resource 9), have group members form teams of two or three. Give each team a card on which you have written one of the thirteen Scripture references used in Step 3. Have each team read the verse(s) on the card, summarize or reword the verse and write the summary on the back side of the card. Then ask that these cards be set aside while you continue with the activity and discussion. At the appropriate place in the discussion of similarities and differences, have a team read its summary of the verse to support that point.

STEP 4

Ask for volunteers to match the words you've written on the board. Then ask group members to suggest ways to show respect and acceptance. After several suggestions have been given, ask for volunteers to roleplay one or more of the suggestions.

STEP 1

Divide into two teams for "Eastern religion baseball." Ask a question of the first batter. If he gets it right, he gets a hit; if he gets it wrong, he gets an out. Use the questions on Repro Resource 9. You will need to expand the questions by using the multiple-choice information. For example, for question #2, besides asking the multiple-choice question, you could ask, **Who founded Buddhism? Who was Siddartha Gautama? What does the title "Buddha" mean?** Or you could form true-false statements like **True or false: No one knows who started Buddhism.**

STEP 4

Say: **Less than one percent of the population of the United States and Canada is Buddhist or Hindu. So why bother learning about these religions?** You could mention at least three reasons. (1) Many people in the western world, though not specifically Buddhist or Hindu, are interested in various forms of eastern religious philosophy. Reincarnation, channeling, yoga, and many other popular beliefs and practices stem from these religions. Understanding more about the root religions helps us better understand these offshoots, many of which are associated with the New Age movement. (2) Even though followers of these religions aren't a majority, their numbers in this country are growing. Reaching just one of them for Christ could make a huge difference as that person interacts with others. (3) Find out if your church supports any missionaries who work primarily with Hindu or Buddhist people. Knowing more about these religions will help you better identify with the challenges these missionaries are facing, and help you pray more specifically for their needs.

STEP 1

Before they work on Repro Resource 8, have your group members play a game to "break the ice" and get them thinking about their similarities and differences. As you call out a category, kids should form groups with people who like the same thing they do. Here are some categories which you can use: favorite food, sport, Old Testament character, kind of music (or group), movie, hobby. Afterward, discuss how we often group with and accept people according to what we have in common. Explain that in this session you will explore similarities and differences between Christianity and Buddhism and Hinduism. (You may want to keep this activity in mind at the end of the session when you talk about accepting people in spite of certain kinds of differences.)

STEP 4

Part of accepting a culture is exposing ourselves to what makes it different. Since eight out of ten people in India are Hindus, give kids a flavor of the foods that many Hindus would eat. An Indian food store or a store specializing in international foods can give you the best ideas for refreshments. You might try serving a curry dish, at least enough for kids to taste. You might also want to provide *barfi* (toffee), which comes in pink coconut and green pistachio, *laddos* (sweet balls) or *halwa*; they are all favorite sweets. Another possibility is *roti*, a round, flat, pancake-like bread, which many Indians eat once a day.

STEP 1

Help raise your group's awareness of the countries in which Hinduism and Buddhism are practiced by showing some video footage from travelogues of India, China, Burma, Laos, Vietnam, Nepal, Taiwan, or Thailand. These videos are often available at libraries or larger video stores. If you can't locate appropriate video footage, consider playing some Indian music as kids arrive. It's possible that your local library will have videotapes about Buddhism and Hinduism. If so, consider showing selections from them.

STEP 2

Before the session, record an interview with a Buddhist or Hindu. Focus on the person's beliefs, particularly regarding the human predicament and how his or her religion addresses it. Also, have the interviewee explain the ultimate goal of his or her religion and how it's reached. After listening to the interview, discuss with your group members how the religion's ultimate goal and the path it offers toward that goal compare with Christianity.

STEP 1

Condense this activity by eliminating the jelly bean portion. Distribute "What Do You Know about Eastern Religons?" (Repro Resource 8). Tell kids to ignore the instructions about jelly beans and instead to circle the answers they think are right. Afterward, discuss the correct answers. You might want to give kids some jelly beans anyway, so they don't feel like they're missing out.

STEP 3

Cut up one copy of "Similar Yet Very Different" (Repro Resource 9). Distribute the slips among your group members. Have one of the kids stand up and read the statement on his or her slip. If the rest of the group members think the statement is similar to Christianity, have them go to left side of the room. If they think it's dissimilar, have them go to the right side. If there are disagreements, have volunteers from both sides explain their reasons. After everyone has voted, get a volunteer to read the passages suggested in the session. Then ask if anyone wants to change his or her vote.

STEP 2

Since Christians are "people of the Book (Bible)" and followers of Eastern religions are greatly a "people of meditation," hold a "Knowing God" contest. Have group members form two teams: the "Bookies" and the "Meditates." Distribute paper and pencils to each team. Assign different Bible passages about God to the Bookies. Instruct the Meditates to sit in their chairs with their eyes closed. Members of both teams will reflect for five minutes on who God is. When the time is up, give the teams two minutes to write everything *new* they learned about God in their five-minute reflection time. Collect the papers in two separate piles. Then write the two lists on the board. The Bookies should have the longer list. Discuss how Christianity's emphasis on learning prepares us better to *know* God.

STEP 3

Have group members make a case for Eastern religions. Form three teams: attorneys for Hinduism, attorneys for Buddhism, and the jury. The attorneys must study Repro Resources 8 and 9 and come up with arguments to present to the jury concerning whether *God is found deep in the individual (Hinduism)* or *through freeing one's mind from worldly suffering (Buddhism).* Explain that this case is crucial. Your state has decided to endorse only one religion, and these are the finalists. The winner is the team that the jury decides presents the best case. Afterward, with the "trial" still fresh in their minds, have all three teams make a case for Christianity's superiority over both Eastern religions.

STEP 1

Have your junior highers play the "give and take" game on Repro Resource 8 against your high schoolers. Let each member of each team take the given number of jelly beans. If you want to even up the sides a bit, you could secretly tell the junior highers two answers for each question that *aren't* correct. This increases their odds to 50-50.

STEP 2

Before discussing the ultimate goals of Buddhism and Hinduism, have group members write down what they consider to be the ultimate goals of the following:

• school

• baseball

• dating

• General Motors

• life

• Christianity

This will give group members something to contrast Buddhism and Hinduism with.

STEP 1

If "What Do You Know about Eastern Religions?" (Repro Resource 8) is too difficult for your sixth graders to work on individually, ask them to look for two or more other kids to work with on this resource. Although they will be working in teams to decide which answers to mark, tell them to individually take or give back the jelly beans so that everyone on the team ends up with the same number of beans.

STEP 4

After the kids have matched the words "accept," "reject," and "respect" with the other phrases, talk about ways we can show respect and acceptance. Write the kids' responses on the board and then ask them to give examples of those responses in action. Then discuss ways to reject others' beliefs without rejecting them as persons.

DATE USED:

Approx. Time

STEP 1: *Give and Take* _____
- ❏ Small Group
- ❏ Fellowship & Worship
- ❏ Mostly Guys
- ❏ Extra Fun
- ❏ Media
- ❏ Short Meeting Time
- ❏ Combined Junior High/High School
- ❏ Sixth Grade

Things needed:

STEP 2: *Ultimate Goals* _____
- ❏ Large Group
- ❏ Heard It All Before
- ❏ Little Bible Background
- ❏ Media
- ❏ Urban
- ❏ Combined Junior High/High School

Things needed:

STEP 3: *Comparison Shopping* _____
- ❏ Extra Action
- ❏ Small Group
- ❏ Little Bible Background
- ❏ Mostly Girls
- ❏ Short Meeting Time
- ❏ Urban

Things needed:

STEP 4: *Accept, Respect, and Reject* _____
- ❏ Extra Action
- ❏ Large Group
- ❏ Heard It All Before
- ❏ Fellowship & Worship
- ❏ Mostly Girls
- ❏ Mostly Guys
- ❏ Extra Fun
- ❏ Sixth Grade

Things needed:

Responding to People of Other Religions

Choose one or more

☐ To help kids see that Paul showed a respectful attitude toward people of other religions and shared Christ without being obnoxious.

☐ To help kids understand that friendships with people of other religions are not unwise, but they have limits.

☐ To help kids choose ways they could best influence people of other religions whom they know.

☐ Other: _____
_____

Your Bible Base:

Acts 17:16-34
II Corinthians 6:14
Ephesians 4:15

STEP 1

Invisible Ball

OPTIONS

LITTLE BIBLE BACKGROUND

FELLOWSHIP & WORSHIP

EXTRA FUN

MEDIA

JR. HIGH / HIGH SCHOOL COMBINED

SIXTH GRADE

As group members arrive, have them sit in a circle on the floor. As they get settled, pretend that you're playing with an invisible ball. You could toss it up and catch it, bounce it against a wall, or simply roll it around in your hand.

Explain: **I found this ball a few minutes ago, and I thought we could have some fun with it.** Pretend to throw the "ball" to one of your group members. As you do, yell: **Think fast!**

That person should catch the ball and then pretend to throw it to someone else in the circle. Give group members a minute or two to practice tossing the ball around.

Then say: **I'm going to start giving directions about what the ball is like or about the way it should be tossed. Change the way you toss or catch it to follow my directions.**

Use as many of the following directions as you like. You may also want to make up some of your own.

- **The ball is very hot.**
- **The ball is slimy.**
- **The ball is made out of sweaty gym socks that haven't been washed in a month.**
- **The ball is made out of feathers—don't let it fall apart!**
- **The ball is very heavy.**
- **The ball is filled with helium.**
- **The ball is very sticky.**
- **Be very polite as you pass the ball.**
- **Be rude and crude as you pass the ball.**
- **Twirl the ball on your finger and count to four before you pass it.**
- **Be as secretive as possible as you pass the ball.**
- **Throw the ball as hard a you can.**

After a few minutes, explain: **Today we're going to be talking about styles. Each of you had a different style for tossing and catching the ball. In the same way, we all probably have different styles when it comes to talking and responding to people of different religions.**

Before you go on to the next section, you might want to ask for the "ball" back "so group members won't be playing with it during the session."

STEP
2

Other Religions and You

(Needed: Copies of Repro Resource 10, chalkboard and chalk or newsprint and marker)

Ask: **How many of you have ever had contact with someone of another religion, such as Islam, Judaism, Hinduism, or Buddhism?**

How many of you *personally know* people of other religions?

How many of you have *good friends* who follow other religions?

You're not looking for specific names here. You just want to get an idea of how much contact your group members have with people of other religions.

Have group members form pairs. Distribute copies of "Encounter with Another Religion" (Repro Resource 10) to each pair. Instruct the members of each pair to read through the sheet and then decide how they would respond to Kerry. Encourage the pairs to think about how they would *really* respond, not how they think they're *supposed* to respond.

After a few minutes, have each pair share its responses. Write the responses on the board as they are named. Don't discuss the pairs' answers now, but keep them in mind and refer to them when appropriate during the next step.

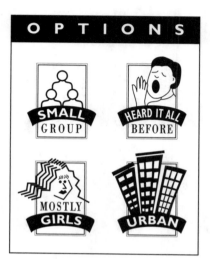

O P T I O N S

SMALL GROUP

HEARD IT ALL BEFORE

MOSTLY GIRLS

URBAN

STEP
3

Faith-Sharing Foibles

(Needed: Copies of Repro Resource 11, Bibles, pencils)

Ask: **On a scale of 1 to 10, how important would you say it is to share your faith—what you believe about God, Jesus, eternal life, etc.—with people of other religions?** (Some group members may say it's very important to share the Gospel with everyone. Others may say that people of other religions have the right to believe whatever they want, and should be left alone.)

On a scale of 1 to 10, how comfortable would you say you are when it comes to sharing your faith with people of other religions? Get responses from as many group members as possible. For those who indicate that they're uncomfortable with sharing their faith, ask them to explain why they're uncomfortable.

Distribute copies of "What's Right? What's Wrong?" (Repro Resource 11) and pencils. Instruct your group members to complete the sheet based on what they think is true about sharing their faith.

Give group members a few minutes to work. When everyone is finished, have volunteers share their responses.

Afterward, say: **It's hard to make rules about sharing your faith because every situation is unique. Some of the statements on this sheet could be true in some situations; but for the most part, they're false. Let's take a look at a particular situation in which Paul witnessed to people in Athens, Greece.**

Have group members reassemble into the pairs they formed in Step 2. Instruct the pairs to turn in their Bibles to Acts 17:16-34.

Explain: **As you read these verses, look for examples in which the statements on Repro Resource 11 are shown not to be true. For instance, verse 32 says that some of the people listening to Paul "sneered" at him. That disproves the first statement. So, next to #1 on the sheet, you'd write "Verse 32."**

Give the pairs several minutes to work. When they're finished, use the following information to guide your discussion of the sheet.

(1) God will make sure that no one ever makes fun of you or rejects you for sharing your faith. Verse 32 talks about people sneering at Paul while they listened to him preach. Any time we share our faith with someone, we risk rejection.

Ask: **Do you think God might ever protect you from rejection when you share your faith?** (If rejection in certain circumstances may be very painful, God might intervene to protect you.)

(2) When you share your faith with people of other religions, it's best to focus on differences, not on similarities, so people will understand why Christianity is better. Verse 23 shows how Paul started out by focusing on something familiar to the Athenians—an altar to an unknown god. Paul then talked about this unknown god—the one true God of the Old Testament. Paul found a common starting point to arouse curiosity.

Ask: **When you're sharing your faith with people of other religions, how might it be helpful to focus on similarities?** (Focusing on similarities is a respectful, positive attitude that works better than blasting people with comparisons and saying that Christianity is "better.")

Is it ever OK to focus on differences rather than similarities? (Yes, perhaps when people insist that some other world religion— Hinduism, for example—and Christianity are the same.)

(3) When you share your faith with people of other religions, you should focus on what they're doing wrong so they'll look up to you. In verse 22, Paul shows respect to the Athenians by focusing on their love for religion. He didn't act as if he were "better" or "more religious."

Say: **Some people might think that Paul was flattering the Athenians by saying they were religious; but the Athenians were religious in their own way. What does the passage say that tells us they were religious?** (The Athenians "spent their time doing nothing but talking about and listening to the latest ideas" [vs. 21]. In their own way, they were trying to "seek [God] and perhaps reach out for him and find him" [vs. 27].)

Have someone read aloud Ephesians 4:15. Then say: **The key to sharing our faith is speaking the truth "in love." We should never act as though we're better than people of other religions. Our attitude should always be one of love and respect.**

(4) When you share your faith with people of other religions, you should not waste your time learning about those religions (reading books about them, watching films about them, etc.). Acts 17:28 shows that Paul was well-versed in Greek poetry. The quote he used, "We are his offspring," pointed to the truth of how God relates to us as a parent, not as a selfish tyrant as many of the Greek mythological gods were portrayed.

Ask: **Are there ever times when it might not be a good idea to study materials of other religions?** (Perhaps it wouldn't be a good idea if you were in a situation in which you were outnumbered by missionaries from another religion. Otherwise, understanding the culture and practices of other religions helps us respect and appreciate people who follow those religions.)

(5) When you share your faith with people of other religions, you should avoid talking too much about the topic that really sets Christianity apart—

Jesus' resurrection. Verses 18 and 32 show how Paul focused on Jesus' resurrection.

Ask: **Why do you think Paul focused on Jesus' resurrection?** (Jesus' resurrection is the central proof of His divinity. Christianity has a living Savior, instead of a dead founder as other religions have.)

STEP
4

Friendship Factors

(Needed: Chalkboard and chalk or newsprint and markers, Bibles)

Some of you may be thinking, *You're crazy if you think I'm going to share my faith with people of other religions. I don't think I should even talk to them!* This is an extreme attitude. And extreme attitudes can get us into trouble when it comes to people of other religions. Let's look at two extremes. Write the following two headings on the board: "When You're Too Close" and "When You're Snobbish."

What are some examples of getting too close to people of other religions? Write group members' answers on the board as they're named. Responses might include the following: Frequently going to their religious services with them; hanging around with a group of kids in which you're the only Christian and everyone else is from another religion; having as your very best friend a person from another religion; etc.

Have someone read aloud II Corinthians 6:14. Then ask: **What's wrong with being best friends with someone of another religion?** (Friends are "yoked together" because they usually spend money and time in similar ways; they have similar heroes; they laugh about the same things; and they talk to people in similar ways. Friends need to have the same values because they rub off on each other.) You might want to mention that this verse also applies to marrying non-Christians.

What are some examples of being snobbish to people of other religions? Write group members' answers on the board as they're named. Responses might include the following: Refusing to be even casual friends with someone because he or she follows another religion; becoming friends with people so you can "show them that your faith is right"; criticizing people for their faith, instead of showing love to them; etc.

OPTIONS

EXTRA ACTION

LARGE GROUP

MOSTLY GIRLS

MOSTLY GUYS

URBAN

STEP
5

Tuning in to God

(Needed: Copies of Repro Resource 12, pencils)

Explain: **In the first session of this study, we talked about how people have a built-in hunger for God. Often God uses us in different ways to help people know Him better and satisfy some of that hunger.**

Distribute copies of "I Can See Myself ..." (Repro Resource 12) and pencils. Give group members a few minutes to complete the sheet. When they're finished, ask volunteers to share their responses.

Encourage group members to keep this sheet handy, as a reminder of their responsibility to share their faith with people of other religions.

Close the session in prayer, thanking God for His great love for people, and asking Him to help you and your group members demonstrate His love to people of other religions.

OPTIONS

SMALL GROUP

HEARD IT ALL BEFORE

FELLOWSHIP & WORSHIP

EXTRA FUN

SHORT MEETING TIME

ENCOUNTER WITH ANOTHER RELIGION

A few months ago, a guy named Kerry moved with his family into the house next door to you. Kerry's in eighth grade, and he seems like an interesting guy. He's very smart; he even helped you with your homework a couple of times. He's got a lot of books in his room and he reads all the time.

As a favor to your parents, you invited Kerry to youth group a few times, and he came. But the last time your parents sent you over to see if he wanted to go to youth group, Kerry said he wasn't interested in Christianity anymore.

"No offense," he said, "but Christianity seems too … basic. I've been doing some studying on Eastern religions, and Hinduism sounds really interesting to me." He said some other things about Hinduism that you didn't really understand, but that sounded really deep.

The next time you saw Kerry was when he came over to borrow a video from you.

"How's the Hinduism going?" you asked.

"Well, the more I studied Eastern religions," he said, "the more I realized that Buddhism is my type of religion. It's much more advanced than Hinduism." He paused for a moment, and then asked, "Would you like to borrow a book on Buddhism?"

The question caught you off-guard and, without thinking, you laughed out loud. You could tell Kerry was offended by your laughter, so you tried to explain that you weren't really laughing at him. You were laughing because you figured you wouldn't be able to understand the book!

"You spend so much of your time going to church and doing church things," Kerry said. "But with Buddhism you don't need to go to church to find 'God' or peace or happiness."

You don't want to hurt Kerry's feelings again, and some of what he says sounds logical to you. But you're not sure whether you should read a book on Buddhism. What do you do?

NOTES

What's **R**ight? **W**hat's **W**rong?

Write "T" or "F" next to each statement to indicate whether you think it's true or false.

_____ **1.** God will make sure that no one ever makes fun of you or rejects you for sharing your faith.

_____ **2.** When you share your faith with people of other religions, it's best to focus on differences, not on similarities, so people will understand why Christianity is better.

_____ **3.** When you share your faith with people of other religions, you should focus on what they're doing wrong so they'll look up to you.

_____ **4.** When you share your faith with people of other religions, you should not waste your time learning about those religions (reading books about them, watching films about them, etc.).

_____ **5.** When you share your faith with people of other religions, you should avoid talking too much about the topic that really sets Christianity apart—Jesus' resurrection.

i Can See MYSELF...

Underline the correct word(s) in parentheses and circle any of the statements below that are true for you.

(If, When, Now that) I know someone who is (Jewish, Muslim, Hindu, Buddhist, _____), I can (never, maybe, almost, really) see myself reaching out to this person in one of these ways:

• praying for this person to come to know the one true God and His Son, Jesus Christ;

• showing this person Christian love, instead of the usual crude behavior—calling him or her names or saying dumb things about his or her religion;

• asking this person about his or her faith;

• looking up information about this person's religion in an encyclopedia so I'll know more about the person;

• telling this person why I believe in Jesus and His resurrection.

STEP 3

If your group is small, divide into pairs; if it's large, divide into groups of three. Have each of these pairs (or groups) read Acts 17:16-34 and come up with five questions (and answers). One question should deal with the events in the passage; two questions should deal with the teaching that Paul does; and two should deal with the witnessing principles that he displays. On separate slips of paper, the members of each pair (or group) should write the category, question, answer, and reference. Collect the slips and put them into piles by category. Then have group members form two teams. A player from the first team will choose a category. You will then ask a question from that category. If the player answers correctly, award his or her team a point; then go to the next team. After you've finished the game, discuss the principles that group members found. Suggest other principles that they didn't come up with. Use Repro Resource 11 as a guideline for review.

STEP 4

Hold a "Too Close/Too Snobby" contest. For Round 1 ("Too Close"), have group members form pairs. Instruct the members of each pair to stand back-to-back with their arms interlocked. Give the pairs a challenge, and see which pair can perform it first. Among the challenges you might issue are running around the perimeter of the church building, picking up five paper wads and throwing them away—without unlinking arms, or participating in some kind of race. For Round 2 ("Too Snobby"), have the members of each pair look straight up (noses in the air) and perform some task without lowering their heads. Among the tasks you might use are catching a foam-rubber ball five times or pouring two glasses of water. This activity will visibly demonstrate the problems of being too close or too snobbish toward those of other religions.

STEP 2

In a small group, it's possible that kids' experiences with people of other religions will be limited. Before going through Repro Resource 10, spend some time talking about ways your group members could have more contact with people of other religions. Brainstorm a list togther. Ideas might include the following:

• Visit a synagogue or some other place of worship.

• Visit a restaurant that serves some type of international cuisine.

• Write letters to missionaries, asking them for the names of kids willing to become "pen pals."

• Become friends with an international student.

• Pray that God would bring you into contact with people who need to hear about Him.

STEP 5

As a group, commit to perform a specific task together that will help you better understand another religion. In addition to the ideas listed in the "Small Group" option for Step 2, here are two other suggestions for group projects:

• Create a pie chart showing the percentage of the world that claims each major religion: Christian (33.2%); Muslim (17.7%); nonreligious (16.4%); Hindu (13.3%); Buddhist (6.1%); various Asian/Chinese religions (5.4%); Atheist (4.4%); tribal religions (1.4%); Judaism (0.4%); all other religions (1.7%). Each section of the pie could be decorated with symbols or pictures cut from magazines, depicting that religion.

• Make a series of posters to display in the church. Each poster could list some things you've learned about a certain religion. Each poster might include a summary of the religion's beliefs, its major differences from Christianity, information on when it started, and an estimate of the number of followers it has today. Decorate the posters with pictures or drawings.

STEP 3

After discussing how your group members feel about witnessing, have them form teams of four or five. Provide the members of each team with newsprint and markers so they can make murals of the events in Acts 17:16-34. Instruct them to read the passage, focusing particularly on how Paul goes about sharing his faith with people of other religions. They should consider his attitude toward the people, the people's beliefs, and the Gospel message. Have them draw their murals in such a way that these views come through clearly. When they're finished, have the teams show and discuss their murals.

STEP 4

Depending on the size of your group, have group members work in pairs or teams of three. Have half of the pairs (teams) think about examples of getting too close to people of other religions; have the other half think about examples of being too snobby to people of other religions. After the pairs (teams) have come up with several examples, have each pair (team) act out one of its examples for the rest of the group. Discuss the examples that the kids act out, focusing on what is wrong or dangerous about the situations and how they could be avoided. As you do so, help your group members develop some biblically based guidelines for relating to people of different religions.

STEP 2

The basic session is such that kids who have "heard it all before" will know the answers long before you ask the questions. Why not set up a scenario in which group members have to identify with someone from another religion? Say: **You were born into a Muslim family and you've been a devout follower of Allah all of your life. You learned the disciplines of Islam as a young child, and you practice them religiously. You think you will earn eternal life by following these practices. You've also learned to hate people from the United States because your parents and all of your relatives have told you about how evil people in America are. One day, a kid transfers to your all-Muslim school. He's a Christian from America! He tells you that Jesus loves you and died for your sins. How do you feel? What do you say to him? The next day, he wants to give you a Bible so that you can read about Jesus. What do you do? What questions do you have for the kid?**

STEP 5

After wrapping up the session, spend a few minutes reviewing the entire course with your kids to see what they've learned. Set up several large graffiti sheets around the room. Label each one with a different religion (including Christianity). Place some markers near each sheet. Instruct group members to write or draw things on each sheet to indicate what they've learned. Each group member must draw or write at least one thing on each sheet. Group members may not copy anything that someone else has already written. After about five minutes, review what's written on each sheet. You might want to keep the sheets hanging on the walls for the next few weeks to serve as reminders of what your group members learned about other religions.

STEP 1

If you know that some of the kids in your group aren't Christians, this session may be tough to teach. The topic of sharing faith assumes that there's faith to share. Consequently, many of the questions and the Repro Resources assume that kids are Christians. You will need to use the kind of sensitivity to nonbelievers that this session emphasizes. Avoid making inclusive statements that won't be true for all of your group members. For example, don't use "we" in a way that refers only to Christians. You may want to mentally edit some of the questions and comments so that you talk about how *Christians* (rather than "we") should or shouldn't share their faith.

STEP 3

Before discussing the foibles of sharing the Christian faith, you may need to explain why sharing one's faith is important. Have group members look up some passages that command us to share our faith or that stress the importance of faith sharing. Some passages you might include are the Great Commission (Matthew 28:19, 20), Peter's admonition to be ready to give an account of our hope (I Peter 3:15), and the need for people to tell about Christ since people can't believe in Him if they haven't heard of Him (Romans 10:14, 15). You can also have kids consider the example of the early disciples, such as Peter's sermon on the day of Pentecost and Paul's many missionary journeys. Wrapping up the discussion by talking about Paul will lead you into the study of Acts 17:16-34 outlined in the session.

STEP 1

Instead of having group members play with an imaginary ball, use the following activity to demonstrate group members' individual styles. Write the following sentence starters on the board:

- If I were a car, I'd be a . . .
- If I were a circus performer, I'd be a . . .
- If I were a magazine, I'd be . . .

Have group members write out their answers, putting all three of them on one sheet of paper. Collect the papers, shuffle them, number them, and read them aloud. Then have group members write down who they think each paper belongs to.

STEP 5

After group members have filled out Repro Resource 12, have them reflect on their reasons for being thankful that God loves people and for wanting to praise Him. At the bottom of their sheets, have them complete one of the following statements: **"I'm thankful for God's love for people because . . ."** or **"I praise God because . . ."** Begin your worship time by having someone read the Great Commission (Matt 28:19-20). Then have as many volunteers as possible share their statements of thanksgiving and praise. Next, have a time of silent prayer during which group members, using their sheets, can confess their weaknesses, lack of faith, and need for growth. Close the prayer time by asking God to make us bold witnesses. End the session with a song about sharing the Gospel, such as "O for a Thousand Tongues to Sing."

STEP 2

Have your group members perform "Encounter with Another Religion" (Repro Resource 10) as a pantomime or a role-play with a narrator. Ask for volunteers to participate. Give them a few minutes to prepare (and perhaps even create a few props). After the pantomime or roleplay is completed, have the entire group contribute ideas about what one could or should do in that situation.

STEP 4

After talking about being "too close" and "too snobbish," ask for two or three volunteers to respond to this statement: **"Religion is only one part of a person's life, so it doesn't have to be a factor in a friendship."** After the volunteers have responded, ask for discussion from the entire group.

STEP 3

When you ask your group members how comfortable they are with sharing their faith, focus on the extent to which being a guy affects this area of their lives. Ask them if they think being a guy makes it more difficult to share their faith and, if so, why. (Some group members may say that being a guy does affect their faith sharing because being a Christian isn't considered "cool," and religion is seen as a weakness.) Point out that all of us are weak and imperfect and in need of Christ. As a group, discuss ways to overcome these preconceived notions about guys sharing their faith. Point out that it takes real bravery to stand up for Christ.

STEP 4

You might be able to get your guys talking about the information in this step by having them discuss what they'd do in each of the following situations:

• **A beautiful girl at school really likes you, and you like her. You invite her to a school basketball game, and she accepts. After that, you start studying together once in a while. You've both met each other's family. One day, you ask her to come to a youth group event at church. You're shocked when she tells you that she's Jewish. What do you say to her? What do you do next?**

• **A guy at school is Hindu. His family is from India. You can tell he doesn't have many friends, but you're hesitant to reach out to him because many of your friends have joked about the way he dresses, talks, and smells. One day, he asks you, "Why do your friends laugh at me?" What do you say? What do you do?**

STEP 1

Instead of having your group members play with an invisible ball, try the following activity to get across the point that we all have different witnessing styles. Write the words to a simple song (perhaps "Three Blind Mice," "Are You Sleeping?" or Mary Had a Little Lamb") on the board. Have group members form teams. Instruct each team to sing the song on the board to the rest of the group in one of the following styles: country, rock 'n' roll, opera, rap/hip-hop, or blues. Give the teams a few minutes to practice their songs. Afterward, talk about how a person's style affects the message he or she is trying to convey.

STEP 5

Have group members form two teams—the "Heads" and the "Tails." Have the members of each team develop a chant or ritual to demonstrate the team's uniqueness. Then give each person a coin. Instruct each team to send one representative to the front of the room to try to "convert" his or her opponent. To do this, the two players flip their coins. If both coins come up heads, the players both join the "Heads" team; if both coins come up tails, the players join the "Tails" team. Any time a team gets new converts, the members should perform their chant or ritual. If the players don't match heads or tails, they should remain at the front of the room while a second pair of players joins them. All four of the players will then flip their coins and join a team—or remain at the front—depending on whether the coins come up heads or tails. Continue play until one team has completely "converted" the other. Afterward, point out that there's a lot more to choosing a religion than flipping a coin. There's also a lot more to "winning converts." It takes prayer, courage, sensitivity, understanding, patience, and love.

STEP 1

Before the meeting, select a one- to two-minute scene from an old movie or TV show in which two people are talking. Try to select something that your kids won't be familiar with. The more action in the scene, the better; but the people must be engaged in conversation. Show the scene to your group—with the sound off. Have group members write down what they think the characters are talking about. You could have group members do this individually or in small groups. If you want, replay the clip several times, and have volunteers supply the dialogue they wrote. This can be a lot of fun. Then play the clip one more time with the sound on. Explain that in this session, you're going to wrap up the series on other religions by discussing how to talk to people of other religions.

STEP 3

Provide group members with a video camera or tape recorder so that they can make a training tape on how to witness to people of other religions. On their tape, they should provide a principle, a supporting scriptural example (perhaps Paul's actions), and an illustration of a wrong way and the right way to witness. Ideally, the tape should cover the principles suggested by questions 2-5 on Repro Resource 11. (If you want group members to work in teams, provide more video cameras or tape recorders and assign one question to each team.) For example, for question 2, the principle would be that we should begin with similarities rather than differences. A scriptural example would be Paul, who, while in Athens, began his speaking by focusing on the statue to the unknown god. A wrong way to witness would be to say, "Mr. Hindu, your religion causes people to foolishly seek God within themselves." The right way would be to say, "Mr. Hindu, you obviously are very concerned with finding God. Christianity says that we can find God through Christ."

STEP 3

You could condense this activity to save time. After discussing faith-sharing foibles and completing Repro Resource 11, assign one of the questions from the sheet to each group member (or to five teams). Have group members (teams) read Acts 17:16-34 and find the verse that applies to their question. After a few minutes, have them share their findings.

STEP 5

Close the session by reading aloud Psalm 96 and John 1:1-14 in an attitude of prayer. These verses challenge us to share the good news about Jesus to all people, to bring light to the darkness, and to help people recognize who Jesus really is. Hand out copies of Repro Resource 12 to group members as they leave. Challenge the kids to fill out the sheets sometime during the next week. Ask them to bring the completed sheets to the next session. (You may want to reward those who bring back their completed sheets.)

STEP 2

Distribute paper and pencils. Ask group members to write down one question they hope they'll never be asked by a member of another religion. Collect the papers; then write group members' questions on the board. As a group, choose a few questions to answer together. (You may want to choose questions that more than one person wrote down.) The purpose of this activity is to help group members answer some of these questions *now* before someone from another religion tries to answer them according to that religion's theology.

STEP 4

Use the following activity as an aromatic demonstration that getting too close to people of other faiths can rub off on you—literally. Get a volunteer who is willing to go into another room and douse himself or herself completely with cologne or perfume. He or she must stay in that room. Then make a challenge to the rest of the group members that no one can run into the room with the doused volunteer, hug him or her as quickly as possible, and come out without a smell. Have several volunteers try. None should be able to do it. Afterward, discuss the near impossibility of being close to someone of another religion without some of the person's beliefs "rubbing off" on you.

STEP 1

The invisible-ball activity may not go over very well in groups with older kids. If you think that's the case with your group, try the following activity instead. Have each group member write down a simple phrase on an index card (perhaps "The rain in Spain falls mainly on the plain"). Collect the cards. Then have a panel of "experts" analyze the handwriting style of each one. The experts should then make guesses about each writer, based on his or her handwriting. (You could also number the cards, tape them to the wall, and have group members write down which card belongs to whom.) Point out that just as we all have different writing styles, we all have different styles when it comes to talking with others about Jesus.

STEP 3

You might want to skip using "What's Right? What's Wrong?" (Repro Resource 11). Instead, have your group members form teams of three. Instruct each team to read Acts 17:16-34 and come up with a set of guidelines (at least four) for sharing one's faith with someone of a different religion. Provide the teams with paper and markers so that they can make their guidelines into pamphlets (illustrated, if they like). After a few minutes, have the teams display their pamphlets and discuss their guidelines. Use the information in the session and on Repro Resource 11 to review the passage and supplement the teams' ideas.

STEP 1

This entire session might be a bit over the heads of many sixth graders. Some are not quite ready to share their faith with members of other religions. Therefore, you might want to take the emphasis off of "you" and focus instead on how Paul and other Christians shared their faith. Go through the Bible study; then spend the rest of the session reviewing the major religions of the world. (See the "Small Group" option for Step 5 for some ideas.)

STEP 3

Have your sixth graders complete "What's Right? What's Wrong?" (Repro Resource 11). Briefly discuss their answers. Then, instead of having them work in pairs to look at Paul's experiences in Athens, have them form teams of three or four. Instruct half of the teams to read Acts 17:16-23 and look for examples in which statements 2, 3, and 5 on Repro Resource 11 are shown not to be true. Instruct the other teams to read Acts 17:24-34 and look for examples in which statements 1, 4, and 5 are shown not to be true. After a few minutes, have the teams share and explain what they found in Scripture.

DATE USED:

Approx. Time

STEP 1: *Invisible Ball* _____
- ❏ Little Bible Background
- ❏ Fellowship & Worship
- ❏ Extra Fun
- ❏ Media
- ❏ Combined Junior High/High School
- ❏ Sixth Grade
Things needed:

STEP 2: *Other Religions and You* _____
- ❏ Small Group
- ❏ Heard It All Before
- ❏ Mostly Girls
- ❏ Urban
Things needed:

STEP 3: *Faith-Sharing Foibles* _____
- ❏ Extra Action
- ❏ Large Group
- ❏ Little Bible Background
- ❏ Mostly Guys
- ❏ Media
- ❏ Short Meeting Time
- ❏ Combined Junior High/High School
- ❏ Sixth Grade
Things needed:

STEP 4: *Friendship Factors* _____
- ❏ Extra Action
- ❏ Large Group
- ❏ Mostly Girls
- ❏ Mostly Guys
- ❏ Urban
Things needed:

STEP 5: *Tuning into God* _____
- ❏ Small Group
- ❏ Heard It All Before
- ❏ Fellowship & Worship
- ❏ Extra Fun
- ❏ Short Meeting Time
Things needed: